THE COEN BROTHERS

RAISING ARIZONA

MILLER'S CROSSING

  O Brother,

WHERE ART THOU?

FARGO

The BIG Lebowski

BARTON FINK

THE COEN BROTHERS

THIS BOOK REALLY TIES THE FILMS TOGETHER

by Adam Nayman

Abrams, New York

Contents

An Introduction

by Adam Nayman

N 2009, AFTER seeing *A Serious Man* at the Toronto International Film Festival, I went to have coffee with a friend who had also been at the screening, and who had enjoyed the film considerably less than I did. What I saw as a riotously funny update of an Old Testament parable—the book of Job by way of *The Twilight Zone*—was for him a mean-spirited exercise in misanthropy. At one point, after nearly forty minutes of increasingly animated debate, he told me that my praise for the film was getting far too "abstract"; he said that the difference between us was that I was trying to look at the film in terms of the "bigger picture." I laughed and said that I thought that the "bigger picture" was what *A Serious Man* was all about, suddenly feeling very much like the film's protagonist, Larry Gopnik (Michael Stuhlbarg), standing meekly beneath a massive chalk scribble—a proof so long and convoluted that it looks like an entire vast galaxy swirling above him.

The shot of Larry at the blackboard is, for me, the single most indelible frame in any movie by the Coen brothers. It is a microcosm of a cinema that's always gesturing toward the bigger picture. One of the occupational hazards that comes with writing about the work of Joel and Ethan Coen is that it's easy to

feel dwarfed by the sheer size, scope, and cosmological complexity of their cinematic universe. It's equally difficult to try to narrow your focus on any single movie hovering somewhere within it. No sooner have you started talking about one of their films than you start circling back to another, and then another, a daisy chain of associations held together by the certainty that, for all their focus on random mischance, nothing in the brothers' vise-tight, magisterially engineered movies could possibly be happening by accident. This is true on a film by film basis, but also collectively; the moments of resemblance, resonance, and recognition across their filmography are many. Even the most apparently incidental detail—a low-angle shot of a highway; a fleeting reflection in a television set; the name of a nightclub mentioned in passing—can be angled to connect in several directions at once, both within the shape of the film and beyond it, toward some Grand Unified Theory of Coen-ness.

For instance, the image of a Soviet submarine surfacing off the coast of California to receive a delegation of blacklisted Hollywood screenwriters in the 1950s-set *Hail, Caesar!* has a deliriously double-edged resonance. It nostalgically hyperbolizes Cold War era paranoia (the Russians are coming! The Russians

are coming!) while also signifying strangely within a post-Trump zeitgeist (they're already here!). But it also finds the Coens, in their sixteenth feature, calling back directly to the opening scene of their debut–a monologue by the corrupt private detective Visser that kicks off the Texas-set neo-noir *Blood Simple* (1984).

"The world is full of complainers. But the fact is, nothing comes with a guarantee. I don't care if you're the Pope of Rome, President of the United States, or even Man of the Year–something can always go wrong. And go ahead, complain, tell your problems to your neighbor, ask for help–watch him fly. Now in Russia, they got it mapped out so that everyone pulls for everyone else–that's the theory, anyway. But what I know about is Texas ... and down here ... you're on your own."

The contrast between the U. S. of A. and the Evil Empire hinted at in Visser's voice-over plays out more fully in *Hail, Caesar!* It's a contrast manifested in the swank, Burbank backdrop of Capitol Pictures and the contents of Marx's Das Kapital, which has become the reading material of choice for a group of backlot dissidents. Their plan to kidnap the studio's biggest star and send the ransom money to the motherland permits *Hail, Caesar!* to pivot on a perfectly circular conceptual gag, which is that the Hollywood Communists need Capitol's capital in order to honor Das Kapital. But the joke also spins 180 degrees on its other axis: *Hail, Caesar!* is a film of uniquely vexed contradictions. When Capitol's fixer, Eddie Mannix, retrieves the semi-brainwashed matinee idol Baird Whitlock and goes to slap the socialism right out of him, he ends up sounding suspiciously Soviet: "The picture has worth, and if you have worth, you serve the picture!" Is he describing the top-down mandate of assembly-line moviemaking, or the utopian possibilities of a system where "everyone pulls for everyone else"? Would that it t'were so (blood) simple . . .

A diabolical comedy of ideas masquerading as old Hollywood pastiche, *Hail, Caesar!* is structured as an ideological feedback loop, and it encircles several of its predecessors in the process, including *Barton Fink*—which was also set at Capitol Pictures, in the 1930s, and thus functions unofficially as a prequel—and *Burn After Reading*, which unfolds in Washington long after the Cold War has thawed out into a lukewarm pool of leftover paranoia. "You are not ideological?" asks the Russian apparatchik incredulously of the civilians who've come to his office looking to sell what they think are state secrets. Placed as a question, it's also a commentary on a willingness to undermine their country's national security in exchange for financial gain (even as their greed confirms them as capitalists through and through). With its opening and closing God's-eye-view shots—a wry reminder of the bigger picture—*Burn After Reading* also has a perfectly circular structure, and the stolen computer disc containing (worthless) CIA data that catalyzes its plot is an emblem of the characters' hopelessly circuitous reasoning. Just as the quarter being flipped throughout *No Country for Old Men* by the contract killer Anton Chigurh is a symbol of the heartless profit motive he represents.

To move back and forth through the Coens' career is to get caught in the loop, like riding a merry-go-round through a house of mirrors. A Venn diagram of their filmography would just be one big circle with smaller spheres orbiting it like planets. In addition to *Burn After Reading*'s burned CD and the fateful coin in *No Country for Old Men*, there's also the tumbling tumbleweed rolling through the opening credits of *The Big Lebowski*; the spherical set design of "America's Funniest Divorce Videos" in *Intolerable Cruelty*; the sailing, dislodged hubcap that mutates and levitates into a UFO in *The Man Who Wasn't There*; and the whirling vortex that swallows the suburban universe of *A Serious Man* whole. *The Hudsucker Proxy* fully revolves around the Hula-Hoop dreamed up by the idiot-savant "idea man" Norville Barnes, which gets echoed in the rotating halo of the angel who flies to his rescue in the final scene–a zero that's also infinite, circles within circles. The loop also rolls all the way back to *Blood Simple*, in the sequence where each of the characters making up the three points in the script's tainted love triangle is glimpsed either sleeping or seething beneath ceiling fans, which just keep recirculating all that body heat sweltering between them.

It is a measure of the Coens' meticulous M.O. that everyday objects become freighted with portent. These include ceiling fans and Hula-Hoops, but also asymmetrical items like hats, hatchets, briefcases, and typewriters. If these films frequently touch on the metaphysical, it's via a tactile presentation that renders the material world with startling solidity and clarity. Like no director since Stanley Kubrick—"one of the few filmmakers whose shadow falls over Joel and Ethan's playground," says the American critic and programmer Kent Jones—they are obsessives who calibrate their frames and soundscapes down to the millimeter. The next visibly imprecise camera placement or sloppy dialogue cue in their work will also be the first.

The brothers' absolute control of the medium is a source of dual tension: They are rigorous craftsmen who know exactly what they're doing, and yet they sculpt characters who rarely have a clue. They also produce artworks that seem perfectly formed and impenetrable, and yet also prove—like Kubrick's superficially anal-retentive masterpieces—to be wide open to rigorous analysis and desperate speculation alike. When Larry Gopnik is writing his blackboard equation, we hear him muttering under his breath as if he's trying to convince himself more than his students that his equation effectively represents the complexity of the "Uncertainty Principle" he's trying to drill into their heads. But all he can do at the end of his epic scribbling is stammer that "it proves that we can't ever really know what's going on."

Larry's confession of confusion in the face of such a daunting paradox is a sign of humility even as it suggests that the filmmakers may also be giving their audience–to borrow a phrase from the perpetually apoplectic Johnny Caspar in *Miller's Crossing*—"the high hat." In interviews and press conferences, the brothers tend to laugh off the idea that their films require intellectual investment to be understood, much less enjoyed. This general unwillingness to explain themselves is the Coens' prerogative, although as a defense mechanism against interpretation, it mostly succeeds in egging their critics on (which may in turn be the real point of the exercise). Does the Coens' recurring obsession with the Uncertainty Principle represent their own principled uncertainty? Does it mark them as artists working through genuine ambivalence about the world around them? Or is it just a built-in escape hatch leading them (and us) away from any sort of meaning at all? "Why does he make us feel the questions if he's not going to give us any answers?" moans Larry to his rabbi, who cheerfully tells him that God doesn't owe him anything. Quoth the holy man: "The obligation runs the other way."

With this in mind, consider the book in your hands an attempt to repay the Coens for the priceless pleasures of revisiting their movies by a critic who fully admits to being trapped in the loop and thus is willing to wrestle with a massive, muscular body of work that explicitly cautions against wrestling (well, maybe a little bit, for the critics). I want to untangle the Mentaculus (the mind-bogglingly complex probability map of the universe created by Arthur, Larry Gopnik's deeply depressed brother), instead of accepting the mystery, to find the things–including, naturally, The Dude's rug—that really tie the films together. And if it fails, it'll be in the best Coen tradition of strivers who wanted it all and came up short, from Barton Fink to Llewyn Davis. The fact is, nothing comes with a guarantee.

A Serious Man

BURN AFTER READING

TRUE GRIT

Out of Nowhere

1984 – 1991

THIS IS A true story: In the early 1980s, two filmmakers emerged from a barren cultural wasteland as a fully formed filmmaking force. Watch the scene from *Raising Arizona* (1987) where the jail-breaking Snoats brothers erupt up out of the prison-yard mud and start bellowing madly into the sky and you have a perfect visual representation of the arrival of Joel and Ethan Coen onto the scene of American cinema. The Coens came out of nowhere (actually St. Louis Park, Minnesota, a suburb of Minneapolis); there were two of them (Joel Coen was born in 1955, three years before his younger sibling); and they made too much noise to be ignored. Between 1984 and 1991, they created four films that fixed their reputations as auteurs in America and abroad: the crime thriller *Blood Simple* (1984), the screwball chase comedy *Raising Arizona*, the period gangster pastiche *Miller's Crossing* (1990), and the existential puzzle film *Barton Fink* (1991).

The directorial credit on these titles belongs to Joel Coen, with Ethan cited as a producer, and yet as has been pointed out many times, this distinction was primarily cosmetic. "The division of labor suggested by the credits is pretty arbitrary," said Joel Coen in an interview with *Positif* in 1991, while the Coens' longtime collaborator John Turturro has called them "a two-headed monster."

Most accounts of the Coens' directorial process between 1984 and 2004 (the year that they first officially shared the directorial credit, for *The Ladykillers*) emphasize their synchronicity on set, as well as in the editing suite, where their collaboration is so close that they morph into a separate, third filmmaking entity, "Roderick Jaynes," whose fictitious, pseudonymous existence is a running joke as durable as any of the recurring camera moves, character types, or plot twists in the movies themselves. In fact, the consistency of the Coens' artistic output is matched only by the unerringly repetitive behind-the-scenes narrative regurgitated nearly word-for-word in the proliferation of profile pieces that have been published over the years.

The slightly unnerving sense of sameness in these articles could be taken as a by-product of dutiful, double-sourced journalism or as evidence that these filmmakers have always seemed more determined than most to keep their off-camera stories straight. The mundanity of the biographical details is part of the legend: There's the upper-middle-class upbringing by parents who worked as university professors; references to a mysterious and mostly absent older sister named Debbie; and the brothers' shared, mocking reminiscence of the bedroom community of St. Louis Park as "the United States' equivalent of Siberia." It's been well-and-widely reported in books and magazine articles that the pair spent their childhoods imbibing movies on local television—everything from cable broadcasts of Fellini films to tacky late-night B movies—before starting to experiment with their own Super 8 camera, collaborating with friends from the neighborhood on remakes of their favorite titles.

From there, it's just a hop, skip, and jump through a familiar series of salad-days anecdotes, including Joel's journey to film school, first at NYU, where he met and befriended fellow fledgling director Sam Raimi, and then the University of Texas, where he absorbed some of the regional inspiration for *Blood Simple*; Ethan's sojourn studying philosophy at Princeton, which included a thesis on Wittgenstein and several incidents of acting out, such as a forged note to his registrar citing a disfiguring hunting accident as the cause of an extended absence; the brothers' fateful meet-ups with Yale School of Drama graduates Holly Hunter and Frances McDormand (the latter of whom would marry Joel in 1984 after finishing her star turn in *Blood Simple*) and their reunion in New York City in 1980, where Ethan worked as a typist at Macy's to pay the bills and they started co-writing screenplays, including the script that would be used for their debut feature.

This portrait of the Coens as slightly maladjusted smart alecks working patiently but industriously on their own terms has endured due in equal parts to its truth and its romance. In 1981—the year that Joel Coen began lugging a projector and film reels containing a homemade, two-minute trailer into the homes of potential investors sourced from a list of Minnesota's hundred wealthiest Jews—American cinema was in a period of intense stratification, during which the combined financial and artistic gap between the kinds of movies being made by major studios and those being produced via independent channels grew wider than ever before. The Coens' obvious love and appreciation for the movies of an earlier era was consistent with the cinephilia of their predecessors in the New Hollywood. But as figures like Martin Scorsese, Francis Ford Coppola, and Michael Cimino gradually succumbed to gigantism—with Cimino's *Heaven's Gate* (1980) unofficially sticking a fork in the corpse of what had started as an anti-establishment movement—it was the Coens' agility that positioned them as film-culture warriors. "You can't get any more independent than *Blood Simple*," said Joel Coen in an interview with *Film Comment*'s Hal Hinson in 1985. "It was done by people who have had no experience with feature films, Hollywood or otherwise."

The contrast between the charmingly lo-fi circumstances of *Blood Simple*'s creation (it has credits for 168 separate

investors) and the stark, implacable brilliance of the finished film itself has been used to frame the Coens simultaneously as interlopers and innovators—outsiders who saved time, energy, and sanity by slipping through the industry's back door rather than banging their heads against the front gate. Unable to locate a distributor in Los Angeles, the brothers trawled the international festival circuit with their debut, winning critical plaudits (*Time*'s Richard Corliss called it "a debut film as scarifyingly assured as any since Orson Welles") and eventually the support of the influential independent distributor Ben Barenholtz, who set them up with a deal at his company Circle Films that would carry them through their next three projects.

The Coens' agreement with Barenholtz was predicated on their having complete artistic freedom, a precious commodity that seemed even more so after the troubled production and reception of *Crimewave* (1985), the horror-movie parody that they had scripted for Sam Raimi, whose own thrifty triumph with the early splatter masterpiece *The Evil Dead* (1981) wasn't enough to keep Embassy Pictures from mutilating his original cut. "The priority was never the money," Barenholtz told Ronald Bergan. "They wanted to work without interference. So I created a context." Whatever pressure the Coens may have felt to replicate *Blood Simple*'s splash, their deal with Circle Films meant they could approach the task from whatever angle they liked. "After having finished *Blood Simple*, we wanted to make something completely different," explained Ethan Coen in 1987. "We wanted it to be funny, with a quicker rhythm."

Speed was definitely of the essence in *Raising Arizona*, a hyper-stylized fable about a childless trailer-park couple that clumsily kidnaps a baby belonging to a nouveau-riche furniture salesman to raise as their own child. *Blood Simple* had been an unknown commodity that nobody in Hollywood would touch, but *Raising Arizona* sparked a bidding war among top-tier distributors (the film was released by 20th Century Fox, which supplied half of the $6 million budget). Critics compared it to Preston Sturges's mile-a-minute screwball comedies as well as Warner Bros. animator Chuck Jones's famed Road Runner cartoons (a connection strengthened by having the characters played by Nicolas Cage and Randall "Tex" Cobb both sport matching Mr. Horsepower tattoos). *Raising Arizona*'s healthy box office (more than $20 million in rentals in the United States), coupled with its softer comic sensibility—a cornpone cuddliness far removed from *Blood Simple*'s cold, calculated nastiness—seemed to promise a full-on mainstream breakthrough, which was in turn stymied by the comparatively strange and cerebral movies that followed.

Arriving in the same year as Martin Scorsese's exuberant gangster drama *Goodfellas, Miller's Crossing* appeared icy and remote by comparison, and failed to recoup its $10 million budget. Reviewing the film on the eve of the New York Film Festival, the influential *New York Times* reviewer Vincent Canby tallied up the Coens' dutiful references to noir cinema and literature before concluding "so what?" The slightly enervating aspect of *Miller's Crossing* reflected the circumstances of its creation: The film's plot was so complicated that the Coens took a break during the year it took to write it and whipped up the script for *Barton Fink* in three weeks. "In order to get out of the problems we had with that story, we began to think of another one," said Joel in an interview with Michel Ciment and Hubert Niogret, and *Barton Fink*'s focus on a writer in the agonized throes of writer's block is suggestive indeed. Just a few months after *Miller's Crossing*'s commercial flop, *Barton Fink* showed amazing polarity as an awards magnet at Cannes, winning an unprecedented three major prizes: Best Film (Palme d'Or), Best Director, and Best Actor (John Turturro).

If the Coens' career can be divided neatly into early, middle, and late-middle periods (with of course more work to come), *Barton Fink* is the film that bridges the first and second sections. It was the last movie they made as part of their deal with Circle Pictures, and the first with British cinematographer Roger Deakins, who replaced Barry Sonnenfeld behind the camera. There is also something self-referential about its story, which finds a proudly independent, critically acclaimed playwright placed on retainer by a Hollywood studio and bristling against the assembly-line mentality he finds there. At the time of its release, *Barton Fink* was interpreted by some critics as a distress signal fired up by filmmakers sweating over their unexpected success and fantasizing about its potential pitfalls. That fantasy would be realized soon enough as the Coens decamped to Los Angeles to shoot their most expensive movie to date at Warner Bros. under the guidance of hotshot producer Joel Silver. The $25 million budget set aside for *The Hudsucker Proxy* offered proof of the Coens' ascent into the top tier of American filmmakers even as the film's opening scene offered a vivid illustration of an old maxim: that what goes up must come down.

Blood Simple

RELEASE DATE

January 18, 1985

BUDGET

$1.5M

DISTRIBUTOR

Circle Films

CAST

John Getz

Frances McDormand

Dan Hedaya

M. Emmet Walsh

Samm-Art Williams

Deborah Neumann

Raquel Gavia

Van Brooks

WARNING!

THIS FILM CONTAINS

Love triangle	22%
Double crosses	16%
Motown	13%
Rotting fish	10%
Impromptu grave-digging	9%
Ceiling fans	8%
Jump scares	7%
Groin trauma	6%
Sweat	5%
Cold War dialectics	4%

IT BEGINS WITH a thesis statement of sorts: Over a series of slow dissolves of West Texas landscape, the corpulent ten-gallon mercenary Loren Visser (M. Emmet Walsh)—a private detective who's willing to do even dirtier work if the price is right—lays out a bit of life philosophy that's as nasty, brutish, and short as he is. "Go ahead, complain, tell your problems to your neighbor, ask for help—watch him fly." His point is that empathy and charity are for suckers, to say nothing of good intentions and the best-laid plans that go with them. Don't bother being prepared, because "something can always go wrong." It's tough talk from a lowlife who knows of what he speaks because he exists as a wrench in the gears rather than a cog in the wheel. If something goes wrong, it's because he wants it to.

In most noir narratives, the role of the detective is to solve problems rather than cause them. In *Blood Simple*, Visser dishonors this tradition even as the Coens deliberately place him on a continuum of shifty private eyes playing both sides against the middle. The title *Blood Simple* is taken from Dashiell Hammett's novel *Red Harvest*, a pungent slice of pulp fiction that was originally published in 1927 and 1928 as a series of excerpts in the American magazine *Black Mask*. "This damned burg is getting me," says the book's narrator. "If I don't go away soon, I'll be going blood simple like the natives."

The speaker is a private detective who's right to fear losing his mind, because his job requires him to live by his wits. Hammett's story is about how this

"WHAT I KNOW ABOUT IS TEXAS"

—

In the first sequence of their first feature, the Coens cut together a series of landscape shots to establish a sense of place; the spareness and desolation of the images support Visser's every-man-for-himself philosophy.

PEEPING TOM

—

Throughout *Blood Simple*, living characters are taken for dead; the Polaroid of Ray and Abby sleeping will be manipulated by Visser to give the appearance that they've been murdered.

unnamed investigator–who is referred to only as "The Continental Op"—decamps from San Francisco to Personville, Texas, to investigate the murder of a newspaper publisher. He ends up in the middle of a turf war in which his outsider status becomes an advantage, switching and ditching allegiances as the situation requires. The outpouring of violence that follows the Op's arrival is a "red harvest" whose perpetrators reap what they sow. Hammett's antihero gets away clean because he's smarter than the locals. Despite winding up in several very compromising positions, he never once goes simple.

Red Harvest is a foundational work for the Coens, serving as an inspiration for two of their films: not only *Blood Simple*, but also *Miller's Crossing*, which borrows certain key plot points from Hammett's book and operates more or less transparently as an homage to the author and his work. *Blood Simple* actually owes more to the novels of one of Hammett's major contemporaries: Reviewing the film for *Time*, Richard Corliss wrote that "the setting is a town off the dirt road from Southwest Nowhere, but the emotional topography bears the mark of James M. Cain." As with movie adaptations of Cain's work, such as *The Postman Always Rings Twice* and *Double Indemnity*, *Blood Simple* is

about the complications arising from the affair of an unhappily married woman. The Coens surely aren't shy about their references (*The Man Who Wasn't There* is even more explicitly indebted to Cain), but it's telling that when the film was released in 1984, fans and detractors alike seized upon these comparisons and refused to let them go.

The thinking may have gone something like this: that the only way to reckon with how a pair of neophyte filmmakers could whip up something as accomplished and assured as *Blood Simple*, working with limited resources and outside the studio system, was to say that they were standing on the shoulders of giants. The Minnesota-based duo were prankish undergrads cribbing from longer-tenured masters. "Film students looking at old movies seem to find it exciting when a cheap B thriller or an exploitation picture has art qualities," wrote Pauline Kael in *The New Yorker*, "and they often make draggy, empty short films that aren't interested in anything but imitating those pictures . . . *Blood Simple* is that kind of student film on a larger scale."

Kael's skepticism may now appear excessive in the wake of *Blood Simple*'s canonization, but it does hit on the view of the film as a postmodern hybrid. The Coens are credited mostly for having capitalized on the early-eighties vogue for movies modeled (or remade) from vintage film noirs, including Lawrence Kasdan's *Body Heat* (1981), Taylor Hackford's *Against All Odds* (1984), and Jim McBride's *Breathless* (1983). They would then crossbreed those already secondhand conventions with the gory sensibility of the then emerging subgenre of "splatter flicks," an example of which is Sam Raimi's similarly threadbare, independently produced hit *The Evil Dead* (1981), which Joel Coen worked on as an assistant editor straight out of film school at NYU. This calculus adds up insofar as it accounts for *Blood Simple*'s initial notoriety and cinephile appeal. It also, however, reduces the film to a set of cannily synthesized scenarios and textures, with the Coens cast as crafty opportunists. Rather than simply inventorying its (undeniable) influences, it's more rewarding to look at *Blood*

Simple as a kind of ground zero–a wellspring of the Coens' stylistic and thematic originality. It's a film that points the way ahead for its creators even as they're undeniably glancing backward at the same time.

Visser's opening monologue serves as an overture, a tactic that the Coens will repeat several times throughout their career, beginning with *Raising Arizona* and including also later in films like *The Big Lebowski*, *The Man Who Wasn't There*, and *True Grit*. It reflects a fondness for specific, regional vernacular. The Coens' use of voice-over is always personal and never omniscient, as it is in the films of Stanley Kubrick, where disembodied narrators describe (and, in the case of *Barry Lyndon*, comment on) the action. Like Kubrick, the Coens are often criticized for looking down on their characters. *Blood Simple* shows them working smartly and insinuatingly to the contrary: Rather than simply condescending to the infinitely obnoxious Visser, they use him as vessel to express a worldview that their film will simultaneously vindicate and critique.

The idea that *Blood Simple* is a movie told from Visser's point of view—if not literally through his eyes, then from the punitive perspective he represents—is developed shortly thereafter, when the detective presents his client with a set of photographs that he's taken as part of his new assignment. Roadhouse owner Marty (Dan Hedaya) has hired Visser to follow his wife and determine if she's cheating on him. His disgusted reaction to the tacky snapshots of Abby and Ray (who also works at Marty's bar) sleeping in each other's arms in a motel bed suggests he's seeing more than he wanted to. Visser's resourcefulness in locating the couple and taking the photographs is one thing; his amusement in rubbing his handiwork in Marty's face—"I know where you can get those framed," he laughs—is another. The photographs are irrefutable proof that Marty's life is at a crossroads. Something has gone wrong. But as the story moves on, they will also serve as evidence of how easily truth can be manipulated or obscured. In *Blood Simple*, the

The dead fish on Marty's desk during his meeting with the crooked private eye Visser are a perfect emblem for *Blood Simple*'s cold, morbid tone and predatory worldview. Strategically foregrounded in the frame, their appearance anticipates the pile-up of human corpses to come—Marty and Visser included.

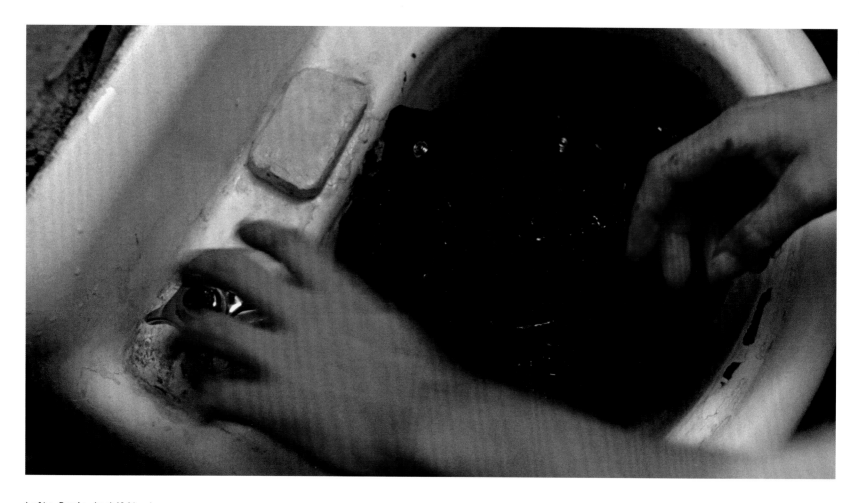

Left: Ray's inability to
clean up the mess after
finding Marty's body riffs
on the film's title; his
panicked ineptitude makes him
"blood simple."

Right: This striking aerial
view of Ray's car, parked
alone in the middle of a
field, suggests that the
character is in an ethical
no-man's-land after burying
Marty alive.

Coens show that it can be dangerous to trust your eyes. Don't believe in anything that you can't see directly for yourself.

The meeting between Visser and Marty is also the first instance of a recurring Coen setup: a fateful conversation between two characters at either end of a desk. In most of these cases, it's a way of dramatizing the main character's encounter with power, which is always embodied by the man sitting behind the desk. In *Blood Simple*, however, Marty evinces no advantage on Visser, not even as his employer, and his confident posture belies his utter gullibility. This blocking strategy is repeated a second time after Marty has arranged to have Visser kill Abby and Ray in exchange for more money. Arriving in Marty's office, Visser hands him nearly identical photographs, hastily doctored to make it seem like Abby and Ray have been shot to death. Marty is convinced of their authenticity. Whether this is because he has—as Visser has already warned

him—"gone simple" out of rage and frustration or it is a reflection of some inherent mental block is ambiguous. Ironically, his inability to recognize faked gunshot wounds immediately precedes his falling victim to the real thing. "Who looks stupid now?" asks Visser as the smoke clears, as if it's not a rhetorical question. By pretending to kill Abby and Ray as a setup for murdering Marty–and in doing so, making off with a healthy fee for services not-actually-rendered–Visser seems pretty smart indeed.

Financially motivated double crosses are commonplace in the Coens' films. They figure into the plots of *Fargo, The Big Lebowski, The Man Who Wasn't There, Intolerable Cruelty, The Ladykillers, No Country for Old Men, Burn After Reading,* and *Hail, Caesar! Blood Simple* begins this tradition with a bang: Marty's death is staged as a shock moment, and the eerie silence that follows offers the audience a chance to catch its collective breath as the implications of

Visser's betrayal set in. *Blood Simple* is also the first example in the Coens' films of how even the keenest schemers are always undone by their own carelessness. Visser's plan is to implicate Abby in Marty's murder by using her pistol, which he then intentionally leaves at the scene of the crime. But in the process of deliberately planting evidence, he also accidentally leaves behind a cigarette lighter bearing his initials. It's a rookie mistake that once again begs the question, "Who looks stupid now?"

This is the first sign that Visser has himself gone (or simply is) simple. His sense of superiority, and the feeling that he's wormed his way into a bad situation and exploited it fully for his own gain, disappears. He succumbs to the same contagious, feverish paranoia that has infected the other characters. The resulting pileup of reckless misperceptions in the back half of *Blood Simple* represents the most sheerly complicated plotting of any of the Coens' films. While the impression is of escalating, bloody chaos, the screws are in fact turning in perfect synchronization, like the rotors of those ceiling fans, or the circular refrain of Carter Burwell's piano score.

There are four major characters in *Blood Simple*, and by the end of the film, three of them (Abby, Ray, and Visser) will be murderers. The fourth (Marty), meanwhile, winds up a corpse several times over. At different points in the story, each of them believes that they've killed Marty. Only Ray, unexpectedly finishing the job that Visser started by burying his badly wounded boss alive, is correct in this assumption. Visser's one true victim is Ray, whom he shoots with a high-powered rifle before trying to do the same to Abby. But instead, she survives the assault and kills Visser, thinking that he's Marty, a bit of mistaken identity that comically undermines her heroism as the last woman standing.

Frances McDormand's performance as Abby is one of the most compelling aspects of the film, and while she's far from an admirable character, the Coens consistently juxtapose her strength against the weaknesses of the three men circling around her. In one loaded bit of staging, she kicks Marty in the groin after he tries to attack her at their house, a calculatedly below-the-belt assault. Later, when Marty is having dirt shoveled on top of him by Ray, he tries to fire an

In its final sequences,
Blood Simple embraces a form
of abstract expressionism,
using the image of a wall
gradually punctured with
bullet holes to inject visual
drama into a narratively
suspenseful situation

empty gun in self-defense, recalling his earlier symbolic emasculation. Abby's seduction of Ray is the event that catalyzes the drama, but she is the only person in the film whose motivations are not driven by vengeance (Marty), avarice (Visser), or a foolishly guilty conscience (Ray). Recognizing that Abby's implication in the intrigue around her has nothing whatsoever to do with money is important. It introduces the generally ethical relationship of many of the Coens' distaff characters to money, including several played by McDormand. She is not only the morally inviolate Marge Gunderson in *Fargo*—an example of the sort of competent authority figure that never once manifests in *Blood Simple*'s frighteningly amoral, basically lawless universe—but also Doris in *The Man Who Wasn't There*, a very different sort of cheating-wife archetype who takes the fall for her husband's embezzlement scheme. (The exception would be McDormand's Linda Litzke in *Burn After Reading*, whose greed knows no bounds.)

The moment that Abby decides to stand up to her bullying, cruel husband and tell him that she's not afraid of him is also when she realizes—after hearing Visser's voice reply to her claim that she is no longer afraid—that she'll never have the chance. It's a satisfyingly unsatisfying irony driven home by the ingenious nature of the Coens' mise-en-scène, which plunges the action into patches of pitch-blackness. Abby has been "in the dark" for the duration of the film about what the men around her have been doing. She's oblivious not only that Marty has discovered her infidelity, but also that he'd hired Visser to follow her and Ray, and that Visser has framed her for the murder, and that Ray has actually killed Marty, and even that her life is in danger right up until the moment that Ray has been shot dead in front of her. The film's signature image is of shotgun rounds blasting through an apartment wall and creating shafts of light cutting through the black. It indicates Abby's dawning understanding about the life-or-death stakes of her situation.

It also hints at the impotent futility of the man firing the gun. Stuck in the bathroom adjacent to Abby's position, Visser can't hit his hidden target, even with multiple shots. It's the last in the film's series of references to diminished

THE FINAL GIRL
—
Abby is the last woman standing in *Blood Simple,* and the first of several uncommonly complex characters played for the Coens by Frances McDormand.

RED-HANDED
—
The brutal, gory violence near the end of *Blood Simple* admits the influence of eighties splatter horror films like *The Evil Dead*—a shock tactic that gives the climax a visceral kick.

THE WRONG MAN

—

Visser's killing by Abby is a case
of poetic justice delivered entirely
by accident; she thinks she's stood
up to Marty but she's really just
finished off a stranger.

THE LAST DROP

—

The first question-mark ending of
the Coens' career: Will Visser live
long enough to drink the droplet of
water pooling on the underside of
the bathroom sink?

male potency. One excuse could be that he's been wounded, and the shot of Visser being stabbed just above the knuckles by Abby a few minutes earlier is an uproarious visual pun: Following a series of mostly successful deceptions, the detective has been caught red-handed. The juxtaposition in this sequence between spare, abstract stylization and horror-movie gore anticipates the aesthetic balancing acts in films from *Fargo*, with its minimalist, crimson-on-snow-white color scheme, to *No Country for Old Men*, which makes similar use of a silhouetted bullet hole as a graphic element.

The Coens' love of turning their closing shots into existential question marks is also inaugurated here. We see a close-up of Visser lying prone on the ground, staring up at the pipes below a bathroom sink, which is leaking, and then a shot of droplets forming on the metal, taken from Visser's point of view. It's a move that rhymes with the first scene and the suggestion that we're meant to share the character's perspective on events. Mortally wounded, and bemused by Abby's misrecognition of him as Marty, his eyes widen as he realizes he might get one last drink of water before he expires. The film goes to credits

as the droplet starts to fall, which is just as easily interpreted as the filmmakers denying their villain even the tiniest scintilla of relief as it is Visser's consciousness cutting suddenly to black.

Either way, it's an anti–grace note whose viciousness is exacerbated by the upbeat soundtrack selection. The Four Tops' "It's the Same Old Song" plays for the third time in the film (the first time as jukebox background music; the second in ironic counterpoint to Ray mopping up Marty's blood in his office), but its significance is only truly revealed with this final spin. The original VHS release of *Blood Simple* substituted Neil Young's "The Believer" in its place, but the Coens' 2001 directors' cut confirms the song's importance as a thematic statement. The choice of a golden oldie emphasizes the Coens' debts to the older works they're drawing on: a not-so-tacit admission that *Blood Simple*'s bloodred harvest is a throwback to noir traditions. But *Blood Simple* is also a timeless story about the circular nature of violence and betrayal, and the song, like the ceiling fan, becomes its emblem of a constant, whirring, reciprocal cruelty without end.

Ray buries the nearly-dead Marty alive in *Blood Simple*, a clumsy murder that's halfway between righteous revenge and abject cruelty.

The "Short Stop" convenience stores in *Raising Arizona* allude to recidivist H.I.'s inability to stay out of prison for very long.

CRIME SCENES

The aftermath of "the colossal goatfuck out in the desert" sets the morbid, bloody tone for *No Country for Old Men*.

Ed Crane doesn't go to Nirdlinger's department store with the intent to kill Big Dave: when he escapes the scene of the crime without leaving a trace, he becomes *The Man Who Wasn't There*.

The triple-homicide that ends the first act of *Fargo* was not in fact based on true events, as the film's knowingly dishonest opening credits state.

Raising Arizona

RELEASE DATE
April 17, 1987
BUDGET
$6M
DISTRIBUTOR
20th Century Fox
Film Corporation
CAST
Nicolas Cage
Holly Hunter
Trey Wilson
John Goodman
William Forsythe
Sam McMurray
Frances McDormand
Randall "Tex" Cobb

WARNING!

THIS FILM CONTAINS

Paternal anxiety	21%
"Morning in America" skepticism	18%
Chuck Jones cartoons	13%
Road Warrior parody	11%
Huggies	10%
Flash photography	9%
Trailer-park chic	6%
Fireball explosions	5%
Unpainted furniture	4%
Dead bunnies	2%
Polish jokes	1%

THE FILM *RAISING Arizona* begins with a head-on shot of a police station height chart. The space is quickly filled by the convenience store robber H.I. "Hi" McDunnough (Nicolas Cage), who's being processed at the county lockup in Tempe, Arizona, en route to prison. After locking eyes with the female police officer taking his photograph, H.I.'s expression shifts from wry resignation to desperate yearning: It's love at first sight. The same cannot be said for Officer Ed (Holly Hunter), whose own face is an impassive mask, the camera lens serving as a frame for her personal and professional skepticism. This carefully designed introduction forces us to see H.I.—the film's narrator and protagonist—through Ed's eyes. The stark, black-on-white backdrop of the height chart raises a question that can't be answered in inches: How will this goofy dude with a Mr. Horsepower tattoo and unkempt cowlick measure up?

Beginning with Cage's half-sheepish, half-wolfish grin, *Raising Arizona* is fully endearing, a quality marking it as a departure from *Blood Simple* and its unlikable characters, who consistently measure up short. Abby's moment of triumph is undermined by her realization that it's not Marty who's been shot dead on the other side of the bathroom door; Visser's

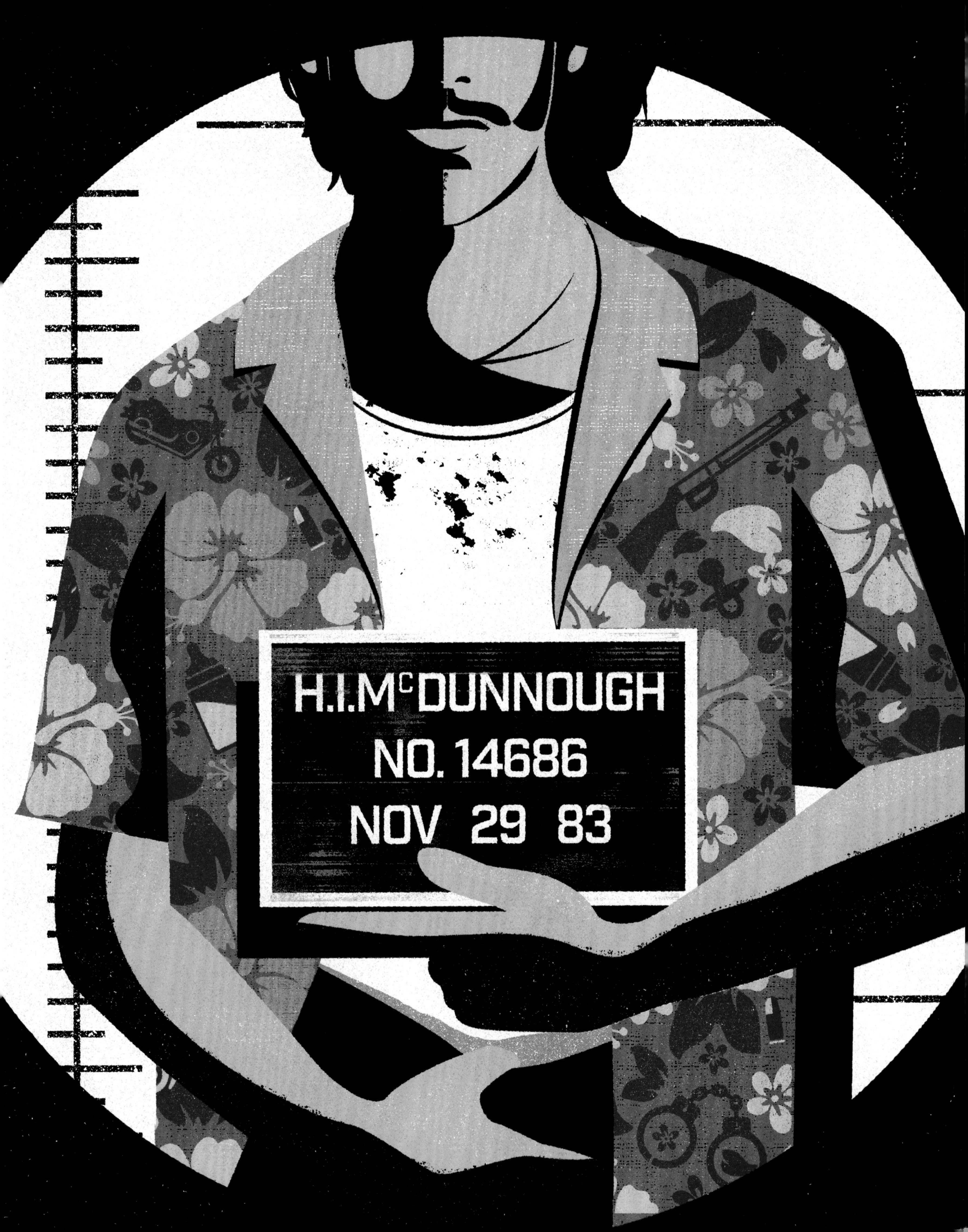
H.I.McDUNNOUGH
NO. 14686
NOV 29 83

DIAPER RUN

—

Where previously H.I. burglarized
convenience stores for money,
fatherhood finds him stealing
diapers. In both cases, the necessity
of theft to keep up with the high
cost of living is foregrounded by
the script and camera work.

MR. HORSEPOWER

—

H.I.'s tattoo symbolizes his
roughness but also an essential,
childlike sweetness; the cigar-
smoking bird Mr. Horsepower was
the logo for the 1950s hot rod
guru Clay Smith.

Top: H.I.'s attempts to confront
his own fears about domesticity
and parenthood generate a wealth
of mirror and doubling imagery in
Raising Arizona; after learning Ed
cannot conceive, he can barely look
himself in the eye.

Bottom: Throughout *Raising Arizona*,
the juvenile behavior of the Snoats
brothers is juxtaposed with H.I.'s
attempts to straighten up and
fly right. Here, they appear as
mischievous greasers in contrast
to their former cellmate's grown-
up grooming.

vindication of a worldview where "nothing comes with a guarantee" comes at the expense of his own miserable life. In *Blood Simple*, every encounter and exchange is a spring-loaded trap, and the Coens are quick to bring the hammer down. *Raising Arizona*'s world is more forgiving and spacious, with a greater freedom of movement for its characters and Barry Sonnenfeld's camera, which whirls and pirouettes through space with unchecked abandon.

Raising Arizona's extended prologue begins as a merry-go-round keyed to H.I.'s own circular trajectory in and out of jail. "Prison life is very structured, more than most people care for," H.I. confides over images of a maximum-security facility filled with slavering grotesques. The Coens duly fill in the blueprint via quick-cut montages connoting monotony: surveys of cellblock corridors; high-angled shots of convicts lying like sardines in their bunks; and slow pans through group therapy sessions that satirize psychotherapeutic boilerplate. The bearded, turtleneck-wearing prison counselor tells H.I. that most men his age are starting a family while the drawing board behind him shows a pie chart labeled "society at large," with a slice cut out representing "the missing piece." Nearly every shot in these passages contains a sight gag, and even the name of the chain of convenience stores H.I. targets nods to the revolving-door rhythm of his life: The neon sign reads SHORT STOP.

H.I.'s lack of self-control is obvious even as he attempts to pawn it off on external factors. "I tried to straighten up and fly straight," he muses, "but it wasn't easy with that sumbitch Reagan in the White House. . . . They say he's a decent man, so maybe his advisors are confused." The Reagan reference fixes *Raising Arizona*'s story in the context of the eighties' "trickle-down economics," and the Coens keep scribbling sociocultural subtext in the margins of the frame.

H.I.'s elderly cellmate sleeps beside a tiny photo of John F. Kennedy, although his stories of living in poverty to the point of having to eat sand don't exactly venerate the prosperity of an earlier era. When H.I., newly employed as an assembly-line worker by a massive manufacturing conglomerate (actually Hudsucker Industries, in a premonitory nod to *The Hudsucker Proxy*), goes to collect his paycheck, the cashier smiles, and says, "The government sure take a bite, don't she?" The action in these passages is syncopated to the sound of Ed, a pristinely uniformed embodiment of law and order, bellowing "Turn to the right!" in a foghorn voice. It was on the Gipper's watch that the US prison population exploded, along with the gap between rich and poor; if the political implication is intentional, it transforms the line into a triple entendre (on top of its sturdier double meaning as a choreographic command and a plea—sincere and quixotic, offered with love—for H.I. to change his ways). Keep turning to the right, however, and you're going to wind up in a circle. *Raising Arizona* finds its shape as a fable of a wayward man abandoning one loop for another. H.I.'s hastily arranged marriage to Ed, and their mutual desire for a child, is his best chance to break out of a pattern of repeat offense—"There's a name for what you are," sneers his parole officer. "Recidivism"— and plunge into the deeper fulfillments of the domestic sphere.

The difficulty of this transition captures a sense of contingency already expounded on in *Blood Simple*, which is that "something can always go wrong." The Coens' own aversion to recidivism at this early stage of their career means that *Raising Arizona* approaches the same idea from a different angle—not the fatalism of film noir but the cheerful recklessness of screwball comedy. Having learned that Ed is infertile ("Her insides were a rocky place where my seed could find no purchase"), the pair plan to kidnap one

of five babies born simultaneously to a wealthy couple upstate who tell the local media they have "more than they can handle." The allusion is to the unlikely octuplets in Preston Sturges's *The Miracle of Morgan's Creek* (1944), and also to the same simmering issues of class warfare and aspiration that animated Sturges's work on the whole; at its core, *Raising Arizona* is about haves and have-nots. There's a blunt rhyme between the shots of the cash-poor McDunnoughs Barcalounging outside their trailer-park "starter home" and the nouveau-riche Arizonas, Nathan (Trey Wilson) and Florence (Lynne Dumin Kitei), relaxing in their lushly appointed mansion, with the divisions between the two couples laid along economic and biological fault lines.

Raising Arizona was released amid a welter of parentally themed Hollywood comedies, including *Mr. Mom* (1983), *Baby Boom* (1987), and *Three Men and a Baby* (1987), all of which feature protagonists unexpectedly thrust into caregiver roles. The common theme of these films is that parenting–even if it's by proxy–unlocks heretofore unknown emotional and spiritual contentment, even as it tests the limits of patience and endurance. *Raising Arizona* follows a similar formula but yokes these tropes to a visual presentation that stylizes and hyperbolizes them to the level of a live-action cartoon. H.I.'s infiltration of the Arizonas' lavishly decorated nursery shows the Coens playing with scale: The infant's room is filmed from low angles and with wide-angle lenses so that spacial relationships are cartoonishly distorted, and the massive-seeming room is strewn with oversize stuffed animals and a gigantic novelty crib built to accommodate all five babies at once. The camera tracks and pans in rhythm with the infants as they crawl across the carpeted floor, blithely eluding H.I.'s grasp and leaving him wrung out and exhausted. Even before he's gotten one of the "critters" home, H.I. is overwhelmed with the responsibilities of his new role, which are heightened by his uneasiness at the paradox of having to break the law in order to achieve the normalcy he desires. Having made it home with Nathan Jr. in tow, he arranges a family portrait with a tripod-mounted camera, but the resultant black-and-white image shows the new father to be considerably less relaxed than in his original mugshot.

Cage's ability to seem frazzled without abandoning his basic, loose-limbed goofiness is crucial to *Raising Arizona*'s comic tone, even if by all accounts the actor didn't fully get along with the filmmakers. An interview with *American Film* in which Cage referred to the brothers' "autocratic" nature on set was widely circulated, and helped to cement the idea of the Coens as monomaniacal auteurs. Hunter, who the brothers met at the same time as Frances McDormand, was actually far more central to the film's conception: After turning down the role of Abby in *Blood Simple* (leading her Yale roommate McDormand to audition and get the part), Hunter remained part of their makeshift clique. A few years later, the role of Ed was written specifically for her. "It was the beginning of the exercise," Joel said in an interview with *Variety* in 2008. "It was us thinking, 'What would be fun to have Holly do?' So we thought: 'A police officer. Who wants a baby.' "

It's easy enough to draw a line from Hunter's work as Ed to McDormand's performance a decade later in *Fargo* as police chief Marge Gunderson; where Ed fears that she'll be defined by her infertility, Marge's pregnancy is the source of her moral authority. Ed's obsession with motherhood catalyzes *Raising Arizona* even though the film rarely privileges her point of view beyond that first look at H.I. For the most part, Ed exists in counterpoint to her husband, whose inner life, by contrast, is wide open to the audience via his voice-over. *Raising Arizona* is only superficially a portrait of a couple: Its real subject is H.I.'s anxiety, and the Coens conjure up a group of

Ed is introduced behind the camera lens, a prop whose presence suggests that she is scrutinizng H.I.'s potential as a husband and father as much as processing his arrest.

In *Raising Arizona*, parenthood is depicted as a life-changing event; a way for its characters to escape their respective ruts and redefine themselves. The perfectly balanced, symmetrical framing as H.I. and Ed watch a television broadcast about the birth of the Arizona quintuplets suggests a domestic stasis that is about to be upended by the arrival of a new (stolen) family member. The small gap between them will simultaneously widen and be filled when they kidnap Nathan Jr.

supporting characters whose major function is to reflect and refract his fears about fatherhood. The first of these are the Snoats brothers, Gale and Evelle (John Goodman and William Forsythe), previously glimpsed as H.I.'s cellmates but given a proper, showstopping entrance in a scene that travesties images associated with childbirth: They emerge—wet, screaming, and covered with mud—out of a hole in the prison yard. The brothers make a beeline for H.I.'s trailer, where Ed is wary of their presence and its effect on her husband, who proves susceptible to their feckless, adolescent outlook; they're like grotesque, overgrown teenagers taunting him for being under his wife's thumb. If the Snoatses represent the life that H.I. is trying to leave behind, his foreman, Glen, and his wife, Dot (Sam McMurray and Frances McDormand), register as a parody of domestic bliss, neglecting their own rambunctious children (they seem to have about half a dozen) and revealing themselves as swingers. Glen's wife-swapping proposal earns him a belt in the nose from H.I., who can't bring himself to tell Ed exactly how he was provoked and falls back on macho platitudes strangely at odds with his sensitive nature. "[You have] a man for a husband," he says firmly, "and that's the only answer."

The assault on Glen is played for laughs right down to the *boom-splat* sound effect when he flees face-first into a cactus, but H.I.'s show of aggression also heralds the last and most spectacular of the Coens' supplementary creations: Leonard Smalls, aka "The Lone Biker of the Apocalypse" (Randall "Tex" Cobb), an impossibly sinister, threatening figure who, in a startlingly assured mid-film detour into magic realism, leaps from H.I.'s nightmare into the real world, sitting tall astride a Harley-Davidson and armed to the teeth. (The Coens make sure to show that Ed is fast asleep while her husband tosses and turns. She may have her own guilty conscience, but we're not privy to it.) Whereas H.I. is a small-time criminal, Leonard is a pumped-up monstrosity, driving his motorcycle past the scene of the crime and all the way to Nathan Arizona's store, where he offers his (extravagantly priced) services as a tracker for the missing infant. The meeting between the furniture magnate and the bounty hunter unfolds beneath a panoply of whirling ceiling fans, a callback to the set design of *Blood Simple* and possibly a joke on the follow-up's increased size and scope. Their back-and-

forth dialogue establishes Leonard as an even more hideous version of Visser—a creature of pure mercenary malevolence—and culminates in a marvelous visual pun: When he leaves, the camera focuses on his still-smoldering cigar, as if to show that this devil incarnate has vanished in a Mephistophelean puff. H.I. switches places from kidnapper to anguished dad when the Snoats brothers steal Nathan Jr. to raise as their own adopted son; after they accidentally lose the baby in the aftermath of a bank robbery, he's snatched up by the biker, forcing H.I. into the unlikely role of action hero.

The frenetic, slapstick pace of *Raising Arizona* belies the complexity of the script's psychological architecture, particularly the way the Coens use Leonard as H.I.'s fun-house double. Both men feature in low-angled shots where they lean down to grab objects (H.I. a box of Huggies and Leonard a baby carrier) off the highway, and their final knock-down drag-out fight can be read as an interior struggle. A sudden close-up shows that Leonard has the same Mr. Horsepower tattoo as his opponent, and it's the last thing we see before the biker gets blown up by his own hand grenade. (It's a measure of H.I.'s essential sweetness that he mouths "I'm sorry" in the moment before the blast.) The impression is not simply of a hero overcoming a villain, but a man forcibly exorcising his own demons. Once Leonard is out of the picture, H.I.'s convulsive panic is replaced by a softer, more nuanced sort of melancholy.

There's a more flattering bit of mirroring in the scene immediately following Smalls's death, when H.I. and Ed return Nathan Jr. to the Arizona mansion and are stopped in the process by his father, who quickly intuits that they were the kidnappers and forgives them an instant later. Upon learning that his visitors are on the verge of separation due to their inability to conceive, Nathan's belligerence fades and he transforms, however improbably, into a sage. "You just gotta keep trying and hope medical science catches up with you, like Florence and me . . . It caught up with a vengeance." Where before the disparity between the two couples was played sardonically, now the Coens close the gap, placing the prosperous patriarch and the scraping would-be daddy on equal footing. Nathan's exit line, delivered by Wilson with a pure and disarming sincerity, is a beauty, unexpectedly reinstating the exultant romance of H.I. and Ed's first meeting: "I'd hate to think

NATHAN ARIZONA

—

At first, self-made salesman Nathan
Arizona projects a blustery, nouveau-
riche arrogance, but emerges as a
concerned father whose fears and
tenderness mirror H.I.'s own.

STICKUP

—

After kidnapping Nathan Jr.,
the Snoats brothers restage H.I.'s
comic diaper heists, reflecting
their temporary assumption of
parental responsibility.

It's never clarified
if H.I.'s hyperbolic,
subconscious fantasy
of domestic bliss is a
prophecy or a projection:
"It seemed real."

of Florence leaving me. . . . I do love her so."
He's able to convince H.I. and Ed to sleep on it,
which sets up *Raising Arizona*'s climactic dream
scene, a montage of possible outcomes for all of
the film's characters. Beneath Carter Burwell's
floating, music-box score, the Snoats voluntarily
go back to prison (an image that suggests a
return to the womb), Glen gets pulled over and
hassled by a traffic cop, and Nathan Jr. grows up
into a handsome blond boy with no memory of
his childhood trauma. We also see H.I. and Ed,
still married and affectionate in their old age,
receiving a gaggle of children and grandchildren
for a Thanksgiving meal at a table that stretches
on into infinity. H.I.'s yearning for normalcy has
been achieved, and his conscience is no longer
violent or unsettled. The life of his mind is serene,
with no demon bikers on the horizon.

It's a blissful vision, but ultimately no less
ambiguous than the antigrace note of *Blood
Simple*. If Visser's beady-eyed stare at the
dripping pipe implies some final, cosmic act
of denial, H.I.'s dream could be its inverse:
wish fulfillment taken to an extreme. Besides
anticipating conceptually similar finales in

Fargo, No Country for Old Men, and especially
The Man Who Wasn't There, the ending of
Raising Arizona introduces one of the Coens'
sturdiest recurring motifs, which is the
prospect of an uncertain future. Even within
the film's gently enchanted reality, there's
no way of knowing if what we're watching
is a genuine prophecy of things to come or
merely a projection of one man's desires.
Raising Arizona ends with a head-on look at
H.I., his reverie suddenly broken, staring up
at his bedroom ceiling. The composition of
the shot hearkens back to the opening height
chart and its implications of personal growth,
but the question of whether H.I. has truly
matured or remains a prisoner of his own
anxiety and naïveté remains very much open.
H.I. imagines a world where "all parents are
strong and wise and all children are happy
and beloved," which, while inspiring and even
moving, is difficult to take seriously in light
of all the comically flawed characters we've
already observed barreling through the film.
What H.I. is describing, even if he doesn't
quite speak its name, is Utopia, which is to say:
no place at all.

SWEET *dreams*

Near the end of *The Man Who Wasn't There*, Ed Crane imagines a UFO hovering over the prison he's been sent to, a teasing vision of escape into some better future.

Norville Barnes's daydream of dancing with a beautiful woman in *The Hudsucker Proxy* symbolizes his aspirations and also the elusiveness of inspiration.

Miller's Crossing begins by showing us Tom's recurring dream; he stubbornly refuses to interpret the meaning of a hat being blown away by the wind.

Raising Arizona shifts into magic realism when the Lone Biker of the Apocalypse springs from H.I.'s nightmare into the real world.

Sheriff Bell's vision of wandering through the wasteland with his father concludes *No Country for Old Men*; it also sets up the postapocalyptic premise of Cormac McCarthy's next novel, *The Road*.

There are numerous comically Freudian allusions in The Dude's hallucination in *The Big Lebowski*; the bowling pins/ball combo is a phallic symbol spurred by viewing a cheap porno.

Miller's Crossing

RELEASE DATE
October 5, 1990
BUDGET
$14M
DISTRIBUTOR
20th Century Fox
Film Corporation
CAST
Gabriel Byrne
Marcia Gay Harden
John Turturro
Jon Polito
J.E. Freeman
Albert Finney
Mike Starr
Al Mancini

WARNING!
THIS FILM CONTAINS

Dashiell Hammett	27%
Headwear	18%
Head shots	16%
Clandestine homosexuality	11%
Symbolic cigars	7%
Shootouts	6%
Punch-outs	5%
Irish ballads	4%
Racist slurs	3%
Godfather parody	2%
Barton Fink in-jokes	1%
Ethics	0%

"**A**LWAYS PUT ONE in the brain." That's the advice offered by mob boss Johnny Caspar (Jon Polito) right before he plugs his associate Eddie Dane (J.E. Freeman) in the back of the head. It's a murder that's been subtly masterminded by Tom Reagan (Gabriel Byrne), the ostensible subject of Johnny's advice but in fact the one who's administering the lesson. The only reason that Eddie Dane is lying prone on the floor in Johnny's office—the victim of a shovel blow to the head from his employer—is because Tom, who used to work for Johnny's archrival, Leo O'Bannon (Albert Finney), has planted the idea that the powerful henchman has been double-crossing his boss. Johnny's got the gun, but Tom, who's secretly trying to bring down Johnny's whole operation, is the one who's guiding the finger on the trigger. The sequence, which occurs late in *Miller's Crossing*, is ingeniously designed around a conceptual pun: Eddie gets his skull blown out entirely because of something that Tom has put in Johnny's brain.

Miller's Crossing is filled with such instances of manipulation. Tom is described as "the man who walks behind the man and whispers in his ear"; he's even introduced in the background of a shot that's focused more intently on Leo, a composition casting Tom as the power behind the throne. The Coens' third feature works with similarly subliminal finesse, planting suggestions in the viewer's mind and letting them expand over the course of its running time and long after the fact. The opening credit sequence ends on a shot of a black fedora being blown gently down an avenue of trees, a terrifically enigmatic image (with a hint of Magritte's surreal 1964 painting *Man in a Bowler Hat*) casting the film

as a kind of interpretive exercise. Or not, if the filmmakers are to be believed. "Everybody asks us questions about the hat, and there isn't any answer, really," said Joel Coen in an interview with Jean-Pierre Coursodon in 1991. "It's an image that came to us, that we liked, and it just implanted itself. . . . It's a kind of practical guiding thread, but there's no need to look for deep meanings."

Getting beneath the surface of *Miller's Crossing* is tricky because of the sheer size and instability of its narrative terrain. There's a lot of surface area to cover and almost none remains stable beneath the characters' feet, and it's made all the more complex to map out by how much of it has been trod before. Even more than in *Blood Simple*, the Coens draw inspiration in *Miller's Crossing* from the novels of Dashiell Hammett— not only *Red Harvest* and its all-out mob war, but also 1931's *The Glass Key*, about a gambler and racketeer trying to exonerate a politician from murder charges. Tom Reagan is a composite of The Continental Op from *Red Harvest*—the unscrupulous manipulator playing both sides

against the middle—and the more principled and loyal Ned Beaumont in *The Glass Key*.

For all his self-destructive flaws (namely drinking and gambling), Ned is a stalwart figure. His every action is undertaken in the hope of helping his embattled friend and boss Paul Madvig, reimagined by the Coens as the powerful and stubborn Leo, a man who can "trade body blows with [anybody] in this city." In *The Glass Key*, Ned and Paul find their firm bond threatened by a woman, Paul's young mistress, Janet; this dynamic is echoed in *Miller's Crossing* through the character of Verna (Marcia Gay Harden), who not only comes between the two men but is also poised to send the entire (unnamed) city around them spiraling into chaos.

In the film's first scene—which precedes the shot of the hat—Leo, who sits comfortably at the top of the city's criminal hierarchy, is approached in his office by Johnny Caspar, who comes bearing complaints. During a long, impassioned speech delivered directly to the

camera (shot to evoke the opening monologue in *The Godfather*), he tells Leo that a crooked bookie named Bernie Bernbaum (John Turturro) has been funneling the profits of fixed fights away from their rightful recipients–namely himself. (Bernie is also the name of the corrupt bookie in *The Glass Key*.)

Johnny believes that killing Bernie is a matter of "ethics," but Leo won't sanction Bernie's murder. Not because of any affection for Bernie: It's because he's romantically involved with Verna, who happens to be Bernie's sister. Tom is aware of the affair because he's also sleeping with Verna, a fact that he keeps hidden from Leo for as long as he can. Johnny is apoplectic, claiming that Leo is giving him "the high hat," a turn of phrase that anticipates the levitating fedora and confirms the importance of headwear within the film's symbolic system. The short-statured-and-tempered capo is willing to go to war over this slight, even though his certainty that Bernie is cheating him stems only from information he's gotten from Eddie Dane, whose motives are themselves deeply personal: "The Dane"

Top left: "Bad play, Leo." In the first scene of *Miller's Crossing*, Tom Reagan tells his best friend and boss that he's handling a volatile situation poorly-an analysis that proves correct.

Top right: The discovery of the body of Rug Daniels-found in an alley without his trademark toupee-draws attention to the importance of exposed scalps in the Coens' script: Uncovered heads are always associated with weakness and death.

The role of Leo O'Bannon in *Miller's Crossing* was written for Trey Wilson, but the actor's death a few weeks before shooting led to Albert Finney taking the part on short notice. Leo's great strength and resourcefulness are underlined in the sequence where he kills a pair of assassins who've been dispatched to his home; Finney's steely, physical performance sells the idea of the crime boss's potency even as the swirl of feathers associates him with a softness that plays out in the script's male romance.

is secretly involved with Mink Larouie (Steve Buscemi), a low-level hood who has recently also "jungled up" with Bernie.

Two-timing is a running motif in *Miller's Crossing*—everything from paying a boxer to take a dive to fooling around behind a lover's back. The concept of two-timing also applies in a different way: nearly every significant scene or exchange in the film is repeated twice, each time from a slightly different angle or with a different outcome. There are two scenes in which Tom storms into the swanky Shenandoah Club to confront somebody and ends up being punched in the face (first by Verna, then by Leo); two sequences where the local mayor and police chief receive marching orders from a mob boss (first Leo, then Johnny); even two monologues about the importance of putting a bullet in the brain during a hit. There are two fateful conversations between Bernie and Tom in the latter's apartment and two pivotal trips to Miller's Crossing, a wooded area on the outskirts of town littered with the bodies of casualties of the ongoing gang wars. In the first, Tom intends to execute Bernie before showing mercy. In the second, he's asked to show the evidence of the murder and is shocked to discover that there's a corpse lying in the spot where earlier, he'd let his quarry run free.

Nearly everything in *Miller's Crossing* has been doubled, and one way to look at the film is as a diagram of two love triangles that intersect at a series of precise, oblique angles, creating multiple planes of paranoia and betrayal. The Tom-Verna-Leo drama has been placed squarely in the foreground, resulting in an archetypal narrative scenario of two men who become divided over a woman. The details of the Eddie-Mink-Bernie arrangement are murkier, owing to the clandestine nature of their affair. *Miller's Crossing* is set in an unnamed American city during Prohibition, a time and place where this kind of desire has to remain safely closeted away, especially in the ruthless world of organized crime. In both triangles, a confident, physically powerful man (Leo/Eddie) is heartbroken to learn that his lover is carrying on with another, weaker figure (Tom/Mink). The parallels are directly strengthened by Verna and Bernie's status as siblings and social outsiders: They're Jewish, which is strongly implied to be a factor in Italian-American Johnny's loathing for Bernie.

The casting of the Roman-Catholic Turturro, whose mother was Sicilian, as a Jewish character is a provocative piece of ethnic masquerade that will be repeated in *Barton Fink*. One of the most troubling aspects of both films is the equivocation of Jewishness and grotesquerie, compounded by Bernie's sexuality, which marks him as deviant to the people around him. (The derogatory nickname of "Schmatte" has a double meaning in Yiddish, connoting both shabbiness and degeneracy.) It's not quite right to say that *Miller's Crossing* is homophobic, however; the gay elements of the film are carefully submerged but surface strategically to recontextualize the material's overwhelmingly masculine thrust. In taking on the gangster film, the Coens have crafted a work that simultaneously exalts and satirizes its traditions, as well as the alpha-male mentality at the center of the genre. Like the secluded stretch of forest referenced in its title, *Miller's Crossing* exists at a slight remove from its milieu, a fertile space somewhere in between homage, parody, and wryly rigorous critique.

Take, for example, the scene where Leo, who has, against Tom's advice, brushed off Johnny's request to hand over Bernie, fends off an assassination attempt by Johnny's goons in his home. It's a virtuoso sequence, scored to a phonograph recording of the traditional Irish ballad "Danny Boy," a soundtrack choice that emphasizes the character's old-world roots; the contrast between the soaring, melodic character of the music and the brutality of the action is humorous and powerful in the best Kubrickian tradition (and predates the "Stuck in the Middle with You" shtick in *Reservoir Dogs* by two years). Leo, who has retired for the evening and is clad in a resplendent red housecoat, is tipped off to the presence of intruders by smoke blowing up through the floorboards (a fire started by the lit cigarette dangling from the fingers of his deceased bodyguard) and snaps into action. The Coens signal Leo's readiness through a series of close-ups showing him armoring himself—bare feet sheathed into slippers; a pistol snatched with purpose off a bedside table; a smoldering cigar extinguished in an ashtray. Leo makes quick work of the gunmen who come to his door, dispatching one with Apollonian restraint—a shot to the ankle to drop him to the floor followed by, in anticipation of Johnny's methodology, one in the brain—and the other with a hilarious excessiveness, riddling his body

During Tom's first visit to Miller's Crossing he has Bernie at his mercy and chooses to spare his life—a decision that endangers his own. On the return trip, he finds himself at gunpoint and survives only because the Dane mistakes Mink's disfigured corpse for Bernie's. In both cases, the man at the wrong end of the gun is hatless, and thus diminished, while the would-be killers retain their headwear and stand tall.

The Coens often use fire imagery
to herald villainous characters.
The massive, exaggerated close-ups
on Johnny Caspar during *Miller's
Crossing*'s most violent sequence
combine with the flames to give
him a demonic aspect.

with machine-gun bullets, causing the victim to dance a "Thompson jitterbug" and in the process sending the proceedings into the realm of all-out pistol opera.

In a 2014 essay for *The Atlantic,* critic Christopher Orr argues that the "Thompson jitterbug" goes too far: "There goes the wall, there goes the chandelier, there go [the gunman's] toes. . . . A few seconds would have been fine, but the joke is prolonged to such bloody, tedious extravagance that it utterly upsets the flow of Leo's great escape." Certainly, the filmmaking here is self-consciously clever. The way the plumes of smoke give way to an all-out five-alarm fire as Tom's house goes up in flames literalizes the idea of a "slow burn." The choreography of the "Thompson jitterbug" nods to famous moments from *Bonnie and Clyde* and *The Godfather* while heightening the bloodletting to a surreal degree–the violence is orgasmically comedic. At the end of Leo's rampage, he retrieves his cigar from his breast pocket and chomps on it

contentedly; the scene is about establishing Leo's potency in the most hyperbolic terms possible. It's only in the aftermath of the shootout that Tom comes clean about himself and Verna, and Leo responds by beating his friend down, a show of power that rhymes with his earlier virtuosity—and plays up Tom's own inability (or unwillingness) to hold his own in the same way.

The late scene where Tom is visited in his apartment by Bernie is staged as a veritable replica of the assassination attempt on Leo, and the most overt instance of the screenplay's "two-timing." It begins with Tom in bed smoking a cigar (like Leo before him), realizing that somebody has broken in, and moving to confront them. The uninvited guest is Bernie, who Tom was supposed to have killed at Miller's Crossing (at Johnny Caspar's behest) but was instead allowed to escape with the condition that he not show his face in town again. Bernie's return puts Tom in a tight spot. And yet when he tries to defend his castle, moving to ambush

Bernie by dropping out his bedroom window just like Leo, he literally trips over himself, ending up helpless on his back in the hallway. Another visual pun: Tom has no slippers, and remains barefoot–he can't fill Leo's shoes.

The original title for *Miller's Crossing* was "The Bighead," a nickname the Coens worked up for their hero, who is acted by Byrne with a permanent furrow across his otherwise regular-size brow. Quiet, thoughtful, and disarmingly soft beneath his sleekly tailored exterior, Tom is a self-effacing punching bag, and in a film filled with hulking, violent brutes and mercenary thugs who tend to shoot first and ask questions (existential or otherwise) later. His contemplative nature is a potentially fatal flaw. He is, as the saying goes, a man who lives inside his own (big) head, and according to the film's production designer, Dennis Gassner, the spacious architecture and precisely ordered décor of his apartment is intended as a visual representation of his inner life. The ease with which Bernie repeatedly sneaks inside in the dead of night suggests the degree to which he's on Tom's mind–an intruder who needs to be cast out before his host can feel safe again in his own head.

No less than *Raising Arizona*, *Miller's Crossing* is a film that accesses its main character's subconscious, but from a far more oblique angle. Tom's feelings and motivations are as clouded—to him and to us—as H.I.'s are open and transparent, and his dreams are more enigmatic. When H.I. imagines himself sitting down at a massive dining-room table with his family gathered around him, it's easy enough to understand what he wants, even if the underlying question of prophecy versus projection remains wide open. Tom's confession to Verna of a dream in which the wind blows his hat away is cryptic right down to his stubborn refusal to interpret what it

might mean. "And you chased it, right?" she says. "You ran and ran and finally caught up to it and picked it up, but it wasn't a hat any more. . . . It changed into something else, something wonderful." "It stayed a hat, and I didn't chase it," he responds sharply, cutting off her attempt to frame the dream as a sign that he's lost something precious. It's as if this bighead doesn't know his own mind–or maybe he doesn't really want to. "Nothing more foolish than a man chasin' his hat," he concludes, summing up his essentially reticent nature.

There is a conspicuous irony here, which is that for the bulk of *Miller's Crossing*, Tom is in fact chasing his hat. Immediately following the opening credit sequence, he wakes up hungover and realizes that his head is bare and trudges over to Verna's apartment to retrieve it; every time he's placed in physical peril, the Coens take pains to show his hat either getting dislodged from his head or being plucked off by one of his enemies, as the Dane does in the second scene at Miller's Crossing, when it seems that Tom's lie about killing Bernie is going to prove fatal. Conversely, whenever Tom is in a position of power, including both times he has Bernie at gunpoint, his hat rests squarely on his brow. In fact, every time a character is killed in the film, he is shown to be hatless, a detail that alludes to the opening of *The Glass Key* and Ned Beaumont's discovery of a bare-headed corpse. "I'm only an amateur detective," he says, "but the hat seems like something that might have some meaning, one way or the other."

In Hammett's novel, the missing hat is a clue in a murder case; in *Miller's Crossing*, the multiplicity of hats has a metaphysical dimension. The most prevalent reading is that the hats in the film are signifiers of masculinity, which explains why the characters all seem

CHASING THE HAT
—
Every time Tom is in a bad position, the Coens show that he's been divested of his hat; here, an insert shot notes the fedora's position on the floor right before its owner gets brutalized by goons.

UNINVITED GUESTS
—
Verna's affair with Tom behind Leo's back carries an illicit charge, as do Bernie's cryptic allusions to sibling incest; as the sole major female character in a film ruled by rigid codes of masculine behavior, she becomes a chaotic, destabilizing presence.

empowered when they're wearing them and exposed or vulnerable otherwise. There may also be a simpler, more emotionally plangent solution. Whenever Tom pronounces "hat" with his Irish accent, it comes out sounding a lot like "heart." And for all the twists and turns of the film's plot—the question of who is working with who, and why—it's the delicate dichotomy between the concepts of "hat" and "heart" that unlocks the syntax of the Coens' poetry like a glass key.

Throughout *Miller's Crossing*, Verna accuses Tom of being cold and indifferent, and even calls into question whether or not he's got anything beating in his chest. "Admit it isn't all cool calculation with you," she pleads at one point. "That you've got a heart—even if it's small and feeble and you can't remember the last time you used it." Verna's words echo in Tom's head (and ours) when he fails to shoot Bernie at Miller's Crossing; like his sister, Bernie appeals to Tom's emotions, pleading with him to "look in [his] heart" over and over until the phrase becomes

an incantation. Bernie is successful in begging for his life, but later confides that it was all so much skillful manipulation. Like Tom, Bernie is a master of getting other people to do what he wants. When Tom confronts Bernie the second time, he's not so easily fooled. "What heart?" he scoffs before finishing Bernie off.

Tom's evolution from "the man who walks behind the man and whispers in his ear" to a man who faces his rival head-on and puts one in his brain for good measure is hardly a conventionally heroic arc, and there's something dubious about this lethal bit of self-actualization. In *Raising Arizona*, H.I.'s showdown with Leonard Smalls plays out as a man confronting the darker side of his personality, and the same is arguably true of Tom's murder of Bernie, which finds him regaining his hat once and for all but at the expense of his heart. *Miller's Crossing* ends by focusing on the Tom-Verna-Leo triangle because Eddie, Mink, and Bernie are all dead. The homosexual characters have been

The shot of Leo walking away from Tom at Bernie's funeral pays off Tom's dream of his hat flying away from him. In the dream, Tom doesn't chase the hat, and he doesn't go after Leo, either; he's too proud to chase his hat, or, given the film's subtle homoerotic subtext, his heart.

eliminated from the story, but Tom's murder of Bernie—and the sexual panic he embodies—hasn't necessarily purged him of his own secret desires. If *Miller's Crossing* is a love story, it's not between Tom and Verna, or even Verna and Leo, but Tom and Leo—a love that both men acknowledge even if they never quite speak its true name.

Coens scholar Jeffrey Adams writes that *Miller's Crossing* frames "the gangster world as a homo-social hideout from the sexual prohibitions of straight society," and cites both Tom's sadomasochism and a string of suggestive turns of phrase ("Gimme a stiff one") as evidence of the film's queer subtext, which is borne out by the staging and implications of the final scene. At Bernie's funeral, Leo, who has figured out that everything Tom did during the film was for his benefit—a way of protecting his interests and his empire—confesses that he's going to marry Verna but that he wants Tom to take his old job back, albeit in language that's anything but businesslike. "I need you," he says, with barely suppressed intensity. "Things can be the way they were."

Tom curtly rejects the offer and watches Leo walk away down the same quiet forest path glimpsed during the opening credits, recasting his dream as a premonition, similar to H.I.'s at the end of *Raising Arizona* but with the possibility and promise replaced by an ineffable sense of loss. The hat has in fact transformed into something else—it's turned into Leo. And Tom, true to his word, does not pursue him. There's nothing more foolish than a man chasing his hat, except maybe for a man who won't follow his heart.

ALWAYS PUT ONE IN THE BRAIN
—

The immaculate entry wound in Bernie's (exposed) scalp is the last of *Miller's Crossing*'s many head shots; after being instructed earlier in the film to "always put one in the brain," Tom makes sure that his first actual murder goes perfectly.

"WHAT HEART?"
—

Facing his rival one more time, instead of "looking in his heart," Tom admits—to Bernie and himself—that he no longer has one.

Michael Miller

EDITOR

FILMOGRAPHY

Raising Arizona (1987)
Miller's Crossing (1990)

A collaborator from the earliest days of the Coens' filmmaking, editor Michael Miller helped to give *Raising Arizona* its relentless screwball velocity and kept the complex narrative of *Miller's Crossing* in perfect balance. In this interview, he reflects on meeting Joel and Ethan in New York in the early 1980s and working with them as their careers were just beginning to take off.

You're unique in that you're the only real person who's been credited as an editor on the Coens' films. I mean, you're not a fictional character like Roderick Jaynes....

Actually, on *The Hucksucker Proxy*, Thom Noble was the editor. He might have been producer Joel Silver's choice; I'm not sure. But yeah, I'm the only editor to work with them on multiple films.

How did you get hired to work on the sound for *Blood Simple*?

My own memories are possibly slightly idealized, but I'll tell you exactly what I recall. It was a hot summer day in the early 1980s, and I was walking in midtown Manhattan. I ran into Skip Lievsay, who has been their sound designer ever since, and he said, "Oh, I'm on my way to meet these brothers from Minneapolis who are making an independently financed feature,"

which today sounds like a normal thing to say but in those days, it was really unusual. And he uttered two magic words that were kind of life-changing for me: "Wanna come?" I thought, "Ah, there'll probably be air-conditioning." So I met Joel and Ethan and they were hilarious. They showed us a scene or two from *Blood Simple*, and they talked a bit about how they raised money for the film, and I remembered thinking as I was leaving: "I have to work with these guys."

And then a couple of years later, they asked you to edit *Raising Arizona*.

I kept badgering them to cut down *Blood Simple*'s run time a little bit. And they went out to Hollywood trying to sell the film, which I think contributed as much to the writing of *Barton Fink* as anything, because people there kept telling them things like "We loved your film; of course, there's nothing we can do with it!" They would be offered, like, a *Weekend at Bernie's* sequel to direct, which I think is where the thing about the Wallace Beery wrestling pictures in *Barton Fink* came from. Anyway, in Hollywood, they kept hearing that they should cut ten minutes or so from the film. So they came back and let me work with them on trimming ten minutes out of it. That was my audition, and I guess I passed.

Did you have a window into their creative process at that time?

On *Blood Simple*, they said, "If you throw out an idea, be prepared to see it in the film because we will entertain the craziest suggestions." And they told a story about Mack Sennett bringing an inmate from the local asylum to story meetings, to throw around ideas that he called "Wildies." They loved Wildies. As for their actual creative process, I know they did a lot of writing in odd places back then. *Blood Simple* was written in Tom's Restaurant on 112th Street and Broadway, which is actually the exterior of the place that became the *Seinfeld* diner. And I remember them writing a scene for *Raising Arizona* in my cutting room one night while I worked on a piece for Twyla Tharp's Broadway production of *Singin' in the Rain*. Joel was lying on the floor smoking cigarettes, and Ethan was smoking a cigarette and pacing, and they starting going back and forth with what sounded like the ravings of two lunatics. But it was the beginnings of the "We ate crawdads" scene from *Raising Arizona*. It seemed like that was their writing process, to act these crazy things out for each other, which Ethan would then write down.

Was there a lot of talk about Preston Sturges during the editing of *Raising Arizona*? His influence on that movie seems almost total to me.

That influence is tremendously there, but it's so transformed by all the other film-viewing and filmmaking experiences they've had. I've always contended, half in jest—but only half in jest—that a lot of their visual framework comes from being downhill skiers in their childhood. So they wound up with this very modern, almost MTV-infused, Sam Raimi–infused version of Preston Sturges. But yes, they would talk about Preston Sturges. In fact, their nickname for me—a variation of Ratzkywatzky—is a reference to *The Miracle of Morgan's Creek*.

When you're talking about that downhill-racer quality, you certainly see that in the way parts of *Raising Arizona* are shot, but maybe you can also talk about that in terms of how it's edited. The cutting is so swift.

I'm very proud of my work on that film, but I have to say in some ways it's one of those films that cut itself. It wanted that pace. Holly Hunter performed at that pace. And it was clear that they had made a screwball comedy, which had to move that fast and the wonderful thing about having all this great coverage that they had is that you could manipulate it to move even more quickly than the actors had.

Is there a particular example?

I think of when Ed says, "Don't you come back here without a baby"—we cut that beat down to one twenty-fourth of a second. Another example of that is, "Son, you've got a panty on your head": The car takes off before Nicolas Cage has finished his last line of dialogue, and it's like you're trying desperately to keep up with the film as it rockets ahead. That kind of cutting is all over the movie.

The opening sequence, with "Ode to Joy," has this breakneck momentum to it, and it's all totally syncopated and controlled. It's hard to tell if the images are driving the music or the other way around.

Most directors use temporary music tracks while they're cutting their films. The Coens don't. For the beginning of *Raising Arizona*, they always wanted to use Pete Seeger's "Goofing-Off Suite" with the Beethoven and the Stravinsky. It was always in their heads, but we didn't put it in during editing. I learned not to use temp score from them. And to this day I try to wait as long as I can to add music because music is very forgiving, and it makes whatever you've cut when you add the music—no matter how loose or imperfect—seem fine. With Joel

and Ethan, we worked scenes to within a frame of their lives because temporary score wasn't in there to forgive anything. For the "Danny Boy" scene in *Miller's Crossing*, even with the song in the script, we didn't use it while we were cutting the sequence.

You anticipated something I was going to ask when I got to *Miller's Crossing*, because that, a bit like the opening montage of *Raising Arizona*, has a self-contained quality. It's something that I think in their cinema has receded a bit, which is the idea of these sort of obviously show-offy set pieces.

I don't want to say it's a sign of maturity because I love the "shootout at Leo's" scene, even though it is almost a stand-alone moment in the film. The Motion Picture Editors Guild did a survey where the membership listed the hundred best edited films of all time, and I'm very proud that *Miller's Crossing* is on that list, even though I know it's, at least in part, because of this very show-offy scene. But the scene is really just a bunch of master shots strung together, all these short little shots: the slippers, the cigar in the ashtray, the chandelier. Short masters. Don't get me wrong. It was a lot of fun to cut. But the opening scene of the film is more interesting to me. Any long

dialogue scene with a lot of coverage is the heavy lifting of film editing.

I've read that the Coens had a very bad time writing *Miller's Crossing* to the point that they actually started *Barton Fink* as a way to get over their writer's block.

I think that whenever they would hit a wall on anything, they would start another screenplay, and continue and then go back to what they had hit a wall on. Interestingly, I was just going through old keepsakes and found my *Raising Arizona* crew jacket. There's a patch on it that says Hudsucker Industries. So they were already well into *Hudsucker* and I guess hit a wall on that when they were writing *Raising Arizona*. *Miller's Crossing*, I'm told, was one of those things that was written in fits and starts.

It's all about dialogue, that movie; the words are more kinetic than the camera.

Yes. One of the things that I find amazing about that film is its insistence, through the use of dialogue, that America was not a melting pot. That Irish stuck with the Irish and they spoke with thick brogues, and the Italians stayed with the Italians, and Germans sounded German, and nothing melted. But one thing that's paramount when you're editing dialogue is clarity; it's always of the utmost importance. So I urged them to get ADR on the landlady in *Miller's Crossing* because when she says "There were shots," it sounds like "They wore shorts." They left it sort of unintelligible, though, because for them that was the point.

In *Miller's Crossing* there's a lot of ethnic stratification and diversity, even though it's a fictional city. Johnny Caspar's problem with Bernie seems to be related to his Jewishness as much as anything else.

Yeah, and maybe my favorite sentence in the entire film, speaking of Bernie's Jewishness, is "They're planting the sheeny." Does it get better than that? I don't think so! There is so much of that. I don't know if you've heard this story but they were asked why they wrote *Miller's Crossing* and they said, "Well, you know, we got a letter from a viewer who had seen *Raising Arizona* and he said, 'Hey, next time you want to make fun of a group of people why don't you make fun of your own, the Jews?'"

I hope that person lived to see *A Serious Man*.

By the way, I think that movie is a complete masterpiece. I mean, I can't say enough good things about it. It's the film that you make after you win the Academy Award for Best Picture because it's the only time you'll ever get a chance to make that movie. And they didn't squander the opportunity; they just made a masterpiece.

Is it worth asking about people's heads–heads and hats and toupees in *Miller's Crossing*? Not to put you on the spot, but can you talk about how central hats were to planning out the structure of the movie? I'm not putting you on the spot, but maybe just in terms of cutting the movie and talking about it in the same way, can you—not verify—but can you talk about how central hats were to planning out how this movie's going to be put together?

Sometimes a hat is just a hat, right? I think one of the huge influences on that film from a visual point of view was *The Conformist*. . . . I mean there's the model for all the hat stuff. It says a lot that Johnny Caspar doesn't wear a hat, and that his bald head is very exposed, which is a sign of vulnerability. The fighter doesn't wear a hat, and when he does he wears a funny hat.

What about the scene at *Miller's Crossing* with Tom and Bernie? That's as spectacular as the shootout in a different way.

That scene is also sort of an example of the Wildie. Performance is one of the things that can get lost in conversations about the Coen brothers, but it's the basis of film editing. You have an almost ethical obligation to use the best takes. If you have a performance like [John] Turturro's in that scene, and you have one take or two or three takes out of fifteen that just knock you on your butt, then you have to ignore match cutting and continuity and use those takes because you can't deprive the audience of the very thing that just knocks you out. And Turturro didn't hold back. The Wildie there is in the excess—he just kept going and going, and

the walk into the woods goes on and on. There are directors who would have wanted to cut it all down, but they didn't.

You have this unique insight into how they edit their films because you say you're one of only two people to work with them in that capacity. Since *Hudsucker*, they've done it all themselves. Do you see a real difference in the way *Miller's Crossing* was edited versus *The Man Who Wasn't There*, or is it negligible?

I see it. I do see a difference. But I have a very specific way that I edit. There isn't a film of theirs that doesn't have exactly the pace it should and exactly the tone it should, which to me are what you need an editor for anyway. I think that they're great editors. Several years ago, and I don't remember which film this was on, more than several years now, quite some time ago, I opened up the Sunday *New York Times* and saw a full page ad for one of their films, and Roderick Jaynes gets a paid ad. And I thought, this has gone on so long, why doesn't it say Roderick Jaynes ACE? And I went to the American Cinema Editors and proposed that we give a membership to Roderick Jaynes, and their board didn't agree. My sense has always been that Roderick Jaynes's name is on *Blood Simple* to give *Blood Simple* production value. They wanted the world to think they could actually afford an editor. And I think it's a sign of respect for editing that they take on a different role and pretend to be somebody else while they do it. I think they're great editors. So great! It's funny to me because they get hired to doctor scripts all the time, but no one ever hires them to edit.

Barton Fink

RELEASE DATE
August 21, 1991
BUDGET
$9M
DISTRIBUTOR
20th Century Fox
Film Corporation

CAST
John Turturro
John Goodman
Judy Davis
Michael Lerner
John Mahoney
Tony Shalhoub
Jon Polito
Steve Buscemi

WARNING!
THIS FILM CONTAINS

Clifford Odets jokes	20%
William Faulkner jokes	18%
Louis B. Mayer jokes	15%
Peeling wallpaper	12%
Anti-Semitic paranoia	10%
Clogged drains	7%
Common men	6%
Existential dread	5%
Kubrickian hallways	4%
Nazi salutes	3%

IN CLIFFORD ODETS'S 1949 play *The Big Knife*, a wildly successful movie star comes to feel stifled by his ironclad studio contract. Having built his celebrity–and fortune–acting in shlock, Charlie Castle decides he wants out, but gets blackmailed back into subservience by his unscrupulous bosses, who, he knows, have got him right where they want him. Odets wrote *The Big Knife* as a reaction to his desultory experiences churning out screenplays in Los Angeles in the 1940s, after he'd already made his name as a groundbreaking, left-wing playwright in New York's famed Group Theater. By this logic, the fatally frustrated but ethically clear-eyed Charlie Castle was his alter ego, a man of principles who can't access them until it's too late, at which point he bravely proves willing to die on their behalf.

In *Barton Fink*, the Coens reimagine Odets via John Turturro's title character as a self-absorbed striver whose only convictions have to do with his own greatness. (His eventual punishment is a fate worse than death—a comeuppance that falls neatly in line with the Faust myth that gave Odets his own inspiration.) The film enfolds the plot and themes of *The Big Knife* into its story of a screenwriter toiling away on assignment for a Hollywood studio in 1941, and its narrative has also been structured to reflect aspects of Odets's real life, opening with a direct reference to the great playwright's penchant for self-dramatization: The story begins at a performance of Barton's new (and, it's implied, celebrated) Broadway play *Bare Ruined Choirs*, an apparent roman à clef about "The Kid," a brilliant writer whose

gifts are going to take him far away from the crowded tenements and modest fishmongers of his native Brooklyn.

Here, the Coens deliberately travesty Odets's work, twisting it into a parody of stolid proletarian drama. Having announced his intentions to depart, The Kid, who is surely Barton's self-portrait of the artist as a young man, is given a fawning send-off by his friends and family, who are delighted to simply serve as inspiration for a visionary writer. The implication is that The Kid will take the "bare ruined choir" of the title and "make it sing," using his position to amplify the working-class cacophony that is his muse, even as he yearns to put as much distance between it and himself as humanly possible.

In his Contemporary Film Directors book on the Coens, R. Barton Palmer points out that the dialogue in *Bare Ruined Choirs* echoes Odets's own play *Awake and Sing!*, originating the string of direct and indirect quotations that give *Barton Fink* its structure as a kind of meta-textual spiderweb. Where *Miller's Crossing* riffed in a very focused way on the narrative and thematic universe of Dashiell Hammett, *Barton Fink* extends its frame of reference well beyond the works of Clifford Odets, and may be the Coens' most densely allusive film (with the possible exception of *The Big Lebowski*). Several of its major characters are, like Barton, stand-ins for well-known figures, including Jack Lipnick (Michael Lerner), the head of Capitol Pictures,

who invites Barton to Los Angeles to write screenplays on retainer and is based in equal measures on Louis B. Mayer and Jack Warner, and W.P. Mayhew (John Mahoney), a white-haired, alcoholic novelist transparently modeled on William Faulkner, who befriends Barton and whose secretary, Audrey (Judy Davis), becomes Barton's lover.

What's startling and troubling about *Barton Fink* is the apparent lack of reverence it has for its reference points–again, in contrast to *Miller's Crossing*, which honored Hammett's style and themes. The script tears into the myth of Clifford Odets with a viciousness that's hard to account for, and it's no less unsparing when it comes to its faux-Faulkner, who, it's implied, hasn't written half of the masterworks bearing his imprimatur. This brashness could be seen as the by-product of the Coens' own ambition circa 1991—the desire of up-and-comers to be taken seriously, on the same elevated playing field as their inspirations. But as *Barton Fink* is also very explicitly a cautionary tale about artistic arrogance and delusions of grandeur, it might be truer to say that the film's irreverence is meant playfully, rather than punitively. It's also the Coens' first real attempt to move beyond mere tropes to engage with actual cultural history: The film goes further in its social and political implications than any of its predecessors, even as it plays out as a claustrophobic psychodrama that never strays too far from its protagonist's addled consciousness.

Like Tom Reagan, Barton Fink is a "bighead." (Quite literally: Turturro's frizzy hairdo is nearly as elongated as Jack Nance's iconic coif in *Eraserhead*.) The throwaway joke in *Miller's Crossing* of a hotel called The Barton Arms cinches the link between the two films. Just as Tom Reagan's spartan but spacious apartment serves as an illustration of his inner life, so too does the eerie, dilapidated interior of the Hotel Earle—Barton's temporary residence after accepting Lipnick's job offer and heading to California—conform to the contours of its new tenant's psyche. When *Barton Fink* won an unprecedented three awards at the 1991 Cannes Film Festival, the president of the jury was Roman Polanski, and it was widely speculated that his admiration for the film was tied, to some extent, to his suspicion that the Coens were paying homage to his so-called apartment trilogy of *Repulsion*, *Rosemary's Baby*, and *The Tenant*—psychological thrillers about characters driven mad by their environment.

The model for this mode is Charlotte Perkins Gilman's chilling 1892 short story "The Yellow Wallpaper," about a disturbed woman who is driven mad by the décor of her rented home;

Left: Barton's play *Bare Ruined Choirs* is based on the socially conscious theater of Clifford Odets; the Coens show the cast's curtain call from Barton's point of view, hinting that he may crave a similar spotlight.

Bottom: Barton's arrival at the Hotel Earle emphasizes his new home's slightly dilapidated luxury, as well as the contrast between its shadowy, interior world and the sunny Los Angeles weather.

The "yellow wallpaper" of Barton's room at the Hotel Earle nods to the title of Charlotte Perkins Gilman's chilling short story of mental deterioration.

the wallpaper in the Hotel Earle is not only yellow, but ripped and peeling as well. Barton has chosen to stay there as a self-conscious act of defiance against his new employers, who would be happier to put him up on the lot. Staying there gives him the sense of distance he needs to feel in his new role as a writer-for-hire. Barton's decision to go to Los Angeles exposes *Bare Ruined Choirs* as a thinly veiled aspirational fantasy and casts doubt on his stated claim that his work—past, present, and future—is intended solely for the edification of "the common man." Everything about Capitol Pictures, starting with its name, points to a mercenary mindset, and Barton's internalized guilt and doubt over selling out has led him to a locale whose architecture is expressive of entrapment (the elevators and corridors are oppressively narrow), paranoia (sound travels easily between the rooms), and psychic anguish (everywhere, there are clogged pipes).

Barton's next-door neighbor at the Hotel Earle is Charlie Meadows (John Goodman), whose given name may be yet another reference to *The Big Knife* and yet exists in crucial counterpoint to Turturro's character. If Barton Fink and Lipnick and Mayhew represent disguised versions of specific figures, Charlie is very much a type: an original creation who's nevertheless immediately recognizable in terms of his appearance and manner. Charlie is a hail-fellow-well-met sort whose massive body is a container for boisterous good spirits, and Goodman's wide smile and hale-and-hearty manner evoke his endearing lead performance in David Byrne's quasi-musical *True Stories*, where he sang the uplifting anthem "People Like Us." That same phrase gets tweaked during Barton's introduction to Charlie, when he informs him that "people like [him]" are his métier—that he wants to create "a theater for the masses that's based on a few simple truths, not on some shopworn abstractions."

The joke, of course, is that Charlie is precisely such a shopworn abstraction, and it's the comic energy that gets charged up between these two characters—the Clifford Odets manqué and his eager muse—that drives *Barton Fink* forward (indeed, Ethan Coen once called the film a "buddy picture"). It's crucial that Barton hears Charlie before he sees him: He calls the hotel's front desk to complain about the sound of weeping bleeding through the walls. The leftist playwright committed to amplifying the suffering of "the common man" is bothered by the sounds of his anguish, which keep him from focusing on the task at hand: churning out a script for a melodrama about a wrestler slated to star Wallace Beery. But Barton's obliviousness runs deeper. Not only does he talk down to Charlie during their initial conversation, but he also won't listen to a word the man says. He doesn't take his neighbor up on his friendly offer to "tell [him] some stories" because he clearly believes that he is the one qualified to share those narratives, or else make new ones out of thin air. This despite the fact that he's struggling with the supposedly rote assignment of the wrestling script, which has already been more or less narrated to him in advance by Lipnick, whose droning inventory of desired elements ("hopes and dreams"; "a bad element"; "a romantic interest") clashes with Barton's desire to be a brilliant original.

THE PRODUCER

—

"I'm bigger and meaner and louder than any kike in town"; Capitol Pictures boss Jack Lipnick bowdlerizes and bewilders Barton from their very first meeting in his office.

CHECK OUT ANY TIME YOU LIKE

—

Barton signs into the Hotel Earle's guest ledger and sees he's just one of countless travelers who've stayed there; the long list of signatures mocks his solipsistic egotism.

The title character of
Barton Fink is a playwright
who knows less about human
nature than he thinks.
While the supposed socialist
Barton can't imagine "the
common man" in more than two
dimensions, his neighbor at
the Hotel Earle actually
contains multitudes.
Charlie Meadows's cheerful
demeanor masks darker, more
frightening impulses, but
he's also a life force.
Smiling and fondling a
pornographic playing
card—a burst of color and
sensuality against the
Hotel's drab, dead aesthetic-
he's everything that the
anal-retentive Barton
has repressed.

Even as *Barton Fink* satirizes Odets's aspirations to socially conscious drama, it styles itself as a social allegory. The first signal moment occurs when Charlie finally convinces Barton to let him give him some advice in the field of wrestling holds, the idea being that a practical understanding of actual maneuvers will give his screenplay some authenticity. In an instant, the initial dynamic between the two men is reversed. Barton's haughty sense of superiority is literally upended as he's crushed beneath Charlie's gigantic bulk. The satisfaction of seeing Barton squirm aside, the scene unfolds as a collage of multiple interlocking contrasts: strength (intellectual versus physical); class (the playwright versus the insurance salesman); and sensibility (the thinker versus the man of action).

Charlie cheerfully lets Barton up off the ground shortly thereafter, but his power has been confirmed. Their roughhousing not only reframes *Barton Fink*'s "buddy movie" dynamic to favor Charlie—now clearly seen as the stronger of the two men—but also inscribes the idea that *Barton Fink* is itself a "wrestling picture," in which the featured combatant's physical frailty is ultimately less of a liability than his moral and intellectual weakness. Barton follows up this literal wrestling lesson with a figurative one: After letting it slip that he's having trouble with his script, he's wrangled by Capitol Pictures producer Ben Geisler (Tony Shalhoub) into a private screening of some dailies from a similarly themed movie. The footage shows a gargantuan grappler advancing menacingly on his opponent, although the Coens' cutting implies that his real target is Barton, whose fevered anxiety is illuminated by the projector bulb burning behind him in the empty movie theater.

This massive, threatening figure contains multitudes: He's an emblem for the monolithic power of the movie industry bearing down on Barton's slender shoulders, pinning him down despite the lightweight parameters of his assignment. He's also a physical double for Charlie, "the common man" who Barton at once fears and resents, and whom he's trying to animate through his own work. Palmer suggests that the wrestler and Charlie are twin versions of a golem, a creature derived from Jewish mythology, molded out of clay by a rabbi trying to save his village from a pogrom. This interpretation holds insofar as Charlie arguably becomes Barton's own private golem as the movie goes on, acting out his darkest impulses and serving as his protector whenever he becomes threatened. There is yet another way to read this sequence, however, and it's also tied to Barton's Jewishness: Each of the rushes is identical, composed of a shot of the wrestler moving toward the camera, bellowing a single line, "I will destroy him!" The choice to give him a heavy German accent—"I vill destroy him!"—adds yet another layer of meaning; whereas Barton condescends to "shopworn abstractions," the Coens work dexterously to prove their potency.

Not only does the image of the heady Jewish intellectual cowering at the sight of a German aggressor evoke one of the darkest chapters of twentieth-century history, but the date on the clapboard for the rushes, December 9, 1941 (two days after the Japanese attack on Pearl Harbor, which led to America's entry into World War II), does as well, and more explicitly. The action in *Barton Fink* never strays from Los Angeles, and even then rarely from the cramped confines of the Hotel Earle, but the terrible events occurring overseas keep manifesting themselves even in this seemingly secure coastal context: It is revealed that all-American Charlie may have a secret identity as a serial killer with the Germanic moniker of "Karl Mundt," and the detectives who give Barton this information are surnamed "Deutsch" and "Mastrionotti," in effect transforming them into avatars of the Axis powers. "Fink. . . . That's a Jewish name, isn't it?" sneers Mastrionotti, redoubling the historically and culturally specific anxiety embedded in the image of the German wrestler.

Cornered by a group of angry Marines at a USO show, Barton argues that as a creator, he does more for his society than the men who fight overseas to protect it; he vainly claims his brain is his weapon.

With the revelation of Charlie's murderous extracurricular activities—his M.O. is to kill victims with a shotgun and then decapitate them—*Barton Fink* begins its uncanny mutation from a sophisticated literary satire to a wildly stylized horror movie filled with gory mutilations and Polanskian paranoia. Having failed to derive creative inspiration from Mayhew–whose status as a pathetic drunken wreck obliterates the idea that a great writer is ultimately any happier than "the common man"–Barton makes a connection with Audrey, who has been ghostwriting the older author's manuscripts for years. They sleep together, and in the morning, Barton awakens to find his lover dead, stabbed to death in bed beside him (the big knife used to dispatch her is never shown). Barton has no memory of committing the murder, and he desperately asks Charlie for help with disposing the body. The latter's enthusiastic assent not only fits Palmer's conception of Charlie-as-golem, but also hints that he may in fact be the guilty party, acting decisively under cover of night while Barton's conscience stays clean.

Perversely, Audrey's death serves as a catalyst for Barton completing his script, and he celebrates by going to a USO dance in honor of servicemen about to ship out to the European theater. Turturro's physical acting in this sequence is extraordinary, as Barton sheds his inhibitions and cuts loose on the dance floor with a beautiful woman in a red dress (a figure of desire that will return in *The Hudsucker Proxy*). Even in a moment of triumph, however, Barton's obnoxious, serious-artiste persona takes over, and he lashes out at the soldiers, suggesting that his work on the home front is more important than their service overseas. "I'm a writer, you monsters! I create. . . . This is my uniform!" The condescension Barton displays here is nearly identical to the way he treated Charlie, and his comeuppance is similarly physical: He gets belted in the jaw and knocked down, then scuttles away while what was intended to be a pageant of military discipline descends into a frantic riot.

The free-for-all at the USO show is an excuse for a series of sight gags, but it also introduces the other major literary influence on *Barton Fink*: Nathanael West's *The Day of the Locust*, written in 1939 and concerning a Hollywood set painter living in a dilapidated hotel—a setting very close to the Hotel Earle. West's protagonist is named Tod Hackett, and while Tod believes he is a great artist, his surname implies that he is anything but; like Odets in *The Big Knife*, West is trying to undermine the self-mythologizing aspect of the movie industry. In the book's climax, a glitzy premiere becomes the epicenter of a violent mob uprising, with the fury directed at the presumptuousness and inauthenticity of Hollywood itself. West's theme is the way that social frustration bubbles up from underneath; the book has been interpreted as a cautionary allegory for an American variant of the fascism that had already taken hold in Germany at the time of its publication. *The Day of the Locust*

Top left: The massive German wrestler observed by Barton in the dailies for Capitol's new wrestling picture is both a double for Charlie Meadows and a symbol of the writer's anxiety that he's up against larger forces.

Bottom left: "Heil Hitler!" The strangest and most suggestive piece of dialogue in Barton Fink positions Charlie as either an avatar of American strength against fascism or a closet Nazi— "Madman Mundt" speaking in his mother tongue.

is filled with voices straining to be heard—a motif that the Coens brazenly borrow for the introduction of Charlie, with his disembodied weeping bleeding through Barton's wall. And, at the end of *Barton Fink*, Charlie transforms into a one-man *Day of the Locust*, except that instead of directing his rage at Barton, he lays waste to the detectives who've come to arrest Barton for Audrey's murder.

Charlie's rampage recalls the rushes of the wrestler, right down to the relentless repetition of a single line: not "I will destroy him," but "I'll show you the life of the mind!" The expressly demonic presentation in these sequences, with the Hotel Earle consumed by flames, implies that to look upon the "life of the mind" is to be immolated; as in West, the repressed anger of "the common man" finds monstrous expression. The Coens complicate things by having Charlie punctuate his murder of the detectives with an enigmatic whisper of "Heil Hitler," which either confirms his essentially fascist nature—that he is in fact "Madman" Karl Mundt—or else is meant sarcastically, in all-American defiance of the German and Italian men tormenting his friend and neighbor Barton Fink. Either way, the

sequence plays out with Barton handcuffed to the bed in his hotel room, helpless to intervene and forced, finally, to receive Charlie's lesson about the "life of the mind," which in this case proves to be well beyond the playwright's supposedly protean powers of imagination.

Barton is freed from his shackles but ends the film in chains. His wrestling script disappoints Lipnick, who responds by informing him that he will remain under contract to Capitol Pictures for the foreseeable future, but that the studio won't produce anything that he writes until he "grows up a little." Certainly, it's a stretch to see the vain, vulgar, pompous Lipnick, who arrives for their meeting done up in a military costume to underline his authority, as a mouthpiece for the Coens' own views on Barton's skills as a writer. The studio boss's condescension toward the mass audience and what he believes they want— "action, drama, wrestling"—displays no more empathy or solidarity than Barton, while his militant support of the war effort suggests a similar insecurity or ambivalence about his own role as a Jewish man on the home front. (His costume is also based a bit on possibly apocryphal gossip: Jack Warner reportedly

roamed around the studio lot dressed as a general.) Still, Lipnick's critique of Barton as an "arrogant sonofabitch" rings true enough that it feels like the last word on the character, whose punishment of well-paid servitude at the expense of his voice ironically fits his crime of broadcasting his selfless virtue to anybody who would listen.

The carefully jerry-rigged enigmas at the end of *Barton Fink*, including Barton's sudden appearance on a deserted beach modeled on a postcard hanging in his room at the Hotel Earle, and his stewardship of a mysterious package bequeathed by Charlie, are, like the hat in *Miller's Crossing*, tantalizing invitations to interpretation. They're also finally less important than the understanding that Barton, whose fantasies of escape were plain enough in the text of *Bare Ruined Choirs*, has, by arriving at his destination, become entrapped for all time. In *Bare Ruined Choirs*, a character prophesies the hero's success by saying, "We'll be hearing from that kid again, and I don't mean a postcard." As Barton wanders along the coastline, we see that he's taken his place inside the postcard, never to be heard from again.

BEHIND EVERY GREAT MAN
—
The alcoholic novelist W.P. Mayhew is as thinly veiled a stand-in for William Faulkner as Barton is for Clifford Odets; the Coens tear into Faulkner's myth by suggesting that Mayhew's secretary, Audrey, is the true author of his books.

AXIS POWERS
—
The detectives dogging Barton at the Hotel Earle are surnamed Deutsch and Mastrionotti—German and Italian monikers that bounce provocatively off Barton's Jewishness.

COENPLEX
CINEMAS

NOW PLAYING

1

2

3
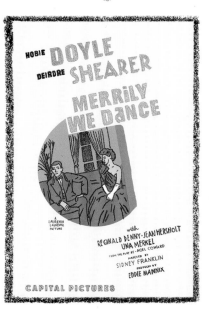

NOW PLAYING

4

5
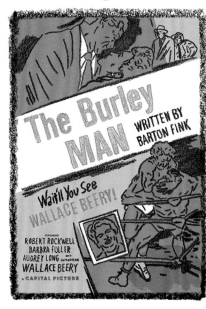

6

Hits and Misses

1992 – 2000

GOD FORBID ANYBODY should ever be enticed into the theater to see one of their movies." That was producer Joel Silver talking about the Coens in late 1993—a few months before the world premiere of *The Hudsucker Proxy* at the Sundance Film Festival. The interview, which was conducted by Dennis Jacobson, professor of cinema studies at the University of Iowa and published in the script for *The Hudsucker Proxy*, hints at the tensions between industry power player Silver and a pair of filmmakers whose early work was both created in and angled away from the mainstream; it suggests that the collaboration between the Hollywood hit-maker and the independent whiz kids was fraught with complication and miscommunication.

It is also a total fabrication: one among many meta-fictional pranks that the Coens have pulled over the years in an attempt to better control, or perhaps directly mock, the wider interest in and reception of their work. At the same time, this ersatz Q and A, which includes such unlikely revelations as Joel pushing for a sixty-year-old Jeanne Moreau to be cast in the role that actually went to Jennifer Jason Leigh and Ethan pushing to play the lead, reflects something of the reality behind the making of *The Hudsucker Proxy*. "They like being quirky artistic filmmakers, but they want to have their movie perform as well," Silver told *Premiere*. "It's kind of hard when you make a picture and nobody wants to see it."

The Hudsucker Proxy was supposed to be the Coens' breakthrough after four consecutive critically acclaimed, commercially niche productions, and if the cast had included the brothers' actual first choices for certain roles—namely Tom Cruise as Norville Barnes and Clint

Eastwood as Sidney J. Mussburger—that may have been the case. Not that the film's ultimate box-office failure rested with Tim Robbins or any of the other actors, or even with the filmmaking, which was as dazzling and precise as ever. Every cent of the much-publicized $25 million budget was on screen in the form of massive sets re-creating 1950s New York, and on a visual level, the film represented some of their most accomplished work to date, with virtuoso camera movements and deft, clever editing. Nor was the culprit a lack of creative control: Now working with Warner Bros.—which co-financed the film in partnership with PolyGram—the Coens retained the same final-cut deal that they'd had with Ben Barenholtz and Circle Films. While the studio did suggest reshoots and re-editing after a disastrous test-screening, these were agreed upon rather than mandated.

The problem with *The Hudsucker Proxy* was, simply, that nobody wanted to see it–and that the critics who had previously done their part to entice audiences into the theater were less impressed this time out. Reading the reception of *The Hudsucker Proxy* now, it seems that in some cases, the knives were out; Roger Ebert's cleverly written pan referred to the "rap" against the Coens, which was that "they're all technique and no heart." In some cases, it was as if writers were holding *The Hudsucker Proxy*'s phenomenally accomplished craft against it, citing it as evidence that the brothers were either desperately scribbling to fill up their biggest-ever canvas or that they were more preoccupied with proposing and overcoming technical and narrative challenges than entertaining their audience. The irony was that by attempting to reimagine elements from some of the most beloved American film comedies of the 1930s and 1940s, the Coens ended up alienating contemporary viewers who didn't share their

frame of reference. The film competed for the Palme d'Or at the Cannes Film Festival, but did not replicate *Barton Fink*'s triumph, instead losing out to the American film *Pulp Fiction* by Quentin Tarantino.

If *Blood Simple* had helped to herald a key chapter of American independent cinema in the mid-1980s, *Pulp Fiction* rewrote the book: It grossed $100 million, made countless top-ten lists, copped an Oscar for Best Original Screenplay, and made a household name of both its writer-director and its distributor, Miramax. And in a way, it's arguable that *Pulp Fiction*'s success had something to do with the Coens making a spectacular comeback two years later with *Fargo*—a film that was by no means derivative of Tarantino but perhaps benefited from being released into a zeitgeist charmed by the idea of profane, violent crime thrillers. The plan had originally been to follow up *The Hudsucker Proxy* with *The Big Lebowski*, a shaggy-dog caper film set in Los Angeles featuring characters and incidents drawn from the brothers' own experiences, including their friendship with the film producer and former activist Jeff Dowd, known to his associates as "The Dude." But because they were insistent that the lead role of the stoner-private-eye be played by Jeff Bridges, they

were forced to wait until the actor was free of prior commitments—a delay that led directly to the creation of *Fargo*.

Besides Joel Silver, the major contacts the Coens made during the production of *The Hudsucker Proxy* were the producers Tim Bevan and Eric Fellner of Working Title Films, who were eager to fund the brothers' follow-up regardless of its predecessors' dismal reception. *Fargo* was actually written before *The Hudsucker Proxy* was released, and had already been conceived as a smaller-scale project: a blood-simple thriller set against a snowy Midwestern backdrop. The generally accepted narrative that the Coens went back to basics in the wake of a box-office catastrophe is thus not quite accurate.

Fargo did represent a return to roots, both in terms of its stripped-down style and geographical setting of Minnesota—the first of two times the Coens made a movie about their home state (the other being *A Serious Man*). Filmed on location in Minneapolis and temporarily re-routed to Grand Forks, North Dakota, when the Land of 10,000 Lakes had its lightest winter snowfall on record, *Fargo* was a smooth shoot, and was brought in at budget without any of the postproduction agonies that had marred *The Hudsucker Proxy*. The flip side to this modesty were doubts about the film's viability in a marketplace that had recently rejected their wares. "You're whittling down your audience from the already marginal subset of egghead art-house moviegoers to the only members of that subset who live in or are familiar with upstate Minnesota," warned one of their longtime friends, William Preston Robertson. "You're making this movie for a demographic of seven people, tops."

These concerns proved groundless. Buttressed by the strongest across-the-board reviews for any American movie since *Pulp Fiction*—and a Best Director prize at Cannes—*Fargo* became the signature independent film of 1996, grossing $25 million in the United States, the most for any Coen film to date, and fully penetrating the popular consciousness: There were debates in the media about its veracity (its based-on-a-true-story title card was quickly debunked) and whether the film's content was offensive to Minnesotans ("It's a little bit strange to us, because there was no intention to lampoon the characters in the movie," said Joel).

Where *The Hudsucker Proxy* had strained to evoke old-style Hollywood glamour, *Fargo* and its killer cast of scraggly character actors was praised for representing something new in their body of work: a persuasive, everyday naturalism, albeit spiked with brutally realistic violence beyond anything in *Pulp Fiction*. *Fargo* was nominated for seven Oscars and won two, for Best Original Screenplay and Best Actress (McDormand). In an interview with *Total Film*, Ethan joked that "they didn't have any other important movies to give awards to that year." This disinterest in the notoriety that comes with prizes and commercial success was a common denominator in the interviews granted by the Coens leading up to the release of *The Big Lebowski*, which went into production during awards season in late 1997. "Why was *Fargo* not a flop?" wondered Joel in the same *Total Film* interview. "Most people don't like *Hudsucker*, and I don't know the reason. It's as much a mystery to me that people went to see *Fargo*."

Because *The Big Lebowski* had already been green-lit and cast (with PolyGram and Working Title once again fronting the budget), it wouldn't be right to say that its wilder indulgences (at a price tag of $15 million, twice the cost of *Fargo*) were by-products of its predecessor's success. Its relatively middling reception, on the other hand, did point to how deeply *Fargo* had touched a nerve.

This view has not held, and *The Big Lebowski* is now perhaps the Coens' most widely beloved film, a cult favorite that has inspired reams of mainstream and academic analysis–as well as a yearly confab called Lebowski Fest that is the cinephile equivalent of Burning Man. The film's slow-burning popularity can be attributed to a host of factors, starting with the fact that its plot—deemed "incomprehensible" by *Time*'s Richard Schickel—takes a few viewings to come into focus. Appropriately for a character study of a pothead, *The Big Lebowski* is a movie that requires viewers to build up a tolerance, and in its way may be the Coens' densest and most rewarding work, a meta-textual monolith to rank with *Barton Fink* and *The Hudsucker Proxy* but suffused with some of *Fargo*'s unexpected warmth.

These good vibes extended to the genesis of *O Brother, Where Art Thou?*, which marked the first time that the Coens worked with George Clooney. In 1997, Clooney was still best known for his role on the popular NBC medical drama *E.R.* and was coming off a string of botched attempts to extend his stardom onto the big screen, including an ill-fated turn under the cowl in *Batman & Robin*. While completing production on David O. Russell's *Three Kings* in Arizona, Clooney was approached by the Coens, who came bearing a new screenplay. The brothers said they'd written the lead role of a dim-witted convict on the lam in Depression-era Mississippi with the actor in mind. "I said yes without even reading the first page," said Clooney, whose instincts proved correct: While it didn't have the critical cachet of *Fargo*, *O Brother, Where Art Thou?* would become even more popular, buoyed by a Grammy-winning soundtrack produced by T-Bone Burnett that became 2000's most unexpected smash.

Shot on location in Western Mississippi and boasting a proverbial cast of thousands (one scene featured 1,200 extras), *O Brother, Where Art Thou?* presented technical and logistical challenges on par with *The Hudsucker Proxy* and was, in its way, as fanatically stylized. In order to re-create the look and feel of the 1930s, the Coens instructed cinematographer Roger Deakins to digitally desaturate his typically crisp color palettes to evoke the sepia-toned photography of the twentieth-century photojournalist Walker Evans. "It's not supposed to be reality," explained Joel. "It's supposed to be a make-believe."

O Brother, Where Art Thou?'s North American box-office gross of $72 million was by far the most for one of the Coens' productions, and Clooney was awarded a Golden Globe for Best Actor in a comedy. Six years after the deflating experience of *The Hudsucker Proxy*, the Coens had not only rebuilt their reputation but exceeded expectations.

The Hudsucker Proxy

RELEASE DATE
March 11, 1994
BUDGET
$30M
DISTRIBUTOR
Warner Bros.
CAST
Tim Robbins
Jennifer Jason Leigh
Paul Newman
Charles Durning
John Mahoney
Jim True-Frost
Bill Cobbs
Bruce Campbell

WARNING!
THIS FILM CONTAINS

Perspiration	99%
Deus ex machina	1%

THE 1952 FILM *Singin' in the Rain* isn't typically included in the massive group of titles whose DNA forms the meta-textual double helix winding its way through *The Hudsucker Proxy*. But the relationship between the two movies is intriguing nonetheless. Both movies are celebrations of Hollywood history that double as satires of the entertainment-industrial complex, and of the fine, imperceptible line between complacency and innovation. And, in both films, the heroes have eureka moments that make them look like visionaries.

Late in *Singin' in the Rain*, silent film idol Don Lockwood (co-director Gene Kelly) lobbies studio boss R. F. Simpson (Millard Mitchell) to help jazz up his DOA star vehicle *The Duelling Cavalier* (a starchy period piece) with an elaborate new scene called "The Broadway Melody." The result of Don's impromptu brainstorm is an all-dancing, no-singing production number that's immediately recognizable as a "dream ballet" akin to the first-act show-stopper of *Oklahoma!* (even though *Singin' in the Rain*'s story takes place fifty years before the premiere of Rodgers and Hammerstein's classic).

"The Broadway Melody" culminates *Singin' in the Rain*'s wonderfully sly commentary on the transition from silent to sound cinema. As a film made in the early 1950s looking back on the 1920s, *Singin' in the Rain* engages in

a hybrid form of homage and critique about the ethics and protocols of the industry, as well as the evolution of the medium itself. It suggests that while aesthetics and technology are constantly developing, showmanship—the shared desire to entertain and be entertained—is its own eternal and unchanging truth.

The dream ballet also evinces Don's conflict about his status as an artist rather than an entertainer, as well as, perhaps, Kelly's own professional anxiety as he was entering middle age. Don (Kelly's alter ego) imagines himself as a small-town kid who wins fame and fortune as a dancer but is forever chasing inspiration, symbolized by Cyd Charisse as a statuesque woman in flowing robes who effortlessly seduces the earnest hoofer before revealing herself as the moll of a mob kingpin (who, it's implied, represents the real source of power on Broadway). Rejected by this avatar of compromised artistry, a heartbroken Don wises up and embraces the fulfillment of creativity for its own sake. At the end of the scene, he bumps into another version of himself—a fresh-faced rube straight off the bus from small-town America—suggesting that the showbiz cycle of ambition, alienation, and acceptance will remain unbroken. Their mutual refrain of "Gotta dance!" affirms the importance of constant movement toward happiness, even if the pattern that's being traced is a loop.

In *The Hudsucker Proxy*, when Norville Barnes (Tim Robbins) first arrives in New York City from Muncie, Indiana, he's a veritable double for Kelly's fresh-faced "Broadway Melody" hero: a rube wide-eyed and overwhelmed by the bustle of the big city. Later, after Norville's unexpected ascent up the corporate ladder of Hudsucker Industries—where he's been celebrated as an "idea man" for coming up with a bestselling retail item—he worries that secretly he may be a fraud. Holed up in his executive suite, he dozes off and finds himself in the middle of his own dream ballet, which is much shorter than "Broadway Melody" but just as central to the film's conception.

Norville imagines himself dancing opposite a leggy woman, whose appearance and wardrobe (a flowing red dress) resemble Cyd Charisse's in "Broadway Melody." His pursuit is awkward and graceless, and as soon as she's in his clutches, he wakes up. It's an intricate roundelay of delusion,

allusion, illusion, and elusiveness, and, like H.I.'s fantasy of family and companionship at the end of *Raising Arizona* or Tom's recurring vision of the hat in *Miller's Crossing*, it reveals Norville as a striver, chasing something just out of his reach. The use on the soundtrack of "O Fortuna" from Carl Orff's *Carmina Burana* during Norville's dream initially seems clichéd, or at best bombastically parodic, but is in fact completely precise. Orff's cantata was inspired by a thirteenth-century Gallic poem about the humility of humankind in the face of the Fates, and Norville's subconscious pursuit of an unattainable ideal is the comic pantomime of a man caught up in what the lyrics call "the wheel of fortune."

It would be an understatement to say that circles are important in *The Hudsucker Proxy*, which is, in plot terms, a film about the invention of a circle—the Hula-Hoop—and features production design by Dennis Gassner that incorporates rounded shapes, objects, and architecture at every turn. These include the massive clock tower atop the Hudsucker Industries building, which looms over the New York City skyline like a second sun, and which serves as a backdrop for the film's opening scene (given the script's perfectly circular structure, this scene actually takes place at the end of the story). As the clock ticks down to New Year's Eve 1959, Norville perches on a ledge, staring down at the street, seemingly contemplating suicide. "How did he get so high, and why is he feeling so low?" asks our narrator, Moses (Bill Cobbs), an elderly employee at Hudsucker whose job is to keep the massive clock tower running. The answer to Moses's riddle is that Norville, for all his delusions of grandeur, is ultimately a passenger on the "wheel of fortune," unable to control its implacable rhythm of ascent and descent—and better off just trying to enjoy the ride.

Even when compared to its fastidiously produced predecessors, *The Hudsucker Proxy* is anything but relaxed. The film's unique and sometimes enervating tension is bound up in how hard, at all times, the Coens work to convince us of the importance of passivity. Like Erich Brenn, the famous plate spinner who appeared regularly on *The Ed Sullivan Show*, they're trying to keep a whole host of elements hovering and humming simultaneously, and in the process can't help calling attention to their own dexterity and sleight of hand. The invention of a godlike

Top left: The design of the Hudsucker Industries building emphasizes hard vertical angles but the looming, circular clock tower predicts Norville's invention of the Hula-Hoop.

Bottom left: "How'd he get so high, and why is he feeling so low?" After introducing Norville Barnes in a moment of despair, the film circles back to trace his interlaced professional ascent and personal decline.

ALL OR NOTHING

In *2 or 3 Things I Know About Her*, Jean-Luc Godard used a steaming cup of coffee as a synecdoche for a whole swirling galaxy. The Coens' jokey homage encodes a universal truth in a circular coffee stain.

character to explain and annotate the action looks a bit like the self-projection of control-freak filmmakers trying to account for every luxuriously detailed inch of an overwhelmingly elaborate production.

More than either *Miller's Crossing* or *Barton Fink*, which neatly sectioned off parts of the early twentieth century, *The Hudsucker Proxy* is an exercise in large-scale world-building: The Manhattan skyline caressed by Roger Deakins's camera is a one twenty-fourth scale model that required its own soundstage. The Coens screened Ridley Scott's 1982 sci-fi thriller *Blade Runner* (1982) during preproduction to get a sense of how to best depict a sprawling, self-contained, and artificial universe, and their vision is no less otherworldly than Scott's. There's something deeply fetishistic about the film's re-creation of 1950s New York, but it is fetishism filtered through anachronism, a deliberate mash-up of aesthetics ranging from art deco and Albert Speer to Frank Lloyd Wright, alongside certain key works of German expressionism, including Fritz Lang's *Metropolis* (1927). The film operates according to the same principle of vertical integration guiding Hudsucker Industries: that everything and anything can be reconciled and repurposed under the auspices of a focused, top-down philosophy.

This ecumenism accounts for how *The Hudsucker Proxy* collapses three decades' worth of classic Hollywood comedies into a single, relentlessly contested narrative space. The characters talk like they're in a movie from the 1930s, dress like they're in a movie from the 1940s, and occupy offices modeled on movies from the 1950s (every executive suite in the Hudsucker building looks like something out of Robert Wise's *Executive Suite* [1954]). As the brazen, Pulitzer Prize–winning journalist Amy Archer, who is assigned by her editor to write a story on Norville and ends up falling in love with him, Jennifer Jason Leigh machine-guns her dialogue like Rosalind Russell in *His Girl Friday* (1940) while torquing her voice into an impersonation of Katharine Hepburn. She's also deliberately reminiscent of Jean Arthur's crusading, resourceful star reporter Babe Bennett in Frank Capra's *Mr. Deeds Goes to Town* (1936); that film's plotline about an unsophisticated "Cinderella Man" who becomes a media star is woven into Norville's arc, along with several other Capra productions: Norville's

disheveled, despondent appearance on the ledge in the opening scene is a direct reference to Gary Cooper's suicidal hobo in *Meet John Doe* (1941), while his unfolding role as a fall guy in a manipulative scheme orchestrated by villainous elites recalls Jimmy Stewart's principled Senator Jefferson Smith in *Mr. Smith Goes to Washington* (1939). There's also a nod to Capra's most famous film, *It's a Wonderful Life* (1946), in the form of a guardian angel who tries to talk Norville out of his despondency, just as Henry Travers's saintly Clarence materializes to soothe Stewart's depressed George Bailey.

The Coens' imitation of Capra is somewhat superficial: Capra's films—especially *Mr. Deeds Goes to Town* and *Mr. Smith Goes to Washington* —are fables about principled idealists who refuse to submit to the forces of corruption and exploitation. Cooper's and Stewart's characters may be good-hearted, but they also have a certain edge. Norville, though, is not a man of principles—as his dream suggests, he's a vessel of pure, unadulterated yearning, and as such closer kin to the dim-bulb dreamers in the films of Preston Sturges, whose ironic, capricious worldview informs *The Hudsucker Proxy* more fully than Capra's forceful moralism. The key to Robbins's performance as Norville is that he makes him fully, recognizably corruptible, which in turn lends pathos to his fears that he might be a fraud.

It also creates an opening for the unscrupulous, cigar-chomping Sidney J. Mussburger (Paul Newman), who is looking for a patsy to run the company in an attempt to drive the price of shares down and initiate a hostile takeover. The character's name nods to Burt Lancaster's villainous publicist in Alexander Mackendrick's *Sweet Smell of Success* (1957), the title of which could serve as a précis of Norville's character arc (the same could be said for Frank Loesser's 1962 musical *How to Succeed in Business Without Really Trying*). "Congratulations, kid," Mussburger growls when Norville presents the board of directors with a drawing of a circle, which he confides he worked on for several years before feeling confident enough to unveil it to potential investors. "You've really outdone yourself.... You've reinvented the wheel."

He can barely disguise his sarcasm, but the lack of originality in Norville's invention is the pivot point of *The Hudsucker Proxy*'s interlaced

Top right: The ever-scheming Sidney J. Mussburger is profit motive incarnate; the stock ticker to his left appears as yet another of the film's significant circles.

Bottom right: Skulking through the clock tower in search of a scoop about "idea man" Norville Barnes, journalist Amy Archer discovers the maintenance staff who really keep Hudsucker Industries running smoothly.

CREATIVE BULLPEN

The *Hudsucker Proxy* is a stylized satire of American capitalism. In this wittily composed image, Tolstoy's great epic novel is paralleled with the efforts of Hudsucker's marketing department: art and commerce in close proximity but ultimately divided. (The joke has another level, as well, as the complex process of naming Norville's simple invention takes long enough that the secretary finishes *War and Peace* and picks up

cultural, industrial, and metaphysical allegory. By simply reproducing a shape latent in nature, Norville has tapped into something potent and elemental: He isn't so much ahead of the curve as riding it, around and around. At one point, Norville explains the concept of Karma to Amy, calling it "a great wheel that gives each of us what we deserve"; later on, a German scientist appearing in a newsreel (patterned after the "March of Time" sequence in *Citizen Kane* [1941]) will espouse a similar philosophy in more scientific terms, referring to "the principle that keeps the earth spinning around the sun."

The rube and the physicist are in agreement, and *The Hudsucker Proxy* fairly revels in such unlikely equivalencies. The running motif of the circle keeps any single character or point of view from occupying the moral or intellectual high ground for too long, and the script is filled with twists of fate: Call it O Fortuna, Where Art Thou? The intricacy of this narrative and thematic design belies the fact that Norville's Hula-Hoop, the circle around which all the others orbit, was a later-breaking addition to the script (the original writing of which dates back to the early 1980s, when the Coens were living with Sam Raimi, who shares a co-screenwriter credit). "We had to come up with something that [Norville] was going to invent that on the face of it was ridiculous," said Joel Coen in 1994. The solution to the problem was to take something that already existed in American pop-cultural history. While he's not as close to an actual person as Barton Fink is to Clifford Odets, Norville is very much a stand-in for Richard Knerr, who founded the Wham-O toy company in Carson, California, in 1948, and roughly a decade later began mass-manufacturing and marketing cheap polyethylene hoops.

The five-minute montage showing the process by which Norville's sketch is transformed into an actual physical product is the film's equivalent to the prologue in *Raising Arizona* or the "Thompson jitterbug" in *Miller's Crossing*: a self-consciously bravura sequence that serves as a sort of stand-alone short film. The sequence was actually shot by Sam Raimi, who was the film's second-unit director, and the presence behind the camera of the director of *The Evil Dead* (1981) accounts for its accelerated kineticism. Having been manipulated by Mussburger into filling the chairman-of-the-board seat vacated by the late Waring Hudsucker (Charles Durning), Norville is allowed to sign off on his own pitch, after which the blueprint is sent hurtling through the corporate wringer, beginning with a set of pneumatic tubes and extending through an absurdly protracted series of conferences, confabs, focus groups, and testing sessions in a "proving facility" that include trying to blow up a prototype with dynamite.

The breakneck speed of the editing is ironic. For all the outward signs of progress, the members of Hudsucker's research and development department are going around in circles, mimicking the movement of the Hula-Hoop itself—and a cycle of industrial production that, at its core, seeks to repackage distraction. The merry-go-round rhythm permits a cartoon stylization that goes even further than *Raising Arizona*, with hurtling camera movements, slapstick physical comedy, and silhouetted shadowplay. One great sight gag among many: Outside the "creative bullpen" where a group of "idea men" are arguing back and forth about what to call the thing, we see a secretary midway through *Anna Karenina*; when we come back to this setup later on in the montage, she's moved

The circle is filled in. No longer a simple abstraction, Norville's invention finds its first user in a little boy whose intuitive, ecstatic experimentation spawns a cross-country fad.

on to *War and Peace*, suggesting both that the process is taking forever and that trying to kick-start a fad is a comparatively mindless endeavor in the context of actual literary (i.e., artistic) accomplishment.

The image of rows of gigantic, rust-gray contraptions squeezing out reams of rainbow-hued hoops is deliriously satiric—a color-coded vision of capitalist mechanisms busily at work. If the Coens have any ambivalence about the system they're depicting (as they did in *Barton Fink*, in which the assembly-line mentality of Hollywood is expressly coded as demonic), it's strategically disguised beneath a veneer of pure exhilaration, especially when Carter Burwell's up-tempo score segues into Aram Khachaturian's careening "Sabre Dance" to soundtrack the moment when a small boy becomes the first person to use one of Norville's hoops. These gyrations are ecstatically intercut with shots of price stickers and stock tickers showing Hudsucker Industries' suddenly soaring fortunes. Nearly wordless and propelled entirely by music and movement, this sequence is itself a kind of dream ballet, one that channels larger cultural forces of the period. The shots of kids and teenagers (and, later, their parents) swinging blithely away suggests not only a society caught up in a consumerist phenomenon, but also the swiveling hips of Elvis Presley on *The Ed Sullivan Show* or Chubby Checker exhorting listeners to do the Twist.

Norville Barnes is no pop-cultural revolutionary, however, nor is he a true "bighead." He is a striver, and it's no coincidence that the dancer in his dream ballet looks a lot like the woman whom Barton Fink spins around at the USO show. Like Barton—or maybe his alter ego "The Kid" from the play *Bare Ruined Choirs*—Norville yearns to rise above his station. *The Hudsucker Proxy* is designed to provide him with a lesson in humility, but only to a point. Unlike Barton Fink, Norville isn't punished for his ambition. Instead, at the end of all the Coens' narrative machinations, he's rewarded, several times over. He's saved by Moses while he's in free fall from the clock tower. He is offered a second chance by the ghost of Waring Hudsucker—whose solidarity with the man who has secretly been his "proxy" all along is signaled by his spinning, Hula-Hoop-style halo

as he hovers in the sky–and invited, in the end, to preside over the company. In Moses's words, to "rule with wisdom and compassion." He gets to live happily ever after.

On the face of it, *The Hudsucker Proxy* is among the Coens' brightest films, rejecting not only the fatalism of *Blood Simple* and *Miller's Crossing*—stories where the protagonists' survival is linked to a high body count—but also the disturbing ambiguity at the end of *Raising Arizona*, which refuses to clarify the nature of H.I.'s dream and contains the possibility that everything won't work out for the best. Everything about *The Hudsucker Proxy*'s finale is calibrated for maximum reassurance. The Coens take pains to show that Norville is saved not only from death, but also from the despair that took hold after the initial success of the Hula-Hoop. His relationship with Amy, which was fraught with mutual suspicion, is locked safely into place. Mussburger is punished for his villainy by being remanded to the very sanitarium he'd hoped to send Norville to as part of his takeover scheme. Norville is even granted a second stroke of genius; his new invention, the Frisbee, has supplanted the Hula-Hoop as the sphere du jour.

There is a slight undercurrent of doubt here: The negligible distance between Norville's two inspirations recalls the way that Barton Fink's wrestling picture simply seems to be a word-for-word rewrite of *Bare Ruined Choirs*. The difference, beyond the Coens' seeming preference here for dreamers over bigheads, is that *The Hudsucker Proxy* allows for the possibility that renewal trumps redundancy. Its worldview is cyclical but not cynical. The motto emblazoned on the clock atop the Hudsucker tower reads THE FUTURE IS NOW! The motto is ironic in light of the way the film fetishizes the real and cinematic past, but it also doesn't countenance the usual anxiety about things to come that figures into many of the Coens' endings. The shot of a Frisbee hovering away into the air affirms that innovation is the flip side of complacency, and that it doesn't matter if there's anything new under the sun so long as the earth (and everything on it) keeps rotating around it. In this elaborate dream ballet of a movie, movement is everything. Gotta dance!

DREAM BALLET
—

Norville's vision of a beautiful woman eluding his grasp visualizes his ambition for success but also his insecurities about failure and being a phony; he fears he may not recapture the elusive muse that led him to the Hula-Hoop in the first place.

HALO
—

The reappearance of the late Waring Hudsucker as a benign deus ex machina references the angelic Clarence from *It's a Wonderful Life* and gives the Coens a chance to include one final, subtle circle: his whirling, luminescent halo.

Fargo

RELEASE DATE
April 5, 1996
BUDGET
$7M
DISTRIBUTOR
Gramercy Pictures
CAST
Frances McDormand
William H. Macy
Steve Buscemi
Peter Stormare
Kristin Rudrüd
Harve Presnell
Tony Denman
Gary Houston
Sally Wingert

WARNING!
THIS FILM CONTAINS

Snow	32%
Blood	25%
Night crawlers	15%
Tru-Coat	10%
Radisson buffet	6%
José Feliciano	5%
Bark beetles	4%
Ungwent	2%
Golden Gophers hockey	1%

"I THINK I'M GOING to barf," says Marge Gunderson (Frances McDormand) after arriving at the scene of a triple homicide. It's a line that cuts two ways, announcing the seven-months-pregnant police chief's constitutional frailty, and also a more general sense of disgust at the bloody mess scattered along the highway. It's significant, perhaps, that she shows up approximately one-third of the way through *Fargo*'s running time—after we've already witnessed a nauseating cast of characters and sickening actions. Embezzlement, extortion, murder: We could use a palate cleanser. "It's just morning sickness," she says while hunched over in the snow, reassuring her deputy that all is well even as the bodies thawing in the wrecked car beside her say otherwise. With her sheriff's hat and bulging belly, Marge radiates authority and vulnerability in a frigid landscape; in *Fargo*'s cold and hostile universe, goodness is a delicate condition.

Marge's goodness is not the same kind embodied by Norville Barnes in *The Hudsucker Proxy*, where the Coens played with the archetype of the holy fool, the savant oblivious to his own brilliance. Marge is clearly intelligent. She puts together the jagged jigsaw pieces of the movie's plot despite a limited perspective on events. But she's no visionary, accidental or otherwise. Nor is she a bighead like Tom Reagan or Barton Fink: Not only does she lack their (masculine) arrogance, but she's never paralyzed by insecurity or indecision. After two straight movies about stifled, would-be creators, *Fargo* presents a competent professional who's happy with, challenged by, and fulfilled through her work. Her spiritual sister in the Coens' canon is Holly Hunter's Ed in *Raising Arizona*, another staunch officer of the law. The similarities between the pair are obvious, as is the major inversion between them. Ed morosely defines herself by her infertility—leading to a violation of professional conduct in the form of the

baby-napping scheme with H.I.–whereas Marge is doing her best to subordinate certain biological realities to the call of duty.

When *Fargo* was released in 1996, the common tactic for critics was to either contrast its lean, wiry presentation against the overweening, Rube Goldbergian construction of *The Hudsucker Proxy* or else capitalize on McDormand's front-and-center presence to pair it off with *Blood Simple*. Both moves make sense in their way. Joel admitted that *Fargo* and its largely static and sedate cinematography (as opposed to *Hudsucker*'s jerry-rigged camera gymnastics) represented a "new start from a stylistic point of view" and that the film was "more naturalistic, generally . . . [with] unembellished sets and real locations." The frozen Minnesotan backdrop is geographically distinct from the sunbaked Texas exteriors of *Blood Simple*, but the sense of regionalism (highly particularized rituals, turns of phrase, and accents) is similar. Even so, and allowing for its uniqueness as the first of the Coens' films set in their home state (anticipating the more deeply autobiographical tenor of *A Serious Man*), *Fargo* is most productively placed in conversation with *Raising Arizona*. The two films are extremely close to each other, and not only in terms of the characters of Ed and Marge. (Remember that McDormand also appeared in the earlier film as a trailer-park harpy who inadvertently tortures Ed with her descriptions of motherhood, and her casting in *Fargo* takes on a trickier and more self-reflexive dimension.)

The Coens have spoken of their fondness for kidnapping plots, calling them "pregnant" dramatic situations that spawn suspense and complications. This metaphor is made literal in *Raising Arizona*, where Ed and H.I. are trying to hijack a newborn baby. In *Fargo*, the dynamic has been twisted so that instead of two married co-conspirators, we have a husband conspiring to abduct his wife. His motivation is not to become a father like H.I., but to pay off a debt incurred as a result of shady business dealings. No less than H.I. McDunnough, Jerry Lundegaard (William H. Macy) is a recidivist: His repeat offense is greed. At the beginning of the film, it's implied that he has taken out a loan from an automobile manufacturer while offering non-existent dealer vehicles as collateral. In order to escape the consequences of one scam, he dreams up another. His plan is to have a couple of thugs kidnap his wife, Jean (Kristin Rudrüd), so that he can extract a ransom from her wealthy, tight-fisted father, Wade (Harve Presnell).

Jerry resents Wade because he thinks Wade believes him to be a failure and is reluctant to offer support, fiscal or otherwise, but Jerry's conduct justifies every one of his father-in-law's criticisms and then some. H.I.'s convenience store robberies in *Raising Arizona* are portrayed as mild, essentially victimless crimes, especially with the understanding that he preys on corporate chains rather than mom-and-pop operations; his stickups, conducted with unloaded guns in the dead of night, let H.I. sew his wild oats. Middle-aged family-man Jerry cannot claim such innocence. H.I.'s wildest dreams—a house, a job, a son of his own—are all things that Jerry has, and it is, evidently, not enough for him. The title sequence of *Fargo* depicts Jerry's drive through the snow from Minneapolis to Fargo to arrange the kidnapping, and the detail that he's towing another car in his wake is perfect. The second vehicle is like an albatross around his neck.

"This is a true story," claims the title card of *Fargo*. The veracity of this opening gambit has long since been debunked: "We made up our own true crime story," admitted Ethan when pressed by a journalist about whether or not the script had really been inspired by a botched ransom plan. But the relationship between truth and fiction is nevertheless central to *Fargo*, which strives for a different kind of authenticity than its predecessors. The inter-textual gamesmanship of *Miller's Crossing*, *Barton Fink*, and *The Hudsucker Proxy* is replaced by a superficially loose (but of course scrupulously controlled) realism that takes advantage of extant, present-tense locations and structures in lieu of elaborate historical re-creations. Like *Raising Arizona*, *Fargo* takes in the spartan spaces of the American heartland. Diverting from Barry Sonnenfeld's alternately saturated and sunblind color palette, Roger Deakins's cinematography emphasizes whiteness to the point of abstraction. At times, the action seems to be taking place within a void where the foreground and horizon are indistinguishable from each other.

The blankness of the canvas is striking in and of itself, but the ingeniousness of the visual scheme is most apparent when all that blinding, negative space gets spattered with other shades. "Not blood, red," said Jean-Luc

Godard, answering charges of violence in 1965's *Pierrot le Fou*; *Fargo* is awash in crimson imagery, almost always heightened by its proximity to paleness. When Gaear Grimsrud (Peter Stormare) and Carl Showalter (Steve Buscemi), the two thugs Jerry has hired to carry out his kidnapping plan, are stopped by a police car while driving back from the scene of the crime (with Jean stashed under a blanket in the back seat), the headlights of the officer's prowler glow an eerie, iridescent white; the blood that lands on Carl's face pops against the pallor of his skin. Later, Carl's own blood will fertilize the landscape after Gaear, following a disagreement over how to split a briefcase full of ill-gotten cash, feeds him face-first into a wood-chipper—*Fargo*'s most famous moment, and a masterpiece of visceral absurdity with the stark, discombobulating clarity of an illustration from a child's fairy-tale book.

That's not an accident or incidental: *Fargo*'s fable-like aspects begin with Carter Burwell's mournful musical score—a folklike dirge with a circular, recursive melody—and carry through its image system, most noticeably in the looming, moonfaced effigy of Paul Bunyan (whose two appearances effectively bookend the film and mark the story as a "tall tale"). Jeffrey Adams writes that "[the film's] false claim to truth finds its visual equivalent in the statue of legendary giant woodsman Paul Bunyan." It's a perceptive reading that can be pushed even further: The visual doubling of the Bunyan statue (which was specially built for the production) with the character of Gaear—a flannel-clad hulk who, in a decisive moment, wields an axe—is richly suggestive of the disparity between cultural myths and their earthbound inspirations. Nobody in *Fargo* is larger-than-life; most characters are quite small—which is to say petty, venal, and frustrated by the sense of their own insignificance. A slow, ominous push-in shot of Gaear staring soporifically at a television set at the cabin where he's holed up with Carl and Jean to await further instructions from Jerry emphasizes this point. He's watching a documentary about bark beetles, which pays

The contrast between Carl and Gaear—one nervy and aggressive, the other dazed and confused—is consistently played up for comic effect, and anticipates the dynamic between Walter and The Dude in *The Big Lebowski*.

EMPLOYEE OF THE MONTH
—
The first glimpse of Jerry in *Fargo* is via his corporate headshot—a perfect representation of his phony, posturing nature and the forced smile that always conceals a hidden agenda.

BREAKING IN
—
Jean's kidnapping is an oddly comic set piece in which the terror of a home invasion is undermined by the intruders' clumsy, amateurish tactics, like walking up to the front door in broad daylight wearing ski masks.

sideways homage to David Lynch's *Blue Velvet* (1986) and its vision of insectoid evil while also hinting that Gaear and Carl—who spends the scene banging angrily on the set-top to improve the reception—are nothing more than tiny specks in the grand scheme of things.

The narrator's disembodied voice as he describes the close-up footage conveys an entomologist's detachment, which could be taken as an echo of the Coens' own point of view: Despite its acclaim, *Fargo* was subject to criticism that it condescended to its Midwestern characters, something that was rarely claimed about *Raising Arizona*'s cornpone dramatis personae. The question of whether a film has "affection" for its characters is almost always loaded, targeted to pick off supposed anti-humanists, and *Fargo* does give its detractors some ammunition. Carl and Gaear's comically abusive treatment of Jean, whom they knock out, blindfold, and drag around like a sack of potatoes over the course of several scenes, is of course cruel; because they treat her like a prop, it's possible to think the Coens are doing so, too. Jean's presence at the edge of the bark beetle scene, however, is affecting in a way that prizes empathy over exploitation. While Gaear is mesmerized by the nature documentary, she's frozen with terror.

The blocking of the actors is like a sick parody of domestic repose, with Gaear, Carl, and Jean as a bizarro family unit. This setup is paid off via a near-subliminal edit to reveal that Marge is watching the same program at home in bed with her husband, Norm (John Carroll Lynch). Half-hypnotized by the image, her glazed expression mirrors Gaear's perfectly. Marge recognizes a tender kinship with the insect on the television screen—the bark beetle being profiled is a new mother providing food for her brood—but is unaware of her shared experience with six-foot night-crawler Gaear. (The visual device of linking the killers with the officer pursuing them via a television screen will be repeated, even more insinuatingly, in *No Country for Old Men*.) At this point, Marge doesn't know who Gaear and Carl are, much less that they're the killers behind the triple homicide in Brainerd. The effect of these characters all watching the same television program is ironic, but also strangely poetic, as if the Coens are allowing for all these different stock types (the lowbrow criminals, the innocent victim, the determined cop) to coexist on a recognizably modest, quotidian continuum.

That there is no place for Jerry in this cross-cut alignment is telling of the peculiar niche he occupies in *Fargo*'s moral hierarchy. Carl and Gaear are low-level goons, and the Coens take pains to underline their stupidity, expressed variably through Buscemi's agitated logorrhea and Stormare's mute stupor. The behavioral contrast between these characters is played, brilliantly, for profane comic effect. (In *The Big Lebowski*, Buscemi's silence as Donny could be a rejoinder to his motormouthed mania here.) Too casual, woefully underprepared, and finally terrible at the task they're being paid for, Gaear and Carl are blood simpletons—more malevolent versions of the Snoats brothers from *Raising Arizona* (although Gaear's dead-eyed lethalness descends from the Lone Biker of the Apocalypse).

Jerry, meanwhile, is a legitimate businessman: An early insert shot of his "employee of the month" photo at his car dealership in Minneapolis shows a poised, smiling professional. But he's also a crook, shown not only in his finagling of that phony loan but also in the way he gouges a customer over the added cost of a special sealant—"the Tru Coat"—to his purchase. "You're a liar, Mr. Lundegaard. . . . a fucking liar"; the way the man hesitates over the curse word italicizes both the deep-seated Protestant reticence of the community as a whole and also Jerry's specific, mediocre, everyday sort of evil. His discomfort in his interactions with Carl and Gaear, as well as Shep Proudfoot (Steve Reevis), the ex-con auto mechanic who brokers their meeting, melds insecurity and arrogance: Jerry is simultaneously intimidated by the roughneck mentality of these other men and smugly certain that he's smarter and more savvy, which turns out to be incorrect. Carl and Gaear's murderous incompetence may screw up Jerry's plan, but the plan itself is so suspect that he's less a victim of fate than its hapless enabler.

This may be the key difference between Jerry and H.I., whose own cockeyed plan (hatched in collaboration with Ed) is less obviously self-serving (and, accordingly, less destructive). In *Raising Arizona*, the conceit of a working-class couple stealing from a wealthy one on the grounds that the latter have "more than they can handle" is politicized and never quite repudiated; the twist that Nathan Arizona has a good heart and effectively gives H.I. and Ed his blessing (once his son has been returned) is in keeping

"I think I'm gonna barf." The framing of this key shot in *Fargo* forces the ugliness of a murder scene in our face, aligning us with Marge's revulsion as she investigates the crime. Her claim of "morning sickness" points to her pregnancy, but the dialogue can be taken as an expression of shock at the aftermath of the criminals' mercenary, expedient cruelty. In a wasteland littered with corpses, Marge seems to be the only one who cares.

with the film's buoyant spirit. Jerry's desire to rip off Wade comes from a similar place (and Wade, who condescends to his son-in-law at every opportunity, is far less likable than Nathan Arizona), but the script and Macy's remarkable seriocomic acting keep the audience from identifying too closely with his desires. Macy was nominated for an Oscar for Best Supporting Actor, but he's as much of a lead as McDormand, and his nervy, squirrelly performance—projected through wide, wary eyes—is the film's primary source of dread and tension. The argument that the Coens are harsh on their characters is probably better applied to Jerry, whose torment is constant and agonizing. Futilely scraping ice off his car's windshield and then throwing a childish tantrum, he's a portrait of impotent frustration; the comic timing as he calms down and resolves to keep scraping (otherwise there's no way he'll be able to drive out of the parking lot) is a thing of beauty.

Marge and Jerry's showdown in the latter's office is another comedic high point, showcasing the Coens' talent for broken-telephone dialogue: As she asks clear, focused questions, he dodges and dissembles until his practiced salesman's patter has melted into gibberish. Jerry flees the scene once he realizes that the soft-spoken but determined police chief is on to him, a choice that speaks to his essential weakness. A few scenes later, when Gaear runs from Marge, who's tracked him (via the "tan Ciera" from Jerry's lot) to the cabin in the woods, Jerry's flight from Marge is interestingly doubled; the parallels between Jerry and his hirelings are

suddenly inverted. Instead of focusing on Jerry's denial that he's anything like the thugs in his employ, the Coens pass his overwhelming sense of helplessness on to Gaear, who's humbled by a well-placed gunshot to the back of the leg, evidence of Marge's trained precision versus her quarry's more brutish violence.

In both cases, it's clear that Marge has power over the men in her midst—see also her strange and fascinating run-in with Mike Yanagita, a Japanese-American man (played by the Korean-American actor Steve Park), whose presence in *Fargo*'s otherwise lily-white Midwestern milieu is automatically dislocating. R. Barton Palmer has written superbly on the significance of Marge's trip to Minneapolis to see Mike, a former high-school classmate who calls her to catch up. What seems like a diversion from the narrative— a distraction from the investigation into the roadside killings—is connected to the script's running motif of weak, dishonest men. It also represents steadfast Marge's one dalliance with the questionable impulses that drive Jerry.

When Marge arrives at the Radisson in Minneapolis for her lunch date with Mike, she's sporting a floral dress and wearing makeup—the only time in the film that she appears stereotypically feminine. Although she quickly rejects Mike's pathetic romantic advances, her choice to see him in the first place is riddled with ambiguity, contextualized even further by McDormand's appearance as a cheating wife in *Blood Simple*. Marge lets

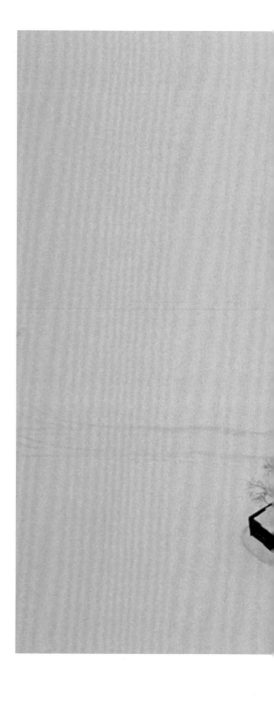

SIGNS AND WONDERS
—
Marge's need to eat throughout *Fargo* is tied to her pregnancy but also marks her as a rapacious middle-American consumer—a connection cinched by this strategically placed commercial signage.

BLOOD SIMPLE
—
Carl's decision to leave a marker where he's buried the money suggests he's gone blood simple. The crimson scraper will definitely be spotted by somebody else driving by long before he returns.

This ingenious shot of Jerry's car sitting alone in an empty parking lot points to the isolation that he's brought on himself with his "malfeasance"; the high angle gives the viewer moral high ground over the story's villain.

Mike down gently, but we never know if she discloses the trip to her husband. There's a conceptual pun in the idea that by driving to the big city to see Mike, she's "straying from the Norm." Palmer's contention that Mike's ethnicity makes him "exotic" is intriguing, compounded by the joke—which borders on racial parody—that he has been completely assimilated in manner, behavior, and accent. (The superficial difference of his skin color becomes a sort of sight gag.)

Mike is—like Jerry—a fucking liar. He tells Marge that he's been lonely since his wife died of leukemia, but a phone conversation with another old high-school classmate reveals this backstory to be a complete fabrication. Marge's desire, however innocent and sublimated, to

step outside the predictable routine of her life—her job, her marriage, and her impending role as a mother—leads her to a man who could be Jerry's double, in effect turning the detour into a premonition. It's one of the film's subtlest points that when Marge does finally confront Jerry, the duplicity and disappointment of her meeting with Mike is in the back of her mind. Marge does not simply solve the mystery at the heart of *Fargo* and bring one of the surviving perpetrators to justice; she's also a vessel of judgment (without overstepping her jurisdiction as a police officer). Her vomiting at the first crime scene prefigures her revulsion at both the discovery of Jerry's villainy and the sight of Gaear stuffing Carl into the wood-chipper, but this time she doesn't barf. She keeps her composure and does her job.

Marge's one-way conversation with Gaear as she drives him to the police station rhymes humorously with Carl's attempts to get the big man to talk: He slumps in the back seat of her cruiser in, to quote Carl, "total fucking silence." Their scene concludes a trilogy of encounters with morally compromised men: the damaged, disingenuous Mike, the all-thumbs puppet-master Jerry, the blunt object Gaear. Mike is perhaps the odd man out of this group since his dishonesty isn't explicitly tied to greed, unless his yearning for Marge—and the normalcy that a relationship with her could entail—counts. Gaear and Jerry (note the similarity of their names) are literally co-conspirators, but they also embody different modes of villainy: the ogre and the wolf in sheep's clothing (or maybe Tru-Coating?).

Marge's admonishment to Gaear that "there's more to life than a little bit of money," a home truth that's perilously close to a platitude and yet delivered with utter sincerity, is meant as a kind of epigram on the action, a way to give the last word to a character who's earned it.

The key line, though, is her follow-up: "I just don't understand it." It's an admirable sentiment in that Marge is not at all driven or seduced by avarice, but it's also haunting, suggesting an innocence that's scarily incompatible with what we've seen over the course of the film. So when the Coens double down on it in the final scene, it's difficult not to feel a little bit concerned. We see Marge and Norm back in bed, in a two-shot identical to the one where they dozed off in front of the nature show. They talk briefly about Norm's modest artistic triumph of having his sketch of a bird selected for a three-cent postage stamp and then refer to their incoming bundle of joy. "Two more months," says Norm, affectionately brushing his wife's belly. Marge answers by repeating: "Two more months."

On the face of it, this is the coziest ending in the Coens' entire repertoire. The triumphant policewoman returns home to her supportive husband—a reversal on the traditional gender roles in life and cinema—and they contemplate a life together with their new family. But the blessings of home and hearth didn't protect Jean Lundegaard or mollify her husband. The only child in the movie, the Lundegaards' son, Scotty (Tony Denman), will grow up without his mother—who was killed by Gaear, off screen, for no other reason than that she wouldn't stop screaming. It's equally possible to see Marge and Norm as avatars of normalcy whose simple, decent ordinariness will keep such tragedies at bay, or to feel anxious or terrified at the risk of bringing a baby into a world ruled by corruption and contingency. Something can always go wrong, and the future at the end of *Fargo* is scarily uncertain. You can feel the final fade-out in the pit of your stomach.

Top: Marge's disbelief at the wood-chipper doesn't rattle her steady hand or moral authority.

SOCK IT TO ME

In a film defined by a stripped-down realism, Carl's foot protruding from the wood-chipper provides a grim surrealist flourish.

The Zellner Brothers

FILMMAKERS

David Zellner's 2014 drama *Kumiko, the Treasure Hunter* riffs on an urban legend about a Japanese girl who travels to Minnesota to find the treasure buried by the side of the highway by Carl Showalter in *Fargo*. (In actuality, the woman, a twenty-eight-year-old office worker, committed suicide.) Co-written by the director with his brother Nathan, *Kumiko* was critically acclaimed, playing at film festivals around the world; the pair's third feature, *Damsel*, premiered at Sundance in 2018.

It's interesting that your film is actually based on a true story, whereas *Fargo*, which is advertised as being fact-based, is a total invention. Can you talk about the relationship between truth and fantasy that's developed in *Kumiko*?

When we first heard about the urban legend that we ending up riffing on for *Kumiko*, it was presented as a true story. While we were deep in developing the script, the story was debunked as a modern myth that took a life of its own online. At first we were alarmed, caught off guard, because the truth was so different from the story we were familiar with. For a moment we wondered if we had to change everything; then we realized that no, it was the myth that drew us to the story and it was the myth we were to be faithful to. As far as our film's concerned, that became the "truth."

Treasure hunting and the hope of discovering a great fortune is a running motif in the Coens' cinema; did you think of that relationship while crafting the story of *Kumiko*?

No, it was the work of Werner Herzog that kept speaking to us in crafting *Kumiko*, particularly his films *Stroszek* and *Aguirre, The Wrath of God*. In the making of *Kumiko*, we intentionally chose not to revisit *Fargo*, partly out of respect for the film (as we didn't want to find ourselves riffing directly on it from an aesthetic point of view) and because we wanted *Kumiko* to be its own thing. For the universe that our story takes place in, we wanted *Fargo* to represent "the movie world" and *Kumiko* to represent "the real world."

What were your impressions of *Fargo* the first time you saw it? It was the first of the Coens' films to touch a seriously mainstream nerve, which is interesting because in some ways it's more self-effacing than its predecessors....

We loved it, particularly its balance of humor and pathos. I don't know what each of our favorites are of their work, but it's certainly up near the top.

Kumiko inverts one of the strangest subplots in *Fargo*, which is when Marge meets the Asian man in a restaurant. In a way, *Fargo* is a film about outsiders in Middle America, and Mike is a very explicit example; *Kumiko* is a visitor rather than an assimilated citizen, but some of that exoticism—about seeing America from her perspective—is what drives your film forward....

That's an interesting point, though to be honest it wasn't anything calculated on our end in the making of our film, or even something we thought about after. Part of the urban legend (which apparently there's some truth to) was that a local cop called local Chinese restaurants to see if anyone could speak Japanese. We took that thread and ran with it.

Is there a way you can reconcile your own practice as sibling directors with what you know of the Coens' working style? Are they a direct inspiration or influence or simply artists whose work you've followed?

We have an enormous amount of respect for them as filmmakers, and it was crucial for us to be respectful to *Fargo* in every step of making *Kumiko*. They've definitely been an influence in general and a source of inspiration; I particularly remember our minds being blown the first time we saw *Raising Arizona* as kids, being introduced to their work through that. However, with *Kumiko* it was the legend, the idea of this modern-day treasure hunter on a delusional quest for fortune, and the blurred lines between truth and fiction, that initially drew us to the material rather than solely because of the *Fargo* connection.

FRIENDS OF THE COENS

"I no longer work with Joel and Ethan Coen. I live with Joel and Ethan Coen. One is my husband and the other my brother-in-law. I enjoy the fact that many people don't know which is which and I think we should keep it that way.

So, basically, it is a family situation. Whenever they begin a new project my first question is: Is there a part for me? The second is: Where does it shoot? The answer to either question gives me an idea of what course my life will take over the following couple of years.

We like to call it The Family Circus.
I alternate between being The Trapeze Artist
and The Bearded Lady."

—

Frances McDormand

FILMS:
Blood Simple (1984)
Raising Arizona (1987)
Miller's Crossing (1990)
Barton Fink (1991)
Fargo (1996)

The Big Lebowski

RELEASE DATE
March 6, 1998

BUDGET
$15M

DISTRIBUTOR
Gramercy Pictures

CAST
Jeff Bridges
John Goodman
Steve Buscemi
Julianne Moore
Philip Seymour Hoffman
John Turturro
Peter Stormare
David Huddleston
Sam Elliott

WARNING!
THIS FILM CONTAINS

Raymond Chandler pastiche	25%
Seventies AM radio staples	16%
Bowling alley etiquette	13%
Porn movie parody	12%
Castration anxiety	10%
Cannabis	9%
Kahlua	8%
Severed body parts	4%
Photos of twentieth-century Republican presidents	2%
Kraftwerk jokes	1%

I N THE PUBLISHED screenplay for *The Big Lebowski*, a character named "The Dude" is introduced in the stage directions as "a man in whom casualness runs deep." Of all the Coens' movies, *The Big Lebowski* is, at least on the surface, the most ambling and aimless. It starts with a tumbleweed that tumbles through its opening shots to the serene sounds of the country band Sons of the Pioneers, which kicks things off at a mellow tempo. The tumbleweed's slow encroachment through the frame is like a cue for Jeffrey Lebowski's own woebegone progress. This is a man who takes it easy to the point that he loses track of the days of the week, and who dresses like every day is Casual Friday. But the film around him has depths to plumb, and then some: There is no bottom.

The Big Lebowski was released in 1998, after the success of *Fargo* had rerouted the Coens' career. It was originally written in the early nineties, around the same time as *Barton Fink*, which accounts for similarities between the characters played in both films by John Goodman (who was not available to shoot closer to the completion of the script because of his commitments on ABC's sitcom *Roseanne*). The film it most closely resembles in the first part of the Coens' career, however, is *The Hudsucker Proxy,* with which it shares several key elements, including a good-hearted simpleton protagonist (The Dude, aka Jeff Lebowski, played by Jeff Bridges, for whom the role was written); a folksy narrator (The Stranger, played by Sam Elliott, whose name was similarly invoked by the Coens in their early screenplay drafts); a general sense of good cheer more indebted to the screwball optimism of *Raising Arizona* than the icy detachment of *Blood Simple* or *Miller's Crossing*; and an overall embrace of wild stylization (in terms of camera movement, set and costume design, and soundtrack curation) in place of *Fargo*'s bloody simplicity.

Where *The Hudsucker Proxy*'s grandiosity arguably smacks of showing off—a feeling consistent with it being the brothers' first foray into studio-subsidized filmmaking—*Lebowski*'s virtuosity serves a sense of modesty. The difference between the films lies in the divergent attitudes of their protagonists, one who embodies skyscraping ambition and one whose aspirations have long since atrophied. It's a fantasy of upward mobility versus a daydream of horizontal stasis. When Norville Barnes drifts off to sleep at his desk, he imagines himself trapped in a tango with a beautiful woman who keeps gracefully eluding his grasp. In The Dude's hallucinations, he's cruising on a flying carpet or floating facedown along the polished length of a ten-pin bowling lane. He is happy to follow the tumbleweed's lead and just roll with the flow.

The Dude's basic malleability is a running (or rolling) joke throughout *The Big Lebowski*, which is constructed more or less as an obstacle course for a character who can barely be motivated to get out of bed in the morning. It's a matter of record that the character—and Bridges's look and basic mannerisms in the role—was based in part on the American film producer and political activist Jeff Dowd, who helped the Coens navigate the distribution market back in the days of *Blood Simple*. Yet there's more to the performance than impersonation. One of Bridges's specialties as an actor is transparency—as in John Carpenter's *Starman* (1984), where he empties out entirely as an alien adopting a human form—and his guilelessness as The Dude is really quite remarkable; not a good-ole-boy tour de force like Nicolas Cage in *Raising Arizona* or Tim Robbins in *The Hudsucker Proxy* but the weariness of a man whose idealism has long since departed and left him running on empty. The claim made by The Stranger that Jeffrey Lebowski is "possibly the laziest man in Los Angeles County. . . . which would place him high in the running for laziest worldwide" is backed up by Bridges's soporific comportment, which suggests a character hypnotized by his own passivity—a waking trance state that leads him to subconsciously absorb information from the world around him.

Paying for a carton of milk at the supermarket on the eve of the first Gulf War, he sees news footage of George H.W. Bush threatening Saddam Hussein and files the president's tough talk away for his own use later on. After being roughed up at his squalid pit of an apartment by thugs who've

PLEDGING THEIR LOVE TO THE GROUND

—

The tumbleweed appearing at the edge of the Pacific Ocean is deliberately out of place: Combined with the drawling narration by Sam Elliott and the song by the Sons of the Pioneers, it suggests a collision of genres— an old-school Western rolling through the middle of a modern LA noir.

HOME INVASION

—

The bowling ball continues the running motif of significant circles in *The Big Lebowski*; when Jackie Treehorn's thugs break into The Dude's house, they use it as a weapon to destroy his living space.

mistaken him for a different, considerably more prosperous man with the same name—who pee on his rug to make the humiliation complete—The Dude goes to the other Jeffrey Lebowski for compensation and, after being rebuffed, tells him that "this aggression will not stand." In lieu of any strongly held beliefs (beyond the fact that he hates the Eagles), The Dude is wide open to suggestion, and hearing saber-rattling Republican platitudes being parroted by an aged hippie is the pivot point of *The Big Lebowski*'s 360-degree sociological satire. It sends up the deflated idealism of seventies leftists via The Dude's two-decade de-evolution from a proud campus radical into a guy who tries to buy a carton of milk with a personal check while also extending its mockery to a flock of hawkish avatars constantly in his hair.

These include The Dude's best friend, Walter Sobchak (Goodman), a Vietnam vet whose PTSD manifests in spasms of psychotically self-righteous rage. This character was rumored to be modeled on the famously militant Hollywood screenwriter John Milius, another example of the film's stranger-than-fiction dramaturgy. Then there's the Big Lebowski himself, acted by the late David Huddleston as a physical and ideological double for Dick Cheney, who proudly displays photos of himself with a host of Republican

power brokers. "This picture was taken when Mrs. Reagan was the First Lady of the nation," explains Lebowski's factotum, Brandt (Philip Seymour Hoffman), channeling the unctuous butlers of 1930s drawing-room comedies by way of Waylon Smithers from *The Simpsons*.

By rejecting The Dude's request for a new rug to replace the soiled one, the Big Lebowski claims to be standing for conservative notions of self-reliance. By the end of the story he will be unmasked as precisely the sort of "bum" he's pegged his guest as, subsisting only on an allowance from his adult daughter Maude (Julianne Moore). The Big Lebowski's presence as the proverbial "man behind the desk" puts him in the company of Nathan Arizona, Jack Lipnick, and Sidney Mussburger. And this archetype of the male tycoon secretly propped up by a woman will recur in *The Man Who Wasn't There* and *Intolerable Cruelty*. It's a ridiculous oversimplification to call *The Big Lebowski* a movie about a man who wants to replace his rug. That would be like saying John Huston's *The Maltese Falcon* (1941)—which along with Howard Hawks's *The Big Sleep* (1946), and Robert Altman's *The Long Goodbye* (1973) comprise the holy trinity of noirs the Coens pillaged to piece together their own plot

As her first name suggests, Maude Lebowski is a figure of unconventional cool in a film filled with losers who are either out of time or out of their element. Her avant-garde artistry challenges and confuses the Dude, but it also marks her as a creative force. Like Marge in *Fargo*, her pregnancy serves as a symbol of the future—one where a "Little Lebowski" is on the way to keep the human comedy rolling forward.

The Busby Berkeley-style choreography of The Dude's dream
sequence is steeped in psychological irony; despite his
disheveled outer appearance, the character's subconscious
landscape is meticulously arranged and patterned.

and dramaturgy—is about a guy trying to get his hands on a statue. And yet it's also a measure of the Coens' cleverness that The Dude's obsession with an incidental piece of floor décor doesn't lie too far from the heart of the matter: The rug is the stuff that dreams are made of. *The Big Lebowski* is a film dominated by circular, reiterative dialogue, and The Dude isn't the only one who absorbs and parrots key phrases from the people around him. Language subdivides and multiplies throughout the screenplay with almost viral efficiency. Brandt implores The Dude over and over again that Bunny Lebowski's (Tara Reid) life is "in his hands." Maude reassures The Dude that the doctor she's recommended to suss out a blow to his skull is "a good man, and thorough." Walter, taking a golf club to a stranger's sports car, howls that "this is what you get when you fuck a stranger in the ass!" Yet it is The Dude's refrain that "the rug really tied the room together" that rings

loudest: This dubious claim becomes a symbol of a slovenly character's latent desire for order and meaning underneath his laissez-faire lifestyle.

The Coens are explicitly riffing on vintage detective fiction, and the main character is styled as a sleepy, distracted stand-in for Raymond Chandler's two-fisted, single-minded private investigator Philip Marlowe. He is played by Humphrey Bogart in the film version of *The Big Sleep* and Elliott Gould in *The Long Goodbye*, although only the latter's influence really shows in Bridges's acting. This leads to a general pattern of unraveling and revelation in the story. And yet the solutions to the mysteries that pile up following the home invasion by the "rug pee-ers" are ultimately subordinate to The Dude's journey of self-discovery, which recalls Tom's interior odyssey in *Miller's Crossing* (except that he's chasing a hat, not a rug) and anticipates the

existential crises of the characters in *A Serious Man* and *Hail, Caesar!* (whose dilemmas are more ephemeral than soiled furniture).

Consider that at the beginning of *The Big Lebowski*, The Dude is a man without attachments. "Does this place look like I'm fucking married?" he asks the henchmen who've plunged him headfirst into his own toilet bowl. His only obligation is to his bowling-league teammates, Walter and Theodore Donald "Donny" Kerabatsos (Steve Buscemi). After being moved by the episode with the rug to rouse himself to action, he becomes a hero (of sorts) by deducing that which none of the other characters in the film could figure out—that the missing "trophy wife" has in fact kidnapped herself for the dual purpose of extortion and emancipation from her foolish, impotent husband. He has also ensured the continuation of his family line

by impregnating Maude, earning himself an authentic heir instead of one of the ersatz "Little Lebowski Achievers" that the Big Lebowski claimed as his own legacy.

In *Raising Arizona*, H.I.'s paternal anxieties drive the action and give the final dream sequence its bittersweet flavor. In *The Big Lebowski*, The Dude's new identity as a father-to-be is mentioned only in passing by the narrator, whose inability to stay on track with his observations points out his own seeming superfluousness to the proceedings. He's as out of place as the tumbleweed that breezes by in the opening sequence: Both are reliable archetypes rendered comically unfamiliar by the coastal setting, as if two dusty refugees from a nineteenth-century Wild West show had followed their manifest destiny right to the edge of the Pacific Ocean. The incongruity of the iconography between Old West and West Coast can be read as the Coens staging a collision between two foundational Hollywood genres—the Western and the noir— but the playfulness has a purpose beyond an initial non-sequitur giggle. Somewhere around the middle of the film, after The Dude has enlisted Walter (or rather been forced to invite him) along on his pseudo-Marlowe-ian quest to retrieve the disappeared Bunny Lebowski, the pair ends up at the suburban home of one Arthur Digby Sellers, the author of 156 episodes of the 1960s NBC Western *Branded*. Walter unsurprisingly idolizes the writer of a show steeped in American hero worship, but is taken aback when he sees that Sellers is ensconced in a comically oversize iron lung—an image of the Old West machismo exemplified by *Branded* (and the narrator)—subsisting fragilely on life support while The Dude's soft-bodied innocuousness is what finally wins the day.

In their BFI monograph on *The Big Lebowski,* J.M. Tyree and Ben Walters have written about the idea that the Coens' oeuvre is fundamentally about interrogating (and parodying) concepts of masculinity. Note that the song that plays over the opening credits of *The Big Lebowski* is Bob Dylan's "The Man in Me," a romantic ballad that doubles as an ode to self-improvement. Variations on this theme abound: The bowling alley is depicted as a homosocial utopia where men avoid or complain about their partners, its equilibrium threatened only by the intrusion of a suspected pederast (John Turturro as the obscene Jesus Quintana). The contrast between Walter's gun-toting mania and The Dude's pot-smoking deference presents different models of manhood, with the meek Donny always caught in the middle. In what may be the film's single funniest throwaway shot, he's glimpsed looking into the middle distance when The Dude and Walter lock eyes with Jesus. The film is also suffused with homosexual panic, again exemplified in the character of Jesus. There's also fear of castration, which starts when the German nihilists pursuing The Dude throw a live ferret on him as he lies naked in the bath and culminates at the end of the showstopping dream

TAI CHI RUG
—
The rug (or the idea of a rug that "ties the room together") is central to The Dude's sense of well-being; here, we see him centered (in his mind and in the frame) against his new prize possession.

MAGIC CARPET RIDE
—
Throughout *The Big Lebowski*, The Dude's dreams and fantasies serve as projections of his inner life; here, Maude and the rug are linked as obscure objects of desire, floating serenely just out of his reach.

WALTER'S GUN
—
The Dude's paralyzing passivity is contrasted with Walter's relentless aggression. The incongruity of a friendship between a former campus radical and a Vietnam vet is the film's sweet, optimistic center—both of these late-sixties axioms find themselves desperately out of time in early-nineties Los Angeles.

BOWLING BALL TILE
—
Even in the 1990s, The Dude can't escape the specter of Richard Nixon; elsewhere, he runs up against avatars of American conservatism in the form of George H.W. Bush and the Big Lebowski himself (a dead ringer for Dick Cheney).

sequence when he dreams that they're chasing him with a massive pair of scissors, echoing an earlier threat (delivered by Peter Stormare in an accent several hundred kilograms heavier than the one in *Fargo*) to "cut off [his] Johnson."

The dream sequence is the place where all *The Big Lebowski*'s superficially mismatched parts come out to play: It's the thing that really ties the film together. As The Dude reels from the effects of a mickey slipped to him by the malevolent soft-core porn producer Jackie Treehorn (Ben Gazzara), he imagines the oasis of the bowling alley being infiltrated by Maude Lebowski, who is dressed as one of the Valkyries from the opera heard blaring earlier from her brother's speakers. She's joined by Saddam Hussein, recast as the guy who rents out lane-appropriate footwear. Meanwhile, The Dude imagines himself as a sexually vital figure out of one of Jackie's low-rent porn films and dances across chessboard floors imported from the Lebowski mansion. He then turns his attention to bowling (the one thing he can believably teach the impossibly worldly Maude to excel at) and, in a true moment of all-American Zen, transforms from the bowler into the ball.

The implicit contrast between The Dude's disheveled, inarticulate exterior and his exquisitely ordered, surpassingly Freudian fantasy world is funny in and of itself, illustrating that the man contains multitudes. It's also an interpretive key to a film in which everything

extraneous can be reconciled, from Midwestern WASP Walter's bizarre embrace of his ex-wife's Orthodox Judaism, which gives him a strange sort of moral authority in the showdown with the evil Germans (as if the embittered Vietnam vet was getting instead to reenact the uncomplicated heroism of World War II); to the Gipsy Kings' cover of "Hotel California" playing behind Jesus's first appearance (The Dude hates the Eagles, and so the film associates them with his deviant rival); to poor, doomed Donny, who is always being reprimanded for being "out of his element" despite never really getting to voice an opinion on anything and ends up as a jar of ashes accidentally scattered to the wind instead of the sea, as out of his element in death as he was in life.

"Donny's Death Scene" is the title of a song by the American rock band Wussy from their 2016 album *Forever Sounds*. In it, vocalist Lisa Walker gives Buscemi's character exactly the sort of star treatment the Coens deny him, paraphrasing lines from Walter's cliff-side eulogy ("like so many others of his generation / taken from the world before his time") and turning a fifth wheel into a tragic hero, complete with a pedal-steel salute. The scene where Donny is mourned by his two best (only?) friends is notable in that it's the only time that Walter and The Dude truly break their cycle of mutual antagonism. The image of Goodman's massive bulk sagging into a desperate embrace is unaccountably moving, even as it's framed by the narrator as just another

rotation among many: "I guess that's the way the whole durned human comedy keeps perpetuatin' itself down through the generations."

The Stranger's final monologue makes essentially the same point about life's circularity as Moses's parting words in *The Hudsucker Proxy*, with the grandiosity switched out for shamefaced self-deprecation: "Aw, look at me, I'm rambling." His confirmation that The Dude is going to have a son, meanwhile, picks up on Marge and Norm's final exchange in *Fargo*, minus that barely suppressed sense of dread. In addition to being the Coens' sweetest film, *The Big Lebowski* might be the only one with an unequivocally happy ending. "I happen to know that there's a little Lebowski on the way," The Stranger says, offering a modest rejoinder to the mock-gigantism of the film's title. And his subsequent promise to "catch [us] further down the trail" instills a sense of comfort that, far from being at odds with the "stupefying" nature of the story we've just witnessed, stems directly from it. The future is uncertain and possibly just as stupefying as everything that's come before, yet it's waiting for us all the same. The tumbleweed rolls on.

FRIENDS OF THE COENS

"Working with the Coen brothers . . . what is it like? Well, it's pretty great! They create a wonderful atmosphere for everyone's best work to surface—a sense of ease. You get the feeling that nothing's a big deal. They are true masters on so many levels, directing, producing, screenwriting, and film editing . . . they just know how to do it right."

—

Jeff Bridges

FILMS:

The Big Lebowski (1998)

True Grit (2010)

Lisa Walker
GUITARIST AND SINGER

In 2016, the critically acclaimed Ohio-based rock band Wussy released its sixth LP, *Forever Sounds*, featuring a song written by guitarist and singer Lisa Walker entitled "Donny's Death Scene." Singing sweetly over a hard, groaning guitar riff, Walker gives Steve Buscemi's hapless bowler an unexpectedly epic testament; her lyrics paraphrase the Coens' dialogue ("A man is down tonight") while generating their own poetic context: "See the camera pan the sky / and pastel stars change color in the light." The sincerity of Walker's tribute elevates the song from a cinephile in-joke into something as textured and moving as *The Big Lebowski* itself.

Can you talk a bit about your fondness for *The Big Lebowski,* and maybe Donny's death scene in particular?

If you work from home and you don't go out a lot, having cable can be a bit of a lifesaver. And *The Big Lebowski* is something that plays fairly regularly on channels like IFC and things like that. Any time I see it on, even if I'm working, it's nice to have it on in the background. It's comforting. It's a very friendly [set of] sounds and images. And I remember being transfixed by Donny's death scene. You don't really choose the moments that draw you in. And that moment, that crane shot I guess, where the camera pans out and he's lying in Walter's arms and you see the lights of the bowling alley, they seem like they're these special lights. The image fades out until it's only those lights. . . .

And it looks like a constellation. . . .

Yeah, it's like they're stars in a sky. This might sound hokey, but it's as if they're his stars, for his spirit. And there's this sound like a woman's voice, a singing voice. Like a wail—not an off-

putting one, but if you watch it you kind of hear it trailing off from the music. It's very haunting, and it's one of those things where it sucked me in in that moment. That scene that I'd seen a million times, that moment kind of haunted me. And I think that that was the image I was thinking of. And I thought [Walter's] "man down" thing, as corny as it is, is also very telling that he is a soldier, and in moments of true crisis Walter goes to that. It's a moment of love. It's a moment of bravery. It's beautiful.

There are a lot of levels to the film. . . .

I mean, it's an art piece to me. It's an art piece; it's like a moving painting that uses *Night of the Hunter* like a Rosetta stone, if you will. It's the way that great authors retell stories, like *The Odyssey* or biblical stories. They tell them as modern stories even though they're as old as time. I know that sounds stupid, but . . .

It sounds like the Sam Elliott narration at the end of the film, actually. "The whole durned human comedy keeps perpetuatin' itself down through the generations."

Exactly. It's like at the end of *Night of the Hunter*, when Rachel says that "the children, they abide." It's to say the spirit of youth lives and thrives despite hardship. And that's exactly what Elliott says when he says, "The Dude abides."

Yes, absolutely. And isn't it beautiful that in a film called *The Big Lebowski* the last thing we learn is that there's going to be a little Lebowski?

I cry every time I watch it. It sounds ridiculous maybe. Honestly the first time I saw it, I didn't get it; it took two viewings to really like it. I watched it the second time thinking, "Oh gosh. I'm an idiot. This is the greatest thing I've ever seen!"

I love that you gave Donny a musical tribute because he's sort of the least developed character in this complicated movie. He exists between the two extremes of The Dude and Walter, in this middle ground. . . .

Not to me! I think Donny represents so much. He's an underdog, and an innocent. Those are the characters who I root for the most. If I'm reading

something or watching a film or a TV show, I'm drawn to those characters. I don't want anything bad to happen to them. There are certain people about whom you're like, "Gosh, you could hurt anyone, but not them!" and it's so tragic that he has to meet his end. It kind of brings some reality to the movie, and it keeps it from being . . .

A total cartoon?

Yeah, and from being too light, because it's a reminder that actions have consequences. And sometimes innocents are caught in the crossfire. And the thing about the eulogy, too—it's as funny as it is beautiful. It's ridiculous and yet it's not. The fact that they've figured that out . . . I thought it needed some applause—without totally ripping it off—and that's one thing I was trying to get across with the song.

Can't Stop What's Coming

2001 — 2006

I N 2001, JOEL Coen shared the Best Director prize for *The Man Who Wasn't There* at Cannes with David Lynch—a split decision that ended up looking curious in the context of the two movies being rewarded. Lynch was tapped for *Mulholland Dr.* (2001), a marvelous, mind-bending melodrama that was hailed by many as its maker's return to form after a decade of underwhelming features; its rich, haunting Hollywood dreamscape and jaw-dropping lead turn by newcomer Naomi Watts put it in the conversation with *Blue Velvet* (1986) as the director's masterpiece. Lynch was rewarded with great reviews, strong box office, and an Oscar nomination for Best Director (losing to Ron Howard). But when *The Man Who Wasn't There* eventually made its way onto American screens, it was with little fanfare or sense of celebration. While no less accomplished an evocation of a hybrid real/cinematic past than *O Brother, Where Art Thou?*, the film's shady noir-isms failed to catch the popular imagination like its predecessor's tuneful screwball humanism; it became their lowest-grossing release since *Barton Fink* (which also won Best Director at Cannes).

Box office is no way to measure artistic merit, and it would be overstating the case to call a film as generally well received as *The Man Who Wasn't There* (which *The Guardian*'s Peter Bradshaw flatly labeled "The best American film of the year") a failure. But it did open the 2000s on a less than triumphant note for the Coens, setting up a half-decade stretch that is generally taken to be their driest period creatively, if not commercially. Their follow-up to *The Man Who Wasn't There* was supposed to be an adaptation of *Deliverance* author James Dickey's 1993 novel *To the White Sea* into an epic action movie. The book is a terse, exciting account of a downed American rear-gunner trying to survive in the Japanese capital during an attack by his own countrymen; the Coens' plan was to film it mostly without dialogue. "Don't set a movie in Tokyo during the firebombing unless you have a lot of money to pay for it," Joel said in 2010 of the scuttled project, which was to have starred Brad Pitt ("He's too old now," added Ethan in an interview with *Time* in 2007).

To the White Sea would have been the Coens' first film set in another country, and also their first time working from an externally generated screenplay: The script for *To the White Sea* was written by the team of David and Janet Peoples, who wrote *12 Monkeys* (1995). It's interesting, perhaps, that the film they took on instead—*Intolerable Cruelty*—was similarly the work of other writers, at least originally. The story of a divorce lawyer who falls in love with the wife of his client was credited to TV scribe John Romano before being finessed by Robert Ramsey and Matthew Stone; in 1994, as they were working on *The Hudsucker Proxy*, the Coens were asked to do a rewrite of the script so that it could be made by somebody else—the prime candidate being Jonathan Demme, who'd done brilliantly with similarly screwball material in *Something Wild* (1986) and *Married to the Mob* (1988).

That the Coens ended up returning, a decade after the fact, to what was essentially a work-for-hire job, did not exactly frame *Intolerable Cruelty* as a passion project. Universal tried to sell the film more as a star vehicle for George Clooney and Catherine Zeta-Jones (the latter having just won an Oscar for Best Supporting Actress for *Chicago* [2002]), and the combination of conspicuously above-the-title talent, casually luxurious production values—including a $60 million budget that doubled the supposedly sky-high cost of *The Hudsucker Proxy*—and a producer's credit for hit-maker Brian Grazer gave *Intolerable Cruelty* the sheen of a mainstream studio release rather than an auteurist vision. "There's plenty of reason for an involuntary recoil toward the Coen brothers' fearsomely titled new movie," wrote Elvis Mitchell at the outset of his (ultimately positive) assessment in the *New York Times*; "more conventional than anything [the Coens] have done in the past," suggested *Variety*'s David Rooney. Debuting at Venice rather than Cannes—a geographic shift that could be interpreted as a step down, prestige-wise—*Intolerable Cruelty* ended up doing very well commercially (more than $100 million at the American box office).

Like *Intolerable Cruelty, The Ladykillers* was also intended for a different director: The Coens wrote a remake of the 1955 Ealing Studios comedy about a group of thieves posing as musicians—and waging war against their oblivious little old landlady—at the behest of their former cinematographer Barry Sonnenfeld. When he bowed out of shooting the script, they decided to take things on themselves.

Shifting the story to the American South—creating a Mississippi diptych with *O Brother, Where Art Thou?*—did put some distance between the Coens' *Ladykillers* and its London-set source material, and casting Tom Hanks as the villains' grandiloquent ringleader seemingly ensured a certain level of box-office performance. But by literally remaking a single well-regarded film rather than their usual method of paying homage to several different sources at once, the Coens were risking critical derision. They seemed to know it, too: In the introduction to the published script, their editor Roderick Jaynes—long established as a fictional character, a phantom conjured up so the brothers could cut their movies without officially taking credit— opens his essay by saying, simply: "I begged them not to do it."

"Listening to the gospel numbers T-Bone Burnett has chosen, you'd think the Coens are trying to repeat the success of the *O Brother, Where Art Thou?* soundtrack," chided *Salon*'s Charles Taylor, sounding a note of exasperation that continued through the majority of the film's reviews. Despite earning a special

jury prize at Cannes for star Irma P. Hall—shared, quite bizarrely, with the experimental Thai director Apichatpong Weerasethakul—*The Ladykillers* was the Coens' most poorly received movie, and while the casting of Hanks paid off with a $75 million US gross (more than enough to recoup its budget), the general lack of enthusiasm in the aftermath of its release suggested that Roderick Jaynes may have known something his longtime collaborators didn't. A case can be made that *The Ladykillers* is underrated, and that the boldness of swapping out a brittle British pensioner for an elderly African-American woman—in effect generating an entirely new sociocultural context for a story of sinners and their divinely ordained punishment—is actually among the Coens' most interestingly idiosyncratic maneuvers. But if *The Ladykillers* is going to be remembered as a landmark, it will be for administrative rather than artistic reasons: It's the first of the brothers' movies to credit both as co-directors. Long after it had been established via interviews and set reports that Joel and Ethan already shared those duties, they decided to make it official, citing the film's convoluted genesis as the basis for declaring shared authorship.

This choice would be significant a few years later when the Coens collected twin Best Director Oscars for *No Country for Old Men*, a film that definitively reversed their early twenty-first-century downward trend. In an interview with *Collider*, Joel explained that producer Scott Rudin had sent them early galleys of Cormac McCarthy's novel. "We'd read [McCarthy's] other books for pleasure and liked him a lot, but this one we thought could make a really interesting movie." On the page, McCarthy's story of a Texas sheriff on the trail of a relentless bounty hunter—himself tracking a Vietnam vet on the run with $2 million of stolen drug money—was terse and propulsive and cinematic; Ethan told *The Guardian* that it made him think of Sam Peckinpah. "Hard men in the Southwest shooting each other," he said. "We were aware of those similarities, certainly."

The parallels between *Fargo* and *No Country for Old Men* as "returns to form" are striking: Both followed studio-subsidized disappointments and adopted a leaner production model; both were lighter on eye-catching style and inter-textual references than the brothers' norm. Co-financed by Miramax and Paramount Classics for $25 million and shot mostly on location in Texas and New Mexico, the film was the brothers' most strictly realistic production since—yes—*Fargo*, and the Coens claimed their creative process was similarly minimal: In interviews, they trotted out variations on the joke that adapting McCarthy's book

was as simple as holding it open and copying dialogue into a word-processing program. ("Paperback novels won't lie open properly!" added Ethan to *The Guardian*. "They flip shut.")

Unlike *The Man Who Wasn't There* and *The Ladykillers*, *No Country for Old Men* left Cannes empty-handed but with an advance guard of reviews hailing it as a masterpiece—a word that popped up with even greater frequency once it came out in the fall of 2007. "*No Country for Old Men* is as good a film as Joel and Ethan Coen have ever made. . . . To make one such film is a miracle. Here is another." Released into an anxious American zeitgeist that seemed to demand antiheroes—2007 also being the

year of Paul Thomas Anderson's demented oil-fields fable *There Will Be Blood*, featuring Daniel Day-Lewis as a sociopathic capitalist—*No Country for Old Men* felt like a movie of the moment: Javier Bardem's hit man Anton Chigurh was the Coens' most instantly iconic character since Marge Gunderson.

No Country for Old Men's global gross of more than $170 million was remarkable considering its stark, bleak, uncompromising tone and viciously depicted violence. Winning four Academy Awards, including Best Picture (defeating *There Will Be Blood* in the process), went a long way toward attracting a wide audience for a movie that plays out like the opposite of a crowd-pleaser.

O Brother, Where Art Thou?

RELEASE DATE
December 22, 2000
BUDGET
$26M
DISTRIBUTOR
Buena Vista Pictures
CAST
George Clooney
John Turturro
Tim Blake Nelson
John Goodman
Holly Hunter
Chris Thomas King
Charles Durning
Del Pentecost

WARNING!
THIS FILM CONTAINS

Old-timey music	33%
Homeric allusions	19%
Preston Sturges allusions	10%
Pomade	9%
White robes	8%
Blind eyes	5%
Imperiled cattle	7%
Barbecued gopher	6%
Grammy Awards	3%
Buried treasure	0%

WRITTEN IN 1928, Harry McClintock's "Big Rock Candy Mountain" is a song about the bitter earth transformed into a utopia—heaven on the ground. McClintock, who lived rough in his youth, based his lyrics on the fourteenth-century legend of "Cockaigne," a place of pure comfort and carnivalesque liberty in which social norms are reversed or upended and the privileged hold no sway over the lower classes. His version of this long-standing escapist fantasy is specifically addressed to the downtrodden and dispossessed, who'd have the most to gain in the case of such a miraculous realm materializing out of thin air: "In the Big Rock Candy Mountain, the jails are made of tin / and you can walk right out again as soon as you are in." The jaunty melody turned the song into an optimistic anthem (and a radio hit when it was rerecorded in 1959 by Burl Ives), but the distance between its narrator's pie-eyed promises and the bare-cupboard reality of the times in which it was written gives it a desperately sad aftertaste: It's the folk music equivalent of whistling in the dark.

A song that transposes an ancient fable into modern times is the perfect ideal for *O Brother, Where Art Thou?* Just as McClintock drew from ancient myth for his hobo anthem, so too did Joel and Ethan Coen reach back to find inspiration for their own Depression-era ballad. Beneath a vintage recording of McClintock singing "Big Rock Candy Mountain," the film's opening credit sequence includes a card claiming that the film's screenplay

Top: Roger Deakins' drained
color palette evokes the
Depression-era photography
of Walker Evans.

Bottom: The convicts are
always under threat, even
from a shotgun-toting child.

was "Based upon *The Odyssey* by Homer," a bold statement with multiple levels of (jocular) implication. First, the Coens had borrowed hugely from other literary works before without footnotes; *Miller's Crossing* did not advertise itself as being "based on *Red Harvest* by Dashiell Hammett." The brothers went out of their way in interviews to crow that they hadn't actually read Homer, but rather integrated his most famous episodes from memory into a script about jail-breaking convicts that had lain dormant since the late 1980s. "Whenever it's convenient," said Joel, "we trot out *The Odyssey*."

The Coens' performative disavowals aside, there is a hint to a less canonical (or acknowledged) reference point in the surname of one of the film's minor villains: Vernon T. Waldrip (Ray McKinnon), who appears late in the film as a romantic rival for escaped fugitive Ulysses Everett McGill (George Clooney). Waldrip is set on marrying Everett's estranged wife, Penny (Holly Hunter). She refuses to recognize her husband, who has returned home dragging a criminal record behind him; her demand is for a partner who is "bona fide." It doesn't take a Classics degree to recognize the significance of characters named Ulysses and Penelope in a work that name-checks *The Odyssey*—the former is Homer's heroic, wandering hero, the latter his steadfast and constant bride, whose home port of Ithaca is his destination after a decade at sea—but Waldrip seems like a nod to the fantasy writer Howard Waldrop, whose 1989 novella

PERFECT HAIR
—
Everett's assertion that he's a "Dapper Dan man" emphasizes his dandyish vanity while continuing the Coens' running theme of characters fretting over what's on their heads.

"WE'RE MASS COMMUNICATING"
—
The relationship of "old-timey" music to the newfangled apparatus that will spread it far and wide is underlined via a striking insert shot of recording technology.

FUNNY LITTLE FROG
—
The magic realism of *O Brother, Where Art Thou?* is judiciously applied; the sirens don't actually turn Delmar into a toad, which keeps the film's action in the realm of plausibility.

A Dozen Tough Jobs humorously relocates the Twelve Labors of Hercules to Depression-era Mississippi, the same setting that the Coens selected for their own Americanized pastiche of Greek myth.

The Coens haven't gone on the record about reading *A Dozen Tough Jobs*, but considering the general magpie-ism of their approach to screenwriting, it might be beside the point to zero in on any one influence. Like *The Hudsucker Proxy* and *The Big Lebowski*—two films it joins on the screwball side of its creators' filmography—*O Brother, Where Art Thou?* is a promiscuously postmodern work. Its postmodern influence begins with its title, which is taken from Preston Sturges's 1941 screwball comedy *Sullivan's Travels*, and extends to its use of real and quasi-authentic figures from 1930s American history as supporting characters. These include the bank robber George "Babyface" Nelson, energetically impersonated by Michael Badalucco, and the blues musician Tommy Johnson (Chris Thomas King), whose apocryphal encounter and subsequent Faustian bargain with the Devil—misattributed years later to the more famous and contemporaneous guitarist Robert Johnson—is recounted in passing. Nothing in the film is "original" except for the reconfiguration of elements, which is why the opening citation is more honest than it seems and, in its way, a signifier not of smarminess but humility. The nod to *The Odyssey* admits that any artist in the Western tradition owes some currency of debt to Homer, and that to mount any story about homecoming is to reconnect with the roots of storytelling itself—to return to the primal scene.

That sense of ancient and hallowed ground is central to *O Brother*. Like *Raising Arizona* and *Fargo* (and, to a lesser extent, *Blood Simple*), the Coens' eighth feature is a landscape film, eschewing urban structures for wide open spaces: forest clearings, back roads, and farmers' fields. It has its own distinctive palette—an old-fashioned photochemical tint achieved, with maximum technological irony, via a digital color-correction process—and a horizontal aesthetic that emphasizes the left-to-right sprawl of its Mississippi setting, using that flatness as a launching pad for a series of sight gags. The first time we see Everett and fellow chain-gang escapees Pete Hogwallop (John Turturro) and Delmar O'Donnell (Tim Blake Nelson), they're popping up over the horizon line before stealthily disappearing from view beneath rows of yellow corn. The staging recalls the up-through-the-muck jailbreak of the Snoats brothers in *Raising Arizona*, where the sight of two large, screaming men emerging from the wet, muddy ground served to parody miracle-of-life piety in a film about wannabe breeders. The visual joke carries a different meaning here: It positions these quixotic convicts as pure products of the rich, fertile Delta soil.

Everything seems to spring directly from the earth in *O Brother*, which features a more organic look than any of the Coens' previous forays into the past. In *Miller's Crossing* and *The Hudsucker Proxy*, the re-creations of bygone eras were largely a matter of stylized production and costume design; that also holds true for *O Brother*, but the sense of pastness is also deeply embedded in the texture of the image itself. Roger Deakins's desaturated color palette hones in on yellows and greens and avoids blues and reds (with one striking, nightmarish exception for the latter). Its slightly sepia look evokes the photographs of Walker Evans and Dorothea Lange, but with the onus shifted away from documentary authenticity toward fantasy—it's the most gilded Dust Bowl in film history. More than any of its predecessors, *O Brother* is enchanted around the edges, rendering a socially and economically harsh historical period in gently fantastical strokes.

This is a provocative and potentially problematic choice, since it runs the risk of not taking the Depression and its devastating effects and legacies seriously. Any movie made under the sign of *Sullivan's Travels*, however, is obviously going to eschew po-faced social realism. In Sturges's classic, a pretentious film director (Joel McCrea) sets out to make a serious drama about the Great Depression and ends up impersonating a penniless hobo in an attempt to "better know trouble"; in an unsurprisingly ironic twist, he is robbed of his money and his identity and ends up truly walking a mile (hundreds of them, in fact) in the shoes of a man less fortunate than himself. Throughout Sullivan's Deep South odyssey, Sturges mercilessly satirizes the liberal impulse toward socially conscious art: The author of the book-within-the-film, also titled *O Brother, Where Art Thou?* is Sinclair Beckstein, whose name kids Sinclair Lewis, John Steinbeck, and Upton Sinclair all at once.

The moral of *Sullivan's Travels*, which occurs to its vainglorious protagonist later than its audience, is that art with a message is less valuable than that which sets out, energetically and unpretentiously, to entertain. "In our minds, [*O Brother*] was presumably the movie that Sullivan would have made if he'd had the chance . . . the one that takes on the big important themes," explained the Coens. Their claim may have been meant sarcastically, but the fact is that *O Brother* doesn't shy away from dealing with darker historical truths amid its lighthearted annotations of *The Odyssey*. This is a film in which the villainous characters are revealed to be white supremacists and members of the Ku Klux Klan, and there is more acknowledgment of racial difference and inequality than in any of their other films except perhaps *The Ladykillers*, which is also steeped in the culture of the American Deep South.

That the Coens treat this material in a broad, stylized way doesn't diminish its potency. *O Brother, Where Art Thou?* is a picaresque, meaning that its scattered, lowbrow humor is deployed in the service of social commentary. In picaresque fiction, ignoble heroes serve as tour guides through imperfect societies; their exclusion from wealth and power grants them moral authority, even though they are fools. The different variations on idiocy wrung by Clooney, Turturro, and Nelson are amusing and specific (Clooney's dandified impersonation of Clark Gable's signature role in *It Happened One Night* is particularly acute), but they derive from Nicolas Cage's work as H.I. in *Raising Arizona* and Tim Robbins' as Norville Barnes in *The Hudsucker Proxy*. The emphasis is not on stupidity, but innocence. Unshaven and with stripes around their shoulders, they give the appearance of hard men, and yet they are, in their way, incorruptible: When Delmar goes and gets "saved" by a congregation of evangelical Christians gathered by a river in the woods, Nelson's puppy-eyed enthusiasm suggests that his character is already one of God's creatures.

In terms of *O Brother*'s supposed engagement with Homeric myth, the Baptists are pretty clearly stand-ins for the Lotus Eaters in *The Odyssey*, a cult of true believers mesmerized by a combination of narcotics and prayer. The conflation of an ancient Greek religious sect with evangelical Christianity is not, in and of itself, especially withering, but the visual link between these benign churchgoers, all dressed in white, and the robes of the Klansmen who gather at the film's climax to try to lynch an African-American character is overt and disturbing. In both cases, "ol' time religion" is tantamount to conformist delirium, heightened by the use of music: a lovely ensemble rendition of "Down to the River to Pray" in the first scene, and a stark, solo version of "O Death" to kick off the latter.

Both of these performances are staged as emanating from within the world of the film—as diegetic sound—as is every other song in the film except "Big Rock Candy Mountain." *O Brother, Where Art Thou?* is, in fact, swathed from beginning to end in music, which is performed within the world of the story rather than being used more conventionally as underscoring. In generic terms, the film is a musical as surely as it is a road movie or a period piece, which is not only its conceptual masterstroke, but also the impetus for its massive commercial success. Released in October 2000, the film quickly became the Coens' biggest-ever box-office hit, buoyed by a soundtrack that topped the Billboard 100—an unlikely champion in a musical moment dominated by pop and hip-hop. (It also won a Grammy for Album of the Year, defeating Outkast, U2, and Bob Dylan.)

The mainstream chord struck by *O Brother*'s carefully picked selection of country, blues, and gospel standards—chosen by music producer T-Bone Burnett in collaboration with the filmmakers and recorded in its entirety before the beginning of the shoot—reflected the novelty, for modern listeners, of being introduced to "old-timey" music, a phenomenon that also plays out, suggestively, within the film itself. In order to earn a bit of money while on the lam, Everett, Pete, and Delmar masquerade as a musical group called the Soggy Bottom Boys. With the help of Tommy Johnson, they improbably perform a flawless version of "Man of Constant Sorrow" that becomes a massive popular success, transforming the trio into recording stars (a twist of fate that helps to save them later in the film, when they're being pursued by members of the Ku Klux Klan). "Man of Constant Sorrow" was the breakout hit from the *O Brother, Where Art Thou?* soundtrack—an emblem of its fetching traditionalism—and yet in the context of the film's 1930s world, it's already "old-timey music": an anachronistic throwback that unexpectedly delights a contemporary audience.

Top: The gradual transformation of Ulysses Everett McGill into his ancient Greek namesake is one of *O Brother*'s best-prepared jokes; the fake beard he dons at the climax gives him a Homeric bearing at last.

Bottom: The seemingly innate ability of O Brothers' characters—including Peter and Delmer—to sing and harmonize on key and at will suggests that music is a natural part of their community and culture; they inhabit the folk melodies of the era.

ON AIR

The enchanted, fairy-tale atmosphere of *O Brother, Where Art Thou?* conceals a subtle commentary on cultural appropriation. African-American guitarist Tommy Johnson sits off to the side while the Soggy Bottom boys—posing as "colored" musicians—record their hit version of "Man of Constant Sorrow." The cluster of circles within the shot frames the idea that this "old-timey music" has continuous appeal, while the reflection of the record executive in the glass hints at the similarly eternal, recursive commodification of culture.

"If it's not new and it never grows old, it's a folk song," quips the hero of *Inside Llewyn Davis*, which is *O Brother, Where Art Thou?*'s spiritual sequel. Taken together, the two films clarify the Coens' relationship to a musical genre founded on familiarity. For filmmakers perpetually interested in circles and circularity, the cyclical proliferation and popularity of folk and bluegrass standards—songs largely without cited authors, passed down and performed by different singers through the generations—serves as a potent analogue to their thematic preoccupations. Jeffrey Adams writes that "all the music chosen for the film is rooted in the southern regions in the 1920s and '30s," which is correct, but several date back even further. "Down to the River to Pray" and "Keep on the Sunny Side"—and "Big Rock Candy Mountain"—were actually originally written in the late nineteenth century. The sense that these are songs that everybody in the film's world already knows helps to

account for why characters not formally trained as musicians—i.e., the Soggy Bottom Boys, as opposed to crack axeman Tommy—are able to conjure up such sweet melodies and harmonies. The Coens' fabulist vision of an older, weirder America where everybody can mysteriously carry a tune gets threaded through a larger truth of "roots music," which is that it is less about creation than interpretation, honoring the past by channeling it.

The overnight success of the Soggy Bottom Boys' recording of "Man of Constant Sorrow" rhymes with Norville Barnes's faddish bonanza in *The Hudsucker Proxy*. In musical terms, Everett and his collaborators aren't doing much more than reinventing the wheel. But where Norville came up with what is essentially a tool of distraction, the Soggy Bottom Boys are touching—however inadvertently—a tender and sensitive collective nerve. The irony of "Man of Constant Sorrow"

The appearance of the sirens provides *O Brother, Where Art Thou?* with one of its broadest, most direct allusions to *The Odyssey*, while their seductive lullaby plays up the heroes' childish innocence.

becoming a hit on the basis of its "old-timey" vibe is that its lyrics describe a melancholy and desperation that's very much in tune with the tenor of the Great Depression. The narrator's claim that he has "seen trouble all [his] days" could be connected equally to the plight of the original Ulysses (whose Greek name, roughly translated, means "son of pain") or to the ever-unlucky Everett (who is the author of some, but not all, of his bad luck) or to Sullivan and his arrogant compulsion to "know trouble"—or to the United States' African-American population in the early twentieth century, whose freedom from the institution of slavery was not an escape from racial prejudice. Because the radio station manager (Stephen Root) is blind, he doesn't realize that the Soggy Bottom Boys, who claim to be "colored boys," are actually, with the exception of Tommy, completely Caucasian, a quick but penetrating dig at the tradition of white artists appropriating Black culture.

The first performance of "Man of Constant Sorrow" is surprising and delightful, but shot through with anxiety (Clooney's wide-eyed acting speaks to Everett's nervousness about hitting the notes). The second time it's sung live is triumphant: Disguised in long, shaggy beards (another nod to *The Odyssey*, and Ulysses's similar tactic of hiding his true identity when he first gets back to Ithaca), the Soggy Bottom Boys play for a large and appreciative crowd who are unaware that their musical heroes are escaped convicts. This time, the song's melancholy is transformed into something raucous and cathartic—not sorrow, but communion. In lieu of the portentous solemnity of the born-again Christians or the psychopathic mania of the Klansmen, the number shows a community united in fellow feeling and, in short order, likewise united against the embittered, racist gubernatorial candidate Homer Stokes (Wayne Duvall), who has all but declared the Soggy Bottom Boys an enemy of the people. Stokes is a complex comic creation, a stout, unassuming figure whose claims to stand up for "the little people" are literalized by his traveling to political events with a midget. The condescension of his persona recalls Barton Fink.

It's a predictable but significant twist that this would-be reformer, whose rallying cry is to "sweep the state clean," is revealed to be the Grand Wizard of the local chapter of the KKK. As with friendly salesman turned avenging angel Charlie Meadows in *Barton Fink*, the Coens sketch the proximity of populist rhetoric and fascist ideology. That the Soggy Bottom Boys end up toppling the state's racist power structure—literally, in the scene where they infiltrate the Klan rally, by tipping a flaming cross onto brutish lieutenant Big Dan Teague (John Goodman)—is a happy by-product of their hapless quest for treasure. Their color blindness, which begins with giving Tommy a lift in their stolen car and culminates in their freeing him from the gallows, is admirable, offsetting their general dopiness and motivation, which is avarice: Everett has promised Pete and Delmar buried treasure, which, in accordance with the Coens' ambivalence toward financial reward, is never found.

Instead, what Everett retrieves—and what further connects him to the original Ulysses—is his wife and daughters. His repeated, flustered claim that he's the "goddamned paterfamilias"

fits in with the lineage of anguished father figures in the Coens' cinema, beginning with *Raising Arizona*, and Hunter's performance suggests nothing so much as a (hyperbolically) fertile variation on her earlier role as Ed. Penny's irritation with her husband stems from the fact that he got himself sent to jail (more than once) when he had six daughters at home; it's as if Ed had given birth to the Arizona quintuplets (and change) and then left H.I. when he wouldn't stop robbing banks. Penny is cruel to Everett, but Hunter's controlled performance makes it clear that she doesn't hate him. She wants him to grow up and take responsibility for his family, the true treasure that awaits him at the end of his odyssey.

Everett's ultimate gratification is delayed by a final twist of the plot: Even after he's reunited with Penny, he and his friends are apprehended by the demonic Sheriff Cooley (Daniel Von Bargen), who has pursued them through the entire film (terse and quiet behind sunglasses that always manage to catch the reflection of flames, the sheriff is in the human-bloodhound tradition of the Lone Biker of the Apocalypse from *Raising Arizona*). It is here that the Coens unleash the trickiest of their Homeric allusions: The Soggy Bottom Boys are saved from hanging by a flood—a deus ex machina in the ancient Greek tradition, even though in *The Odyssey*, it was Poseidon, god of the sea, who did his

best to block Ulysses's passage to Ithaca. The intrusion of divine providence recalls the duel of the Fates at the end of *The Hudsucker Proxy* and looks ahead both to *The Ladykillers*, with its pious heroine protected from harm by a higher power, and to the fully biblical incidents of *A Serious Man*.

The irony of Everett, who styles himself as an intellectual despite his lack of cerebral resources, being saved in this fashion is laid on rather thick during his final monologue. Floating serenely in the wake of the flood, he doesn't express gratitude at being "saved" like Delmar did during his baptism, but begins pontificating that a new mastery of hydroelectric power is going to create a "brave new world…a veritable age of reason." Everett's vision of things to come as a scientifically engineered utopia is as cockeyed as Cockaigne, but its optimism is in keeping with *O Brother*'s picaresque spirit: the hope that things are going to get better overriding the lived experience that they seldom do. Ulysses Everett McGill doesn't fear the future, because he doesn't know any better, and in the film's closing shots, he's permitted the same happy ending as his namesake: His constant sorrow is at an end. As for the "veritable age of reason" he sees on the horizon, it's still yet to come—as faint and far away as the Big Rock Candy Mountain.

UNFRIENDLY GIANT
—
John Goodman's cyclopean Big Dan Teague is a Coen archetype: a hail-fellow-well-met charmer whose gift of gab belies a base brutaity.

BIRTH OF A NATION
—
The use of the Ku Klux Klan as villains shows *O Brother, Where Art Thou?*'s reckoning with the racial tensions of its historical setting.

A 'Coens' Jukebox

Bob Dylan's "The Man in Me" plays over the opening credits of *The Big Lebowski*—a hymn to tender masculinity.

Llewyn Davis makes an earnest, devastating mistake by playing the mournful, old-fashioned "Death of Queen Jane" during his audition at the Gate of Horn.

The Four Tops' Motown classic efficiently expresses the theme of reciprocal violence and cruelty that spins through *Blood Simple*.

A gospel standard about the importance of piety introduces *The Ladykillers'* grim comedy of modern-day grift and greed.

"The Everlasting Arms" plays throughout *True Grit*, culminating in Iris DeMent's stark, unadorned cover version.

In *Miller's Crossing*'s most famous sequence, "Danny Boy" soundtracks Irish mob boss Leo O'Bannon's triumph over two Italian hitmen.

The King's version of "Suspicious Minds" frames *Intolerable Cruelty*'s story of philandering, jealousy, and shady pre-nuptial agreements.

A Serious Man builds toward the moment when the wizened sage Rabbi Marshak quotes Jefferson Airplane's psych-rock hit as if it contains the wisdom of the ages.

The Man Who Wasn't There

RELEASE DATE
October 31, 2001
BUDGET
$20M
DISTRIBUTOR
USA Films
CAST
Billy Bob Thornton
Frances McDormand
Michael Badalucco
James Gandolfini
Katherine Borowitz
Jon Polito
Scarlett Johansson
Richard Jenkins

WARNING!
THIS FILM CONTAINS

The Stranger	19%
Double Indemnity	16%
Lolita	13%
Hair clippings	11%
Beethoven sonatas	10%
UFO sightings	9%
Philandering	8%
Pie-eating contests	7%
Bingo night	5%
Night of the Hunter	2%
Color	0%

"GROOMING, MY FRIEND, is the most important thing in business – after personality, of course." So says entrepreneur Creighton Tolliver (Jon Polito) to Ed Crane (Billy Bob Thornton), the stranger he's trying to embroil in a get-rich-quick scheme. Creighton is a man committed to keeping up appearances; vain and supercilious despite his short stature, he hides his baldness beneath a toupee made of real human hair.

For Creighton, grooming is personality. Ed, meanwhile, is in the business of grooming. He cuts hair for a living, and he's good at it, although he derives no pleasure from it. It's simply a task, prescribed and mechanical. Hence his attempt to shift into business by subsidizing Creighton's plan to start a chain of dry-cleaning stores, a risky but potentially rewarding venture that he thinks might finally get him out of the barbershop that serves daily as his prison – a site of unfathomable, existential boredom bound up in the parade of near-identical heads passing daily beneath his shears.

The Coens first came up with the idea for *The Man Who Wasn't There* while filming *The Hudsucker Proxy*; after seeing a vintage poster displaying different 1940s-era male haircuts, they decided that a story set in a

barbershop was potentially interesting, and then proceeded to undermine that idea in interviews before the film's release. "We're doing a movie about a barber in Northern California in the early 1940s," Joel told Jim Ridley in 2000 during the press tour for *O Brother, Where Art Thou?* "I was in Texas a while ago," he continued, "and I told that to Ann Richards, the former governor. She looked at me for about twenty seconds and said, 'I'm trying real hard to get excited about this.'"

His joke has a measure of truth to it. Despite receiving strong reviews and a Best Director prize at the 2001 Cannes Film Festival, *The Man Who Wasn't There* hasn't endured in the same way as the titles immediately preceding it in the Coens' filmography. It lacks the cultural impact of *Fargo,* the cult bona fides of *The Big Lebowski,* and the surprising mainstream appeal of *O Brother, Where Art Thou?* Taking its cues from Thornton's skillfully inverted lead performance, it is among the Coens' most even-keeled movies, without the wild tonal shifts of several of its predecessors. It's short on eccentric or outrageous touches. In terms of allusiveness, it nods toward a host of filmic, literary, and even scientific sources, including a long monologue about the German quantum physicist Werner Heisenberg and his famed "Uncertainty Principle"—but without the daunting inter-textual density of *The Big Lebowski* or *O Brother, Where Art Thou?* The soundtrack is filled almost exclusively with sparely arranged piano sonatas by Beethoven. Overall, the feeling is one of tight, even suffocating formal control.

This reticence could be taken for a lack of personality, or a surfeit of grooming, as if the Coens were conducting an exercise in technique. Roger Deakins's sterling, hard-edged black-and-white cinematography, which perfectly mimics the textures and lighting values of postwar film noir and earned him an Oscar nomination, is the most obviously outstanding feature. (The film was shot on color stock and printed in black and white.) Whereas in *O Brother, Where Art Thou?*, Deakins played meaningfully with color and hue, here he doubles down on eye-catching compositions. Many of the most memorable moments in *The Man Who Wasn't There* are purely visual: the cracking pane of glass during Ed's fatal struggle with his wife's lover, an optical illusion that makes it seem like the universe itself is splintering behind them; the play of light that

traps an ace attorney in shafts of shadows as he orates in his client's prison cell, which creates the spectacle of a man entrapped by his own rhetoric; the surreal sight of a hubcap dislodged in a violent car crash, spinning lazily off into the forest like a tumbling tumbleweed (or a man's hat caught in an updraft).

It's not all that hard to connect *Miller's Crossing* to *The Man Who Wasn't There*: Both films are period pieces that riff on classic Hollywood genres—the gangster picture and the film noir, respectively—and both feature supremely self-effacing lead performances. Thornton's acting as Ed Crane has some of Gabriel Byrne's soulful reluctance, and this barber, who by his own admission "doesn't talk much" and prefers to express himself through a running internal monologue, is very much a "bighead." Which is not to say that he's all that smart. His plan to get the money for Creighton by blackmailing Big Dave Brewster (James Gandolfini), the department store manager who is sleeping with his wife, Doris (Frances McDormand), is amateur-hour stuff. Big Dave is on to the deception quickly and confronts Ed in his office, where Ed kills him in self-defense. The next morning, Doris is arrested for the crime, with Ed proving incapable of admitting to the deed in any kind of meaningful way and instead blowing Doris's family's money on hiring a fast-talking lawyer, Freddy Riedenschneider (Tony Shalhoub), to act in her defense.

In thematic terms, *The Man Who Wasn't There* offers a reprise, and even a reversal, of *Miller's Crossing.* If the earlier film is about a character who studiously learns to divest himself of all human feeling—to become so comfortably numb that he can murder his rival and walk away from his best friend with the same serene detachment—*The Man Who Wasn't There* concerns a protagonist who wants to fill up his empty life before it's too late. We might even say that Ed Crane, whose job is focused on the heads of others, spends the entire movie chasing his hat.

Just as the spinning hubcap unexpectedly transforms before our eyes late in the film into a hovering UFO (a rare example of a stand-alone special effect from filmmakers who generally prefer more integrated forms of illusionism), the object of Ed's desire keeps shape-shifting throughout *The Man Who Wasn't There*. At

CLIPPINGS

—

A motif of transience runs through
The Man Who Wasn't There; the hair
clippings provide physical evidence
of the customers who pass through
Ed's barbershop before he sweeps
them away.

ONLY HIS HAIRDRESSER
KNOWS FOR SURE

—

Creighton Tolliver's hairpiece hints
at his phoniness as well as his
vulnerability, uncovered scalps also
being a sign of weakness in *Miller's
Crossing* and *O Brother, Where
Art Thou?*

BIRDY

—

Although she's introduced playing
Beethoven on the piano, Birdy is no
piano prodigy. Her musical ambitions
are largely Ed's invention to justify
his attraction to her youth and beauty.

first, it's something abstract: the vague promise
of a better future attached to a start-up dry-
cleaning venture.

Later, Ed will transfer those same aspirations
to cultivate something fresh to the comely form
of Birdy (Scarlett Johannson), the teenaged
daughter of his neighbor. Both the blackmail
plot and the girl next door represent escape
routes—one from his deadening vocation as a
barber, the other from his stale, loveless, sexless
marriage to Doris. Unfortunately, these two
paths are hopelessly interlaced. Birdy's virginal
purity marks her as a human analogue for the
unblemished perfection of the dry-cleaning
technology, but her barely submerged sexual
appeal also makes her a distorted mirror image of
Doris, not to mention a stand-in for the children
that Ed and Doris's union has not yet produced
(a darker version of the paternal anxiety that
runs through *Raising Arizona, O Brother,
Where Art Thou?, The Big Lebowski*, and *Inside
Llewyn Davis*).

Ed shaving Doris's legs in
the bathtub suggests that
the boredom and subservience
he feels at the barbershop
extends into the domestic
sphere as well.

The things that Ed wants—a fulfilling job, an attractive partner, a prosperous family life—mark him as a very conventional man, and yet *The Man Who Wasn't There* draws much of its power from how rigorously it interrogates the idea of its protagonist's normality. Or rather, if Ed Crane is Everyman, then it's frightening to consider the welter of resentment, fear, and denial binding together the social fabric. One of the running motifs in the movie is that of concealment. Nearly all the major characters are hiding something that would reverse other people's impressions of them in an instant, beginning with Creighton's bald pate, which extends also to his (barely) closeted homosexuality. Doris's secrets are myriad; her affair with her boss, Big Dave, is one, and her pregnancy by him, which is only discovered after she commits suicide in police custody (cutting off the film's apparent transformation into a courtroom drama), is another. James Gandolfini's Big Dave represents himself as a war hero but actually sat the conflict out at home. Like the Big Lebowski, he's a superficially powerful man propped up by a wealthy woman—his department store, Nirdlinger's, bears her family's surname. Meanwhile, Dave's wife, Ann Nerdlinger (Katherine Borowitz), maintains a facade as a doting, dutiful wife but, as is revealed during a midnight visit to Ed's house after the death of her husband (a crime pinned on Doris, but for which Ed is responsible), is a deeply paranoid woman who harbors elaborate sexual fantasies involving beings from another world.

Ed's confrontation with Ann may seem like an extraneous digression in a movie that is otherwise extremely tight, but it's actually the film's secret heart. *The Man Who Wasn't There* is set in 1949, two years after the supposed UFO crash in Roswell, New Mexico, that became ground zero for legions of conspiracy theorists. (Northern California was also the setting for Jack Finney's 1955 novel *The Body Snatchers*, a signal text that satirized the creeping conformity of the Eisenhower era.) The Coens audaciously integrate the themes and iconography of mid-century science fiction into their noir narrative. Ann's story about being abducted and probed, along with Big Dave, during a camping trip is her coping mechanism for the fact that their romance had long since waned ("He never touched me again"), a lack of sexual activity that mirrors Ed and Doris's. In conflating her own sexual disappointment with this larger cultural undercurrent, Ann reveals herself as the product of a schizophrenic zeitgeist. She's simultaneously obsessed with and terrified by the large-scale social and technological change around her.

As staged by the Coens and Deakins, who emphasize the black dots of her funeral veil (a reference to "dottiness," perhaps), Ann's visit plays out as a comic torment to Ed, who is dealing with much bigger problems in the form of his wife's murder charge and his unspoken guilt over the fact that he's the one who did the deed. It's also a chilling moment of recognition. Like Ann, Ed wants nothing so much as to rationalize the failure of his marriage and to account for his alienation, even if he stops short of invoking actual aliens in the process. But his patronizing, empathetic response to Ann is also telling. Much later in the film, after he's been arrested for a murder he didn't commit (that of Creighton Tolliver, who was actually beaten to death by Big Dave after Dave discovered his scheme), Ed imagines himself encountering the very same UFO, which hovers above the prison before flying off toward the horizon, leaving him as bereft and alone as Ann Nirdlinger. As *The Man Who Wasn't There* goes on, Ed begins to believe that he can see through the people around him, even as his own motives are utterly transparent. In this, he resembles the perceptive but self-deluding hero of Albert Camus's existentialist classic novel *L'Étranger* (1942), which critic Richard Gaughran persuasively locates as the film's true artistic inspiration, more than the noirs evoked by Deakins's cinematography and the script's numerous references to the novels of James M. Cain (not only in the playful use of "Nirdlinger," but also in allusions to the plots of *Mildred Pierce* [1941] and *The Postman Always Rings Twice* [1946]). Like Camus's Meursault, Ed narrates his tale from prison; both men have a fatalistic view on life that gets confirmed by the savage but seemingly unpremeditated murders that they commit. In fact, quite disturbingly, it is killing Big Dave—and getting away with it—that makes Ed feel, for the first time, like he is not a dupe but a kind of visionary. "It seemed . . . like I had made it to the outside, somehow, and they were all struggling down below."

Ed's emerging self-knowledge does him little good when he's at the mercy of fate, however. The plot of *The Man Who Wasn't There* is organized around long, crisscrossing streaks of deceptively

The laconic gravity of Billy Bob Thornton's presence keeps *The Man Who Wasn't There* grounded amid the script's myriad high-flown ideas; in contrast to other Coen brother protagonists, Ed Crane is not a fool or a hypocrite but a self-deluding striver who makes his own bad luck.

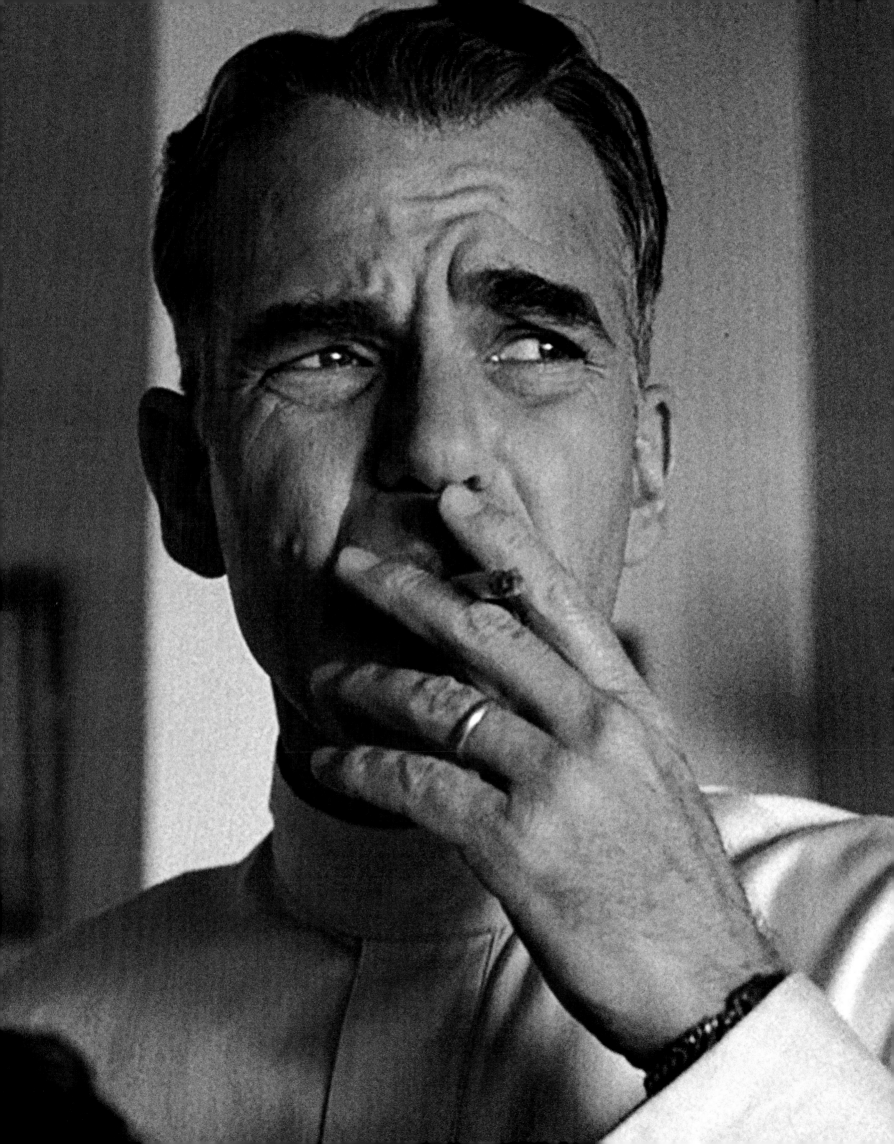

The weave of allusions in *The Man Who Wasn't There* is as intricate as in any of the Coens' other films. The name of the department store where Doris works is a nod to the anti-heroine of James M. Cain's novel *Double Indemnity,* while the use of Nerdlinger's mannequins as witnesses to a murder visualizes Ed Crane's growing dissociation from the people around him (as well as paying homage to Stanley Kubrick's 1955 noir *Killer's Kiss*).

Top: When Big Dave tries to choke Ed, he presses his body so hard against the glass window of the office that it cracks; the framing makes it seem like this sudden violence has created a fissure in reality itself.

Bottom: Division and distance in Ed and Doris's marriage are visualized by the markings on a table in a prison waiting room: Even with life-and-death stakes, they're incapable of reaching out to each other.

good and definitely bad luck. Ed is bypassed as a suspect for Big Dave's murder but has to sit silently as his wife takes the rap; Freddy Riedenschneider's "uncertainty defense" sounds persuasive but becomes a moot point after Doris's suicide; Ed survives a car crash only to awaken in police custody for a murder he didn't commit. Where in *The Hudsucker Proxy*, Norville Barnes is only "fortune's fool" until the powers that be smile upon him, Ed Crane has nobody looking out for him. This cosmic absence is played up in an early scene of him and Doris attending their local church: A slow pan down from the stained-glass ceiling to the pulpit reveals not a priest but a bingo caller in an exquisite visual pun, locating a facile game of chance in a space traditionally associated

with divine certainty. In contrast to the Old Testament–inflected worlds of *A Serious Man*, *True Grit*, and *Hail, Caesar!*, *The Man Who Wasn't There* pretty clearly unfolds in a godless universe (the title could even be taken as a riff on this same absence).

Having long since decided that there is no meaning to search for—that "our reward is on this earth, and bingo is probably the extent of it"—Ed tries to create his own. His involvement with Birdy represents the pinnacle of his ambition, as well as his delusion. For all her studied naïveté, Birdy sees right through the older man's benevolent-uncle act as he attempts to help her fulfill her dreams of being a concert pianist—dreams that she has described in only

The fast-talking lawyer
Freddy Riedenschneider hopes
to exonerate Doris of Big
Dave's murder by applying
the Uncertainty Principle
to her defense; here, Roger
Deakins's use of shadow
suggests a man imprisoned by
his own lofty rhetoric.

the vaguest terms. Pushing her to pursue her aspirations, he becomes something like a parody of a proud parent (and calls attention to his own nonexistent paternity). When she flunks a prestigious music-school audition overseen by a foppish teacher (who is a visual double for Creighton Tolliver) and admits that she'd rather be a veterinarian, Ed takes it badly . . . because what's really being quashed is his own possibility of vicarious success. Her disappointment is muted; his is paralyzing.

The girl's clumsy attempt at making it up to him (offering him a blow job in the front seat of his car as he drives her home) is a parody of a similar scene in *Lolita*, and Ed's flustered, strained, gentlemanly refusal ("Gosh, Birdy!") doesn't fool anybody but himself. In this moment, he's actually getting everything he really wants—sexual gratification and an upending of his routine—but he barely has time to recognize this before the car crashes, plunging both the character and the movie into an extended dream sequence that stands as one of the Coens' very best scenes.

DOMESTIC BLISS

—

Ed's dream while he's unconscious after the car accident with Birdy finds him imagining that he's back home with Doris; whether it's a fantasy or a memory, it offers a double-edged image of marriage as refuge and purgatory.

WHITEOUT

—

The chamber where Ed is scheduled to be executed is a wildly stylized space that pushes the film's old-fashioned aesthetic into a realm of pure, unsettling abstraction: The blinding whiteness of the space fulfills Ed's desire for a "clean start" at the moment of his death.

Top: Ed sees dry cleaning optimistically as "the future," but the Coens' integration of early 1950s UFO panic into the script addresses the era's anxieties about technological advancement.

Bottom: Ann Nirdlinger's funeral veil creates an eerily funny visual effect when she comes to Ed's door: the design makes her look "dotty" as she unravels a far-fetched story of alien abduction.

After Ed blacks out, he awakens into what appears to be a slightly altered replay of the beginning of the movie: He's back at home, placidly looking out at the neighborhood from his porch. A salesman (Christopher McDonald) descends on the house and tries to talk Ed into purchasing some new paving stones—a variation on Creighton's pitch. But before his interest can be too piqued, Doris drives up and tells the vendor, in no uncertain terms, to get lost. The rest of the scene plays out in tableaux, as Ed and Doris move to the living room and sit silently together on the couch, a vision of domestic life that's far from heaven and yet much cozier and more comforting than the nightmare awaiting Ed upon his awakening. Ed will be executed for Creighton Tolliver's murder rather than Dave Brewster's, a wrong-man scenario that nevertheless has the feeling of pieces sliding rightfully into place, but he can hardly plead innocence anyway.

At the end of *Raising Arizona*, H.I. subconsciously conjures up a happy ending for himself and his wife—one that involves children and grandchildren at their feet. It's a rapturous vision of something that he's never had before, whereas Ed's is, hilariously and also hauntingly, a carbon copy of the existence he wanted so fervently to leave behind. It suggests that, in a moment of extreme trauma and panic, he's clinging to his memories of Doris and their entirely functional relationship, which could indicate that he really did love her (as he claimed) or, following his rejection of Birdy, that this would-be escape artist is really the timid, stay-at-home type. As Thornton plays the scene, it's impossible to tell if Ed is irritated or becalmed by the way Doris keeps any possibility of change safely at bay.

There was uncertainty in the Coens' cinema before *The Man Who Wasn't There*, such as the darkly shaded ending of *Fargo*, which is subtly invoked in this scene via the presence of Frances McDormand. But the schizophrenic nature of Ed's dream so resolutely plays down the middle that *The Man Who Wasn't There* seems oddly noncommittal in the end, as if the movie, following its main character's lead, is neatly canceling itself out and leaving nothing behind. The only "fresh start" Ed gets is in the jailhouse chamber where he's sent to be executed via lethal injection, a nasty gag that evokes the chemical nature of dry cleaning, with Ed literally being groomed for execution.

The blinding white of the final shot of *The Man Who Wasn't There* is entirely death-tinged—Ed is heading for the light. It's impossible to read this shot any other way. The earlier image of Doris and Ed sitting grimly side by side in their living room, however (besides anticipating the martial satire of their next film, *Intolerable Cruelty*), initiates a commitment to ambiguity that marks the Coens' finest twenty-first-century work, from *No Country for Old Men* to *A Serious Man*. Those movies don't see the world in black and white, and neither does *The Man Who Wasn't There*, which turns the waking world and the dream life into gray zones.

FILMOGRAPHY

```
Hail, Caesar! (2016)
True Grit (2010)
A Serious Man (2009)
Burn After Reading (2008)
No Country for Old Men (2007)
The Ladykillers (2004)
Intolerable Cruelty (2003)
The Man Who Wasn't There (2001)
The Big Lebowski (1998)
Fargo (1996)
The Hudsucker Proxy (1994)
Barton Fink (1991)
Miller's Crossing (1990)
Raising Arizona (1987)
Blood Simple (1984)
```

The scores that Carter Burwell has written for the Coens over the years are as varied and virtuoso as the movies themselves, integrating folk, classical, and gospel styles (as well as the ambient, minimalist soundscape of *No Country for Old Men*).

Carter Burwell
COMPOSER

You've said that before you wrote the music for *Blood Simple*, you watched *The Birds* (1963) for inspiration.

When I first approached the possibility of writing music for film, I knew nothing about it and had no particular interest in it. But I thought I should probably watch some films and see what people are doing with music. This was in the days of VHS recorders and network television, so I looked at what was going down on television that day, and I saw that Hitchcock's *The Birds* was going to be on. I love that film, so I thought it would be a great one to study. I watched it while I was recording it, and I was so involved in the film that I forgot to actually pay attention to the score. So when the

film was over, I started again and realized that there wasn't anything that you'd call a traditional score. It was more like "musique concrète"; recordings of bird sounds and electronic manipulation. Bernard Herrmann is credited as a consultant on *The Birds*, although I have to admit I don't know exactly what his role was. It was a great lesson in what a film score can be and what it doesn't have to be.

That's somewhat parallel to what you did in *No Country for Old Men*, right? Which is a film that's often described as having almost no musical score, but there's a lot of ambient sound that serves as a kind of music.

It's true. The approach we ended up taking on *No Country* was for the score, such as it is, to come out of sound design. So that film is full of wind; there's wind in almost every scene. That was one place where the music comes from. I created tones to come out of the wind, to create tension and deepen the drama of the situation. We realized early on on that film that music would remind you—and I know it sounds ridiculous—but it would remind you that you were watching a movie. And of course we know we're all sitting in a movie, but music really took you out of the particular reality of that film. I think there are directors who take music seriously and think about its presence in a film, or about its absence. Hitchcock was one of those directors, and I think Joel and Ethan are as well.

In *Blood Simple*, the music is minimal but it definitely has presence. The main pop cut on the soundtrack is very nasty, "It's the Same Old Song," indicating this kind of circular misanthropy. The piano motif of the score is also circular—it goes around and around—but it has some warmth and some soul, in a weird way. It's one of my favorite Coen movie scores.

Concert Score

FARGO
FARGO, NORTH DAKOTA

COMPOSED AND ORCHESTRATED
BY CARTER BURWELL

Molto Bombasto

It's probably my favorite score as well, and one of my favorite movies, too. That and *Fargo* are right up there. That was one of several pieces that I created after having seen a couple of reels of the film. When I first met Joel and Ethan, they were interviewing composers, and I had no film scores to play for them. I hadn't done this before, so I went home and did a variety of things. Some things were more what you would expect for a thriller, for suspense. I can't even say now why that scene relates to me, but it has this quality because the right-hand part is extremely repetitive, a little bit like the clock just ticking away, so it helps with the suspense. And then under that, these chords move again in their own cycle. When we went into the studio to record it, I think we originally planned that this would mostly be done electronically but that that bit would be played on a synthesizer. When Joel and Ethan heard me playing it on piano, and they happened to see what it did against the picture, I think they realized there was some aspect of compassion that it lent to these characters. That film has been written in the cruelest possible way. They

put the characters in really bad situations; the audience sees from the outside how bad the situation is, even if the characters don't. So having music that lends some empathy to them, in a way, makes the audience feel even more uncomfortable, because we actually care what's going to happen to these people. And I think that cognitive dissonance is something that Joel and Ethan jumped at.

What's unnerving about *Blood Simple* is that it's a debut, and yet it's perfectly formed.

I think that the perfection in *Blood Simple* is really in the writing. I think that there are lots and lots of ideas in the way it's directed. Some of them, like Barry Sonnenfeld's camera, when it's gliding down the bar . . . some of these ideas are maybe a bit too full. And at that time, they hadn't gotten to that point where they could reflect on their style and actually throw ideas away, which I think more mature filmmakers are able to do. I think they were all showing off a bit, as people will in their first film. But the writing is amazing, and the cruelty and

humor were there right from the beginning, and it's in all their films.

The score in *Blood Simple* is so wonderfully circular; you're always sort of waiting for it to fill itself out and lock back in. *Fargo* has this big beautiful loop to it, where that folky melody keeps returning to itself. It also seems that this is a theme in the Coens' movies in general—these endless, repetitive loops.

I think you're correct in perceiving that; I think it is something that they like, whether you call it a trope or just a worldview. It's present especially in the films that feel most Coen-esque. It's something that's just in my music; the music that I like to listen to and the music that I like to write is like that. It doesn't typically have an end. I enjoy music in the way it structures time, and I think if you're going to properly structure time, it doesn't have an end. It's just the fact that this may be the music that I like, and I tend to write, and I guess it's just fortuitous that Joel and Ethan and I have a similar formal interest in loops and repetition.

Concert Score

FARGO
FARGO, NORTH DAKOTA

3

In *Fargo*, the music begins simply and then gets really heavy, like we're about to watch an epic. But this feels ironic because everything in the film is so quotidian and banal.

It is meant to be ironic. The story behind that is when they gave me the script before they shot the film, I'm reading it and I was just struck by all the Scandinavian names, and even in the script there are references to the whiteout weather. I know some Scandinavian folk music, so I went back to those CDs and listened to those while they were off shooting and collected a few ideas, a few old folk tunes. And the one that I like the best, and the one that's in the film, is called "The Lost Sheep," which works as a perfect title for Macy's character. It's an old folk tune that eventually became a hymn. I had to elaborate on it because it's a very simple tune; it didn't have a B section, or any kind of development to it, as all folk tunes don't. The main question we had with *Fargo* was: There's going to be violence in the film and we want people to believe it's real. But we also wanted people to be able to laugh, because the killers are also buffoons. If the music laughed at everything, you wouldn't believe the violence. So it was about the music taking things a bit too seriously—the music is sort of bombastically serious. I tried to hybridize the Scandinavian folk tune and the film noir tradition that you have in movies like *The Killers* (1946). I listened really carefully to those scores and how they were composed, with low woodwinds and heavy bass clarinets. I wanted to combine two forms, so the theme begins simply and it's sort of pretty, with this fiddled harp, and then you see this car that's coming through the snow and the music gets big. It gets bigger and bigger, but nothing happens.

It just cuts to this pathetic roadside bar.

Exactly—that's the climax.

Can you talk about the nature of your working relationship with sound designer Skip Lievsay? You've both been there with the Coens from the beginning, and I know that you work simultaneously on the sound mix, which is sort of unusual.

Skip is the person who called me when he was working as a sound editor on *Blood Simple*. We knew each other through the music scene in New York—Skip was a bass player; I was a keyboard player, just playing at clubs in the city. He called, and he said, "I'm working on this film, the first film by these two guys the same age as us, and it needs some music, and the stuff you do seems like it might work. . . . Would you be interested?" And I said, "Yeah, sure. Why not?" So I went by and met Joel and Ethan. They were very honest and said, "This film is probably never going to get distributed; you're probably never going to get the deferred payment you agreed to," but we all went in full speed ahead. When we got to *Barton Fink*, Joel had this idea that maybe they don't even need any music in this movie; it could all be sound effects. He'd been talking to Skip about the sounds of the hotel in things like this; he wanted the sound to be non-naturalistic and very much in the foreground. I thought that there was something music could bring to the script, because I saw a childlike quality in Barton: He presents himself as a man of the world, but he's more naïve. That was my pitch to Joel and Ethan, this little piano theme. They thought it was good, but the sound effects had been designed to be front and center, so Skip, myself, and Joel and Ethan spotted the film together. Instead of meeting up for the final mix and fighting over what's going to be louder than what—which is how it's traditionally done—we'd go into the scenes together. We parceled out the whole sonic spectrum. A good example is when the camera pans from Barton in bed with Audrey over to the bathroom and goes into the sink. It begins with Barton's melody, but once it's in the sink, we don't need music anymore, because this dense sonic collage takes over. So doing the whole thing together worked really well, and we've done it that way ever since.

Do you look at the scripts before you begin composing?

They always give me the scripts before they shoot. With *Burn After Reading*, *A Serious Man*, and *True Grit*, they had all three scripts at once, and told me, "This is what we're doing for the next three years." I do think there are worthwhile conversations to be had based on the script, but I don't specifically start writing based on a script. I don't really write the music until I've seen the picture, because there are so many ways you can shoot the script. So many different movies that can be made from a script. I will say that Joel and

Ethan will show me footage much earlier than anybody else. I think it's easy to feel vulnerable because often composers are the first people to see the footage, other than the director and the editor. But because we've known each other so long, and because Joel and Ethan are cutting their own movie, I can come by and they'll just show me a fraction, so I can get a feeling for it.

Was the use of "Everlasting Arms" on the soundtrack of *True Grit* cued by the script? It feels tied thematically to the rest of the movie, and it's a nod to *Night of the Hunter*; I can't imagine that the screenplay was written without it included in some way.

You're right that it's an early concept, but it was not in the script. We didn't want to do a Hollywood Western score, because it had already been done by Elmer Bernstein for the first version of *True Grit*, so there would be no point. And of course Joel and Ethan had already used country music in their other films. I read the script and went back and reread the book, and I felt that what was in the book but not so obvious in the script was that the whole reason Mattie is out in the wilderness surrounded by outlaws is because of her own sense of self-righteousness. And that comes from her reading of the Bible and her church experiences. In the book, there are page-by-page quotes of the Bible, references that would keep reminding you of this, but in the movie it's not so obvious. There's some voice-over at the very beginning and at the very end, but otherwise it did not dominate the story like it does in the book. And I felt that maybe the music could bring some of the churchy-ness back to the film. And it was really just before Joel and Ethan went to shoot when I called and said, "I've got an idea about the music," and Ethan said that they had the same idea and had been thinking about "Everlasting Arms," because of *Night of the Hunter*. So we both had that same idea, at the same time—it made it seem like I was probably on to something here. Personally, I felt that because it had already been used in this other extraordinary film, it shouldn't be featured in *True Grit*; I was hoping we would find something different, but we went with it. And that's the way it happens sometimes. I didn't personally want to directly reference *Night of the Hunter*, but I think Joel and Ethan

didn't mind. It was the right tune. It was capable of being played so simply, with just a few piano notes.

I always liked that "Everlasting Arms" is playing over a shot of Mattie as she walks away from the camera with only one arm left from her experience, but I don't think that's intentional. . . .

We weren't reaching for that.

In all seriousness, though, people always talk about the Coens' films in terms of intention and deliberate reference, like they're supposed to be decoded or annotated. How much does this come up in the creative process, and how much of it is critical projection?

With something as obvious as the reference to *Night of the Hunter*, of course we're going to discuss it. There are other references in their films that come up as well. What you're talking about, though, is that Joel and Ethan like their films to be full of thought and care. And because they work in genre their films are referential to begin with: They're always referring to an older tradition in filmmaking of one sort or another. And so reference is just built in, and I think they like really layering it up, and it entertains them. Entertaining ourselves is absolutely the highest aspiration we're reaching for when working on these films. I almost never hear anyone talk about the audience, and I've never heard anyone mention critics or film history. We're really trying to entertain ourselves. If we can make ourselves laugh, if we can give ourselves something we really are proud of, that's what we're after. Joel and Ethan have managed to create a system that allows them to do that by having final cut of the film, and by bringing on strong producers who can insulate them from studio influence. They'll have someone like Scott Rudin to stand between them and any external pressures, so we can really make the film for ourselves. That level of detail is something they enjoy: I don't think they're putting clues in there to keep master's students busy for the next hundred years.

What do you think of the Coens' reputation for being aloof or smart alecks when it comes to dealing with the media or talking about their work?

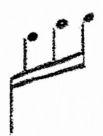

It's not for nothing that they have that reputation. I think that they are, any way you look at it—they are smart-alecky. They are that way on set and in the cutting room, too. In their films, if there are moments that seem to get serious and reflective in some way, you know that there will be a joke right around the corner, because they can't dare to not deflate the balloon. And that is them. That's absolutely them. Ethan studied philosophy at Princeton, and it comes up, in almost all their films, that people keep insisting that life must have meaning when in fact it's so blatantly obvious that it doesn't. The characters are always searching for meaning in the universe, and they get the rug pulled out from under them. So that's truly who [the Coens] are. I think the aloofness comes from them wanting to be recognized as the authors of their work, but that doesn't mean that they want to be interviewed or photographed for magazines. Those are two different things. They've gotten better with interviews over the decades, but it's not something they enjoy. And they don't like talking about themselves, or making themselves the stars of the situation.

Do you reflect on the sheer length and consistency of this collaboration? You've been working with the Coens for almost thirty-five years, which is a really long time.

Yeah. I'm now at the age that when I get together with other composers, people of my generation like Tom Newman will ask me if I'm thinking of retiring. Occasionally I step up to the plate and do Hollywood films, but that's something I could easily leave at any moment. Working with Joel and Ethan is something I'll keep doing until I'm at the edge of the grave. We all really get to do our best. We're never asked to water things down or to try to do anything other than make the best movie possible. It's a special thing. Here's an example of how special it is: We did *Blood Simple* together, and then for *Raising Arizona* they knew perfectly well I didn't know anything about banjo music. When Ethan called me, he said, "You know, this might not be groovy enough, might not be cool enough for you, but would you like to do this?" and I thought, okay, I'll do that. And when it came to *Miller's Crossing*, they also knew perfectly well I knew nothing about orchestral music, had no classical music background at all, and they knew they wanted an orchestral score. Any other director would call an experienced composer. At that point they were well known, and they could have called anybody. But they asked me to do it. And it's crazy, because they knew I would have to learn it all from the ground up, so that's what I did. It's been an amazing opportunity. As long as it keeps going, I'll be happy to muck in.

THE MASSEY PRENUPTIAL AGREEMENT — IT'S — IRONCLAD!

Intolerable Cruelty

RELEASE DATE
October 10, 2003
BUDGET
$60M
DISTRIBUTOR
Universal Pictures

CAST

George Clooney
Catherine Zeta-Jones
Geoffrey Rush
Cedric the Entertainer
Edward Herrmann
Paul Adelstein
Richard Jenkins
Billy Bob Thornton

WARNING!
THIS FILM CONTAINS

"Suspicious Minds"	19%
Ass jokes	18%
Alliteration	15%
Trophy husbands	12%
Very silly men	10%
Designer clothes	9%
Nasty lapdogs	7%
Flossing	6%
Self-inflicted gunshot wounds	4%

AT THE END of *The Hudsucker Proxy*, the Hula-Hoop—that polyvalent symbol of both postwar American ingenuity and assembly-line consensus—keeps spinning on into infinity, as steady and unchanging as the spheres themselves. The Coens' screwball side came full circle a decade later in *Intolerable Cruelty*, where Norville Barnes's orb makes a subtle cameo in the final scene in the set design for the studio set for the popular new reality series "America's Favorite Divorce Videos." The show is an intolerably cruel confection created by a calculating private detective, bankrolled by unscrupulous litigators, and produced by a philandering Hollywood ex-hotshot trying to make it back to the top by appealing to the lowest common denominator. The message in both movies would seem to be that the circle of mindless popular entertainment remains unbroken—for better or for worse.

For better or for worse: The language of matrimony is indeed applicable to a film whose characters spend more time finagling over prenuptial agreements than honeymooning with their spouses. *Intolerable Cruelty*'s opening credits unfold over hyperbolically parodic animated figures of Cupid firing arrows in every direction and underneath Elvis Presley's "Suspicious Minds," a song that acknowledges the essential paranoia underpinning relationships. The Coens' ninth feature is a kind of anti-romantic comedy in which impure motivations pile up with increasingly less pretense down the stretch. In his book *Pursuits of Happiness*, the philosopher and critic Stanley Cavell came up with the term "comedy of remarriage" as a way of grouping the great Hollywood screwball comedies of the 1930s and '40s, from *It Happened One Night* (1934) and *Bringing Up Baby* (1938) to *His Girl Friday* (1940) and *The Lady Eve* (1941).

Cavell's theory was that because the Hollywood Production Code frowned upon depictions of adultery or sex out of wedlock, the makers of these films contrived scenarios where characters got divorced and flirted with strangers only as a way of reaffirming their attraction for each other. The result was that the movies could be chockablock with innuendo without breaking any rules, on top of which the collective impropriety of the characters and their actions served to level the playing field down from both high-class condescension and pious idealism. For all their scandalous, non-monogamous jokes and incidents, the films Cavell filed under "comedies of remarriage" all ended with their central couples together and very much in love—

a mutual affection earned through struggle and self-examination rather than speedily ratified by a priest or justice of the peace.

Ever the clever students of American film history, the Coens take this concept and run with it. *Intolerable Cruelty* is a comedy of remarriage whose hero is a divorce attorney. Like *The Hudsucker Proxy*, it's steeped in screwball allusions: It has a complicated plot and glamorous movie stars; where Tim Robbins stood in for Gary Cooper, George Clooney does his best Cary Grant (moving on from his discount Clark Gable impersonation in *O Brother, Where Art Thou?*). Like *Hudsucker*, it was produced from inside the same Hollywood studio system to which it attempts to pay tribute; and, like *Hudsucker*, it was received largely as a failure. Not in terms of box-office receipts: The combined star power of Clooney and Zeta-Jones—who was fresh off an Oscar win for her song-and-dance act in *Chicago*—led to a worldwide gross of more than $100 million. Critics, however, responded to the film with suspicious minds, suggesting that, after a string of genuinely idiosyncratic follow-ups to the breakthrough of *Fargo*, the Coens had finally phoned one in. "*Intolerable Cruelty*," wrote

BUTT OF THE JOKE
—
Television producer Donovan Donaly takes a photo of his injured posterior as evidence in an upcoming divorce proceedings—the first of several sight gags based on the principle of covering one's ass(ets).

MILLION-DOLLAR SMILE
—
Miles's perfectly polished teeth are indicative of his rapacious, predatory appetites—for money, success, and, eventually, Marylin.

Scott Foundas in *LA Weekly*, "seems the kind of movie that results from two essentially erudite, anarchic talents playing down to the masses."

It didn't help this perception that *Intolerable Cruelty* was the first film that the Coens directed that featured other writing credits, complicating if not undermining their previously unassailable sense of authorship. The script was originally written in the early 1990s by Robert Ramsey and Matthew Stone, and the Coens were hired for a polish, which did not prove definitive. Over the course of many successive drafts, the property generated interest among a slew of mainstream filmmakers—including Ron Howard and Jonathan Demme—before the Coens decided to rewrite and direct it themselves after their planned adaptation of James Dickey's novel *To the White Sea* fell through. The long break between writing and production was not uncommon for the Coens, whose career is filled with examples of delayed projects, but *Intolerable Cruelty* is nevertheless something of a curiosity in their oeuvre. To some extent, it follows their regular M.O. of raiding other sources for inspiration and allusion, but it also reflects some more practical and—for a

Bottom left: In each of his roles for the Coens, George Clooney undermines his leading man stardom by emphasizing narcissism and vanity; Miles's superficial perfection belies a deep insecurity about his job and future prospects.

Bottom right: Marylin's bloodred wardrobe codes her as a "dangerous woman" even as Catherine Zeta-Jones's performance consistently signals the character's loneliness and melancholy.

Intolerable Cruelty is the Coens' version of a romantic comedy—one in which true love is a hopeless illusion. The ironic juxtaposition of a statue of Cupid with a luxury-class poolside location plays up the tension between romantic love and material satisfaction that drives the story towards its viciously cynical conclusion, while the cheap, leopard-print tackiness of the setting indicates the superficiality of the *nouveau riche* characters.

pair of filmmakers used to total autonomy and creative control—daunting challenges, chiefly, how to rework an existing screenplay to their exacting specifications.

Their solution was to overcompensate: *Intolerable Cruelty* is perhaps the most manic Coens comedy after *The Hudsucker Proxy*, lacking the contemplative, landscape-based beauty wedged in between the plot points of *Raising Arizona* and *Fargo* and the deceptively lackadaisical longueurs that slow down *The Big Lebowski*. After *The Man Who Wasn't There*'s terse excursion into noir, *Intolerable Cruelty* constitutes a burst of energy. Its corporate-legal milieu is bustling and fast-paced; its characters are motormouths with tongue-twistingly alliterative names. Clooney's star lawyer is named Miles Massey, while his key client is a Mr. Rex Rexroth (Edward Herrmann). Another change: In stark contrast to the Valley losers of *The Big Lebowski* and the chain-gang fugitives of *O Brother, Where Art Thou?*, the characters in *Intolerable Cruelty* are all mostly pretty smart—sometimes too much so for their own good. Everyone in *Intolerable Cruelty* has ulterior motives and mostly expert poker faces: Catherine Zeta-Jones's Marylin Rexroth is such a good manipulator that she's come into obscene wealth simply by knowing how, when, and to whom to say "I do."

"Obscene wealth becomes you," says Miles to Marylin—a line that takes on the ring of a Zen koan as the film goes on. Wealth as obscenity is the subtext of *Intolerable Cruelty*, as the connection between murderous amorality and material gain developed in so many of the Coens' more overtly serious works gets a comic spin. The film also blends certain thriller-ish aspects into the action: Rex Rexroth's infidelity is captured on video by a seedy private investigator named Gus Petch (Cedric the Entertainer), who's essentially a double for M. Emmet Walsh's Visser in *Blood Simple* (his oft-stated obsession with "nailing asses" pounds the nail on the head, even as it rhymes with Visser's essentially self-serving worldview). Later on in the film, after an endless series of comic reversals, Miles hires a grotesque, mob-connected hit man named Wheezy Joe (Irwin Keyes) to assassinate Marylin, once again recalling *Blood Simple*'s equation of adultery and nasty, retributive violence. When Joe stalks Marylin in her darkened home, it's a callback to the Coens' debut (right down to an unexpected

gore effect that serves as a lone, startlingly cathartic instance of physical violence in a movie otherwise dedicated to verbal barbarity).

That Miles finds Marylin obscene does not do much to stop his attraction to her. Instead, he falls wildly in love with her even as he's trying to block her multimillion-dollar divorce settlement, sparking a chain of events that will see him go from being her courtroom opponent (where he holds the upper hand); to being hired to draft her prenup for a new wedding (where he's being subtly manipulated); to being her eager, desirous husband (where suddenly he finds his "assets" dangerously exposed). *Intolerable Cruelty*'s one-twist-after-another structure is fastidious in the same fashion as *The Hudsucker Proxy*, minus the existentialist gloss. It's a mechanical movie—everything clicks into place—but its best scenes get somewhere fascinating all the same. Three sequences in particular stand out in redeeming *Intolerable Cruelty* from its reputation as an anodyne digression: a pair of dinner dates placed at either end of the story, bookending a seemingly make-do but comically horrific sequence that evokes the same gnawing, masculine terror at the heart of the brothers' other character studies.

The first key scene in *Intolerable Cruelty* comes just before the commencement of courtroom hostilities between Miles and Marylin's lawyer, Freddy Bender (Richard Jenkins). For the second film in a row, the Coens dub a lawyer character Freddy, but Jenkins's character is much less of a virtuoso than Tony Shalhoub's slick out-of-towner Riedenschneider in *The Man Who Wasn't There*; instead of dazzling the jury with talk of the Uncertainty Principle, Freddy Bender is himself uncertain—no match for Miles's practiced show-trial finesse. Dining together in a luxury restaurant (given an extra-plush texture by Roger Deakins, showing off his virtuosity after the stark chiaroscuro of *The Man Who Wasn't There*), Miles and Marylin size each other up simultaneously as potential rivals and romantic partners, with the latter getting in the most vicious dig. She—correctly—sees Miles as a man who is so good at his job that the thrill is gone. She tells him that he's "bored, complacent, and on the way down."

Miles shrugs the criticism off as just another put-down in Marylin's vast arsenal, but we soon see that he's taken her words to heart—the

DIRTY WORK
—

The unscrupulous investigator Gus Petch is a spiritual descendant of *Blood Simple*'s villainous Visser—a mercenary who profits from the philandering and dishonesty of his clients.

"LIVING WITHOUT INTESTINES"
—

Miles's waiting-room reading material mocks his encroaching guilt and anxiety about the direction of his personal and professional life; despite his financial success, he suspects that he's becoming hollowed out by his job.

The gossipy hotel concierge Heinz, the Baron Krauss Von Espy is a caricature of European unctuousness; his lapdog Elisabeta is one of a pair of significant canines in *Intolerable Cruelty*.

same heart that is inflamed with desire for his tormentor. In *O Brother, Where Art Thou?*, the idiocy of Clooney's character was such that self-actualization seemed out of the question, but Miles is yet another of the Coens' "bigheads"—he's cerebral in a way that gradually paralyzes him with doubt. After succeeding in blocking Marylin from accessing Rex's wealth, which he does by humiliating her in open court with proof that she was looking for a man who "would be easily duped and controlled," he's off to a meeting with the senior partner of his law firm. Miles waits outside his boss's office reading a magazine, the cover line of which reads—quite incongruously and hilariously—"Living Without Intestines."

This text is apparently required reading for Herb Myerson (Tom Aldredge), a wizened old monster who looks like nothing so much as the picture of Dorian Gray: a cadaver in a suit. As with the incapacitated screenwriter Arthur Digby Sellers in *The Big Lebowski*, the Coens are deliberately stressing a character's near-death grotesqueness to make a point (and note that Herb breathes in the same halting, iron-lunged rhythm as Sellers). Herb's positioning in the frame, sitting in the shadows behind a massive desk, is also reminiscent of Sidney Mussburger in *The Hudsucker Proxy*—both are corporate

Left: Marylin's dog nips at Miles's overeager hands—a sign that his courtroom victory is going to come back to bite him.

Middle: Miles and Marylin's dinner quickly turns quiet and introspective; in this elegant two-shot, they're positioned as equals, but the lack of eye contact suggests they're both lost in lonely thoughts.

Right: A moment of (seemingly) sincere connection in a film where characters marry and divorce for sport.

monsters who represent profiteering evil in its purest, most undisguised form.

Miles's aspirations to move up in the firm mark him as kin to Norville Barnes. Norville is a rube, and Miles is a shark (a spirit animal evoked by his fixation on his gleaming white teeth, which supplants Clooney's hair-based vanity in *O Brother, Where Art Thou?*), but both are brought up short in the presence of their horrible bosses. When Miles looks into Herb's cold, dead eyes and hears the old man's spiel about working even harder if he knows what's good for him, he understands that he might be looking at himself a few decades down the line. His aspiration changes into terror: The Coens cut to him frozen in panic at his desk and then frantically scanning his face in his office mirror for signs of Dorian Gray–like decay. Thus Marylin becomes doubly attractive to him: not merely as a sexual conquest ("Just for an ass to mount," he confides at dinner) but as an escape route away from a Life Without Intestines.

And so Miles begins to change. In lieu of a keynote speech at a divorce lawyers' convention about "Nailing Your Spouse's Assets" (the nod to Gus Petch's catchphrase indicates that corporate culture and strip-mall detective work have a common denominator), he extemporizes an ode to true love. "Love is good," he stutters,

as the Coens kid (the similarly alliteratively named) Gordon Gekko's "greed is good" speech in *Wall Street*. "I'm here to tell you that cynicism, which we think protects us, in fact destroys—destroys love, destroys our clients, and destroys ourselves." Miles's heart-on-sleeve sentiments are easily legible as a parody of the sorts of summative pleas that come at the end of old Hollywood movies, including and especially the optimistic comedies of Frank Capra like *Mr. Smith Goes to Washington*. There, the assertion of principle in the face of cynicism vindicates the heroes as well as the audience. Miles has learned his lesson, but he's in no position to teach anybody else, because the movie isn't even close to over. Marylin isn't finished with him yet.

Miles's terror at becoming cynical makes him easy prey for Marylin's plan. This involves faking a marriage to a phony oil baron (Billy Bob Thornton as another Man Who Isn't There), annulling it with Miles's help, and then marrying Miles, who doesn't know he's being played and thus tears up his own legendary "Massey prenup," which gives his new wife unfettered access to his (obscene) wealth. Hoisted on his own petard, Miles now has an empty bank account to go along with his broken heart, but Marylin is not fully satisfied by her victory. While she doesn't have a scene comparable to Miles's encounter with Herb Myerson, she's

written and acted by Zeta-Jones to display her own encroaching signs of doubt.

In *Intolerable Cruelty*'s most revealing scene—and perhaps one of the most naked exchanges in the Coens' entire filmography—she confides to Miles (again at dinner) that she finds herself at "that certain point where you've achieved your goals and yet you're still unsatisfied." On the level of plot, this revelation means that Marylin would rather be with Miles than on her own with his money, giving them a matching his-and-hers set of changed hearts. Underneath the narrative machinery, however, the Coens sound almost as if they're talking to themselves. If the through-line of the Coens' career from *Blood Simple* onward was the struggle for financial independence, a movie like *Intolerable Cruelty* simultaneously proves that they've achieved it—because it's a studio film cast with superstars—and points out how tenuous that sense of accomplishment can be—because it's so perilously close to being a job for hire. *The Hudsucker Proxy* was a passion project that spun out of control and nearly derailed the Coens' aspirations to work successfully inside the Hollywood system. By contrast, the knock on *Intolerable Cruelty* was that it slid a little too cozily into a commercial marketplace that its creators had previously always attempted to move through on their own terms.

Considered less as an homage to Cavell's "comedies of remarriage" than as a thinly veiled allegory about the perils and pitfalls of absolute success, *Intolerable Cruelty* takes on the requisite subtext to qualify as "personal" filmmaking. It's hardly a self-pity party, however. Miles and Marylin find their version of true love with each other, but it's not as if they're truly humbled in the process; the Coens' self-examination intertwines with a cruel worldview that recasts "happily ever after" under the sign of the status quo—protected, contra Miles's speech, by a vicious, intractable cynicism.

Instead of building a future together, Miles and Marylin (their first and last names now, finally, perfectly in alliterative sync) go on recapitulating the past. Miles gets out of lawyering (in the hope of preserving his insides) but redirects his money toward underwriting "America's Favorite Divorce Videos," which is not exactly a sea change in vocation. Even outside of the courtroom, he's still profiting from the infidelities of others. And now, he's peddling his intrusions as entertainment, with the help of Geoffrey Rush's odious (but Emmy-winning) producer Donovan Donaly, an ugly Hollywood caricature in the mold of *Barton Fink*'s Jack Lipnick, who proves similarly victorious in the end, with no idealistic artist figure to oppose him.

Intolerable Cruelty's concluding shots of in-studio viewers mindlessly chanting "Nail your ass!" at the urging of the show's cynical host—Gus Petch, who's also given up his original job—are especially unsettling if they represent what the Coens think of their own audience. Or, less nastily, they could be a parody of the idea of "the popular audience," with the joke really being on the Jack Lipnicks and Donovan Donalys of the world. Miles and Marylin may love each other, but the thing that they've created together is truly dubious—another version of Norville's Hula-Hoop, a tool of distraction for the masses. While providing the requisite happy ending demanded by its genre, *Intolerable Cruelty* leaves an impression of eternally unfinished (show) business.

Donovan's ruinous decline after his loss in court gives the Coens a chance to put the big-shot Hollywood producer in the gutter—a comeuppance that will be reversed at the film's conclusion.

Heartbreakers

Abby's rejection of Marty for Ray in *Blood Simple* kick-starts a vicious circle of jealousy and revenge.

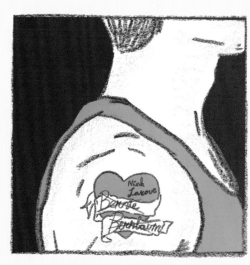

The gay love triangle in *Barton Fink* between Mink, Eddie and Bernie is evoked as a subtle parallel to Tom, Leo and Verna's interwoven romances.

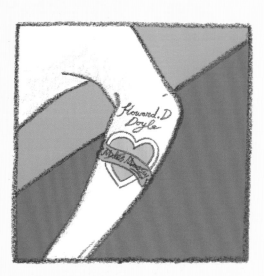

In *Intolerable Cruelty*, Marilyn's sham marriage to fictional millionaire "Howard D. Doyle" (played by a soap opera actor) is designed to get Miles to expose his ass(ets).

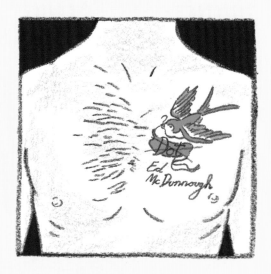

H.I. angrily rejects his co-worker Glen's offer of wife-swapping in *Raising Arizona*; he only has eyes for Ed.

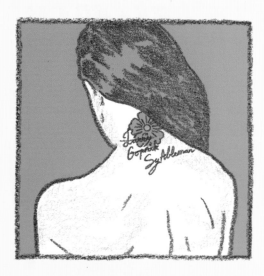

Judith Gopnik wants to leave her husband, Larry, for "serious man" Sy Abelman, but chance (or is it God?) intervenes in the form of a car accident.

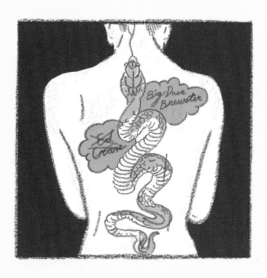

Doris believes that Ed is oblivious to her adulterous relationship with Big Dave in *The Man Who Wasn't There*, but he's on to her almost from the start, with fatal consequences.

FRIENDS OF THE COENS

"The Coen brothers? Yes, they're talented and funny, of course they're very skilled and prolific, probably one of the greatest writing and directing teams of all time, everyone knows that, but what people don't know is that they aren't really related. They just made that up."

—

George Clooney

FILMS:
O Brother, Where Art Thou? (2000)
Intolerable Cruelty (2003)
Burn After Reading (2008)
Hail, Caesar! (2016)

The Ladykillers

RELEASE DATE
March 26, 2004
BUDGET
$35M
DISTRIBUTOR
Buena Vista Pictures
CAST
Tom Hanks
Irma P. Hall
Marlon Wayans
J.K. Simmons
Tzi Ma
Ryan Hurst
Diane Delano
George Wallace

WARNING!
THIS FILM CONTAINS

Ealing Studios	23%
Edgar Allan Poe	14%
Flannery O'Connor	11%
Irritable bowel syndrome	10%
Gospel music	9%
Hippety-hop music	8%
Christian charity	7%
Choking hazards	6%
Post-concussion syndrome	5%
Plastic explosives	4%
Mommy issues	3%

NO LESS THAN the other Jeffrey Lebowski (and I'm talking about The Dude here), Garth Pancake (J.K. Simmons) is a man who left his heart in the 1960s. A garrulous demolitions expert contracted to help out on an elaborate heist focused on a riverboat casino docked in Saucier, Mississippi, Garth is hardly a stranger to the region. In fact, he's fond of recalling his stint with the Freedom Riders, whom he characterizes as "a group of concerned liberals from up north, all working together, just like we are here"—the "we" in this case being a collective of thieves. Even those with a tenuous grasp on contemporary American history would have trouble accepting Garth's equating selfless civil rights activists with mercenaries, but he's too lost in the halcyon haze of his former glory to recognize the stupidity of what he's saying.

Actually, in his combination of oblivious bravado and ex-hippie lingo, Garth suggests a hybrid of The Dude and Walter Sobchak—the campus radical and the reactionary patriot in one lanky, brain-addled package. And, lest anyone who's seen *The Big Lebowski* forget just how incompatible these two attitudes can be when placed side by side, Garth is a character who is literally bursting at the seams. The screenplay for *The Ladykillers* has gifted Garth with a case of IBS (irritable bowel syndrome), which is not only comically symbolic of his vocation—which involves making things explode—but

also alludes to the fact that, like Walter Sobchak before him, he's unable to control himself on any level, physically or verbally.

In a film full of ridiculous characters even by the Coen brothers' standards, the bomber's insistence on painting himself as an aged crusader for social justice (he is an avid reader of *Mother Jones* magazine) makes him the biggest clown around (we might also take Garth's eruptive condition as a sign that he's full of shit). He tries to use his status to bully Gawain MacSam (Marlon Wayans), a young African-American man who, while no smarter than Garth, sees through Garth's patronizing white-savior rhetoric. When asked if he knows who the Freedom Riders were, Gawain's response is succinct: "I don't give a shit who they were. Just tell me when they gonna leave."

There are some obligatory things that can be said about *The Ladykillers*: that it's a remake of the 1955 Ealing Studios comedy by Alexander Mackendrick; that it stars Tom Hanks, then at the peak of his stardom, in a rare villainous role; and that, like *Intolerable Cruelty*, it's considered one of the weaker entries in the Coens' oeuvre, a mere setup for the return to form of *No Country for Old Men*. What goes largely unremarked upon is its sociological satire, which extends and deepens the racial commentary of *O Brother, Where Art Thou?* by bringing it into the present tense. That film's story of villainous, politically affiliated Klansmen defeated by sweet, figuratively color-blind convicts acknowledged America's racial divide while suggesting it could be bridged by the unifying power of folk music. As the Coens' only film to truly foreground African-American

characters (rather than the benevolent narrator figures in *O Brother* and *The Hudsucker Proxy*), *The Ladykillers* risks more in terms of both representation and responsibility, and ultimately stakes out more ambivalent terrain.

On the level of plot, *The Ladykillers* is as convoluted as any of the Coens' crime-story plots. The scheme hatched by Hanks's villainous Professor Goldthwaite Higginson Dorr (a role based on Alec Guinness's Professor Marcus in Mackendrick's original film) to rob the town's casino using the basement of an elderly widow (Irma P. Hall as Marva Munson) as a base of operations is faithful to the source material, as is his cover story: He needs a rehearsal space for his (phony) church music group. As a more genteel version of M. Emmet Walsh's vicious Visser from *Blood Simple*, Dorr is apt to use people for his own purposes. (In an essay on the film in *The Atlantic*, Christopher Orr points out that Visser's famous line after shooting Marty, "Who looks stupid now?" was actually lifted from the script for the Ealing version of *The Ladykillers*.) But like his predecessor, he's something less than a master manipulator: Something can always go wrong. And (as in the original film) the scheme goes haywire almost right from the start, creating a comedy of errors akin to the botched plots in *Fargo* and *The Big Lebowski*, with an even more outlandish set of cause-and-effect consequences.

The complication of *The Ladykillers*' plot would seem to be in support of some relatively simple themes. It's apparent that Dorr and his crew are bad men—greedy, unscrupulous thieves—preying on the kindness and guilelessness of an innocent woman who is too good-hearted at

Like many of the Coens' villains, Professor Dorr talks in circles to avoid saying much of substance. If he's in repose, it's only because he's contemplating his next monologue. The casting of a movie star as beloved as Tom Hanks in the role doubled as a conceptual and commercial hook for *The Ladykillers*; the character's hyper-articulate gentility links him to characters in novels by William Faulkner and Flannery O'Connor, while also playing up the racist legacy of the South in a story with a pious African-American heroine.

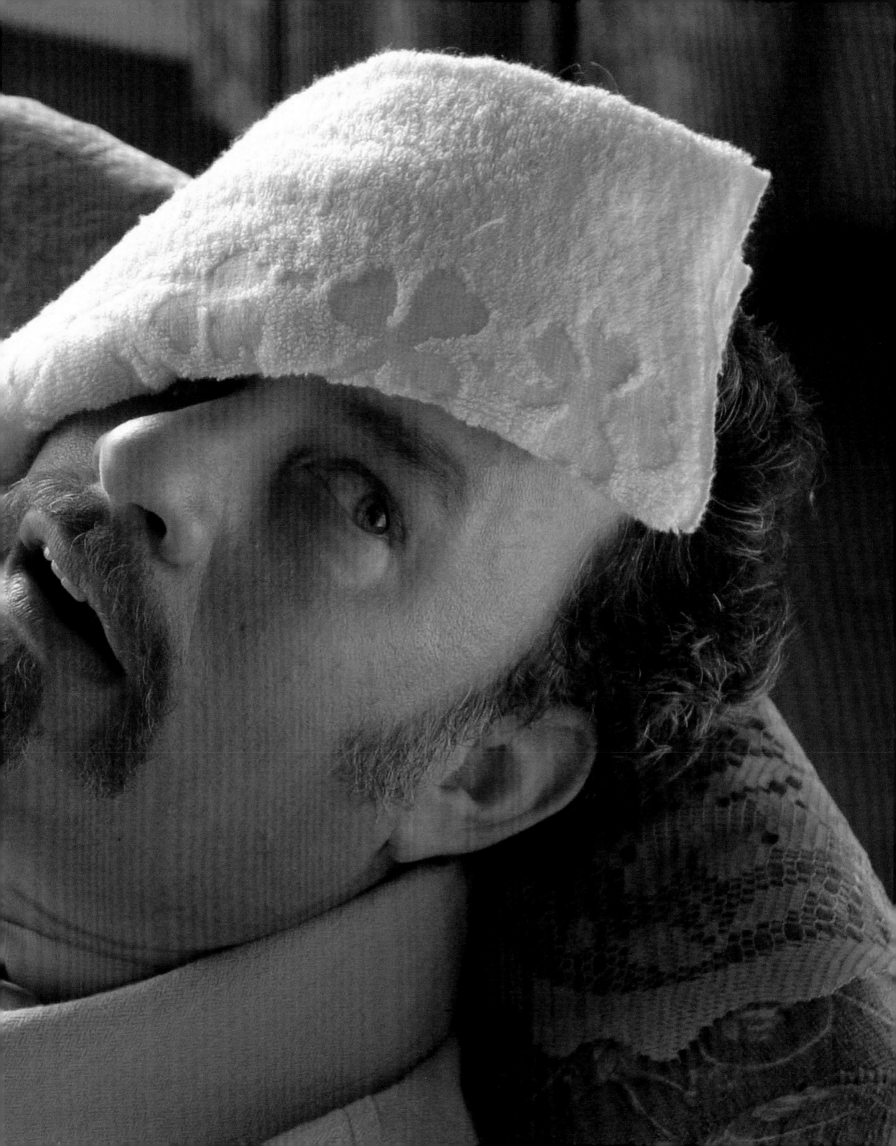

first to recognize their true nature. And, when the crooks are finally forced to contemplate killing their hostess to ensure a clean getaway with the money, they all fall victim to a series of unfortunate events. The ostensible upshot is that of a morality tale in which the universe quietly and righteously sorts itself out according to plan.

Nothing within Coens' cosmology is ever that straightforward, however. *The Ladykillers* is a very slippery movie, especially with regard to religion, which, along with race, is placed front and center (and anticipates the large-scale, Old Testament questioning of *A Serious Man, True Grit*, and *Hail, Caesar!*). The film opens on the strains of what the characters of *O Brother, Where Art Thou?* might recognize as a hymn: "Come, Let Us Go Back to God," as sung by the venerable Texan gospel group The Soul Stirrers. Like "Suspicious Minds" in *Intolerable Cruelty*, this is an overture pointing us toward some embedded philosophy: With its lazy, gentle melody and devotional refrain, "Come, Let Us Go Back to God" is an ideal theme song for Marva Munson, a true believer who takes most of her comfort in the wake of her husband's death from her church congregation.

In the original *Ladykillers*, Mrs. Wilberforce (played memorably and with exuberant comic energy by Katie Johnson) was merely a cranky old biddy—an affectionately ageist creation steeped in regionally specific British stereotypes. In the Coens' version, the character has been reimagined as a fiercely pious lady who feels a need to impose her values on everyone around her. She's introduced barging into the local police station and complaining about a group of teenagers blasting rap music at top volume. "You know what they call colored folks in them songs?" she pleads. "Have you got any idea?"

The song she has a problem with is A Tribe Called Quest's anthem "I Left My Wallet in El Segundo," which is amusing for a couple of reasons. First, A Tribe Called Quest's musical legacy includes critical praise for their progressive politics—for rejecting the then-nascent trappings of so-called gangsta rap and focusing on positive, affirmative messages. It also suggests that even Saucier's youth culture is at least a decade behind the times: the song dates back to 1992. Finally, "I Left My Wallet in El Segundo" is a shaggy-dog narrative about the effort to reclaim lost money—a running motif in the Coens' cinema and very germane to

the plot of *The Ladykillers*. Here, the Coens prove as sophisticated with their soundtrack curation as in any of their more obviously musical movies. Marva's consternation with rap music ("It doesn't make me want to get hippety-hop," she scoffs) is an extension of her old-guard—and in this case, frankly, Old Testament–values: Her dislike of A Tribe Called Quest is suggestive of something more than a fondness for church music. It's one of the script's finest ironies that both Marva and Garth—who, along with Dorr, are the characters who clearly lived through the era of the Jim Crow South—react with contempt to Gawain's brash young-brother act, which is steeped in the sounds and style of "hippety-hop music."

Not that Gawain is any sort of noble hero in line with his Knights-of-the-Round-Table name: Wayans, who got his start on the sketch comedy series *In Living Color*, is a thrillingly unself-conscious physical comedian who's great at playing dumb. But Gawain's status as the low man on the totem pole in the eyes of both the movie's ostensible heroine and also its highest-ranking villains (Dorr is only using him because he works at the casino and can thus be an "inside man") says a lot about the entrenched attitudes of the citizenry of Saucier—and by extension the post-civil-rights-era South, where the movie is set. When Gawain is fired from his job on the "Bandit Queen" for fraternizing with a customer and accuses his boss, Mr. Gudge (Stephen Root), of racism, the older white man's denial gets reconfigured as a vindication: "Everyone on the custodial staff is black, MacSam. Your replacement's gonna be black. His replacement will no doubt be black."

Where *O Brother, Where Art Thou?* ended in a fantasy of racial solidarity, complete with that Ku Klux Klan cross symbolically toppling onto John Goodman's robed cyclops, *The Ladykillers* keeps needling cultural sore spots. Some of the Coens' jibes are obvious: Dorr's bolo tie and faultless gentility mark him as an avatar of the South's old guard—he looks like he could have stepped off the porch of a cotton plantation—and so compound the menace he poses to Marva. The Coens' fondness for having characters who are not as smart as they think they are—and whose verbosity is an attempt to distract from that realization—reaches something like an apex in Dorr's dialogue, which is *The Ladykillers'* true figure of Coen-ish circularity: He's inclined to repetitions and redundancy at every turn,

The conflict between Gawain and Garth comments on the South's ongoing history of racism; time and again, the younger man lashes out against the ex-Freedom Rider's condescending, liberal, white-savior rhetoric.

which makes sense given his old-fashioned self-presentation. His antique appearance and vocabulary give him the demeanor of a man trapped in a time warp. Dorr's professorial bearing and relentless wordiness make him intimidating to Marva, who proves strangely deferential in his presence. She has no problem yelling at the town's police department—actual authority figures—and yet feels ill-equipped to contradict her silver-tongued tenant.

Marva reserves her loathing and skepticism for Gawain and the young, undisciplined black masculinity that she's decided he represents. Her hatred for him is connected to her outsize reverence for her late husband, Othar. "He was some kind of man," marvels Marva of Othar, and the callback to the opening lines of *The Big Lebowski*—"Sometimes, there's a man"—is unmistakable. The Dude is a figure of diminished ideals, and his adventure is spent reclaiming them so that he can pass them on as a birthright to "the little Lebowski on the way." Marva doesn't look to the future. She clings to the things she already knows: her God, her church, and also the lingering goodness of her husband, who she likes to imagine is still watching over her.

Which, as the Coens mischievously suggest, he is. In an homage to *Sullivan's Travels*, Othar's portrait keeps changing expression as the plot thickens. The depiction of Othar as a painting reflects his status for Marva as a Platonic ideal of manhood—an illustration rather than a flesh-and-blood reality. His looming, posthumous presence also opens up supernatural possibilities within the narrative—it gives the film a magic-realist tone that diverges from the original *Ladykillers*. The plot demands that the professor and his henchmen decide, in a panic, to kill the old woman who has helped them, and that their efforts bounce back on them; one by one, Dorr and his men are felled in accidents that suggest some higher power—Othar, perhaps—is protecting Marva like a guardian angel.

The most overt example is when the General (Tzi Ma), a former Viet Cong operative, goes to garrote Marva in her sleep and is startled by the ringing of her cuckoo clock, which features a miniature Jesus figurine. The noise causes the General to choke on his cigarette and fall down the stairs to his death—an absurdist image that reverses the benign deus ex machina of *The Hudsucker Proxy*, with Norville saved from

SOME KIND OF MAN

—

The portrait of Marva's late husband, Othar, presides over the action in *The Ladykillers*, sometimes changing expression in accordance with the plot—a sight gag borrowed from Preston Sturges.

CAT'S EYE

—

The sense that Dorr and his associates are being watched skeptically throughout the film extends from Othar's portrait to Marva's cat, who will eventually be the cause of the General's death.

Irma P. Hall was given a special prize at Cannes by a jury headed by Quentin Tarantino for her performance as the pious, persnickety widow Marva Munson.

BANDIT QUEEN

The change in the story's location means that instead of robbing a railway station, the criminals steal money from a riverboat casino whose name reflects their own mercenary sentiments.

"TROUBLE OF THIS WORLD"

The use of the bouncy, infectious gospel standard to soundtrack the riverboat heist recalls the Coens' wicked use of contrapuntal music in *Blood Simple* and *Miller's Crossing*.

death by the tolling of a clock bell, and renders it wrathful. It's thus possible to believe that Marva's God-fearing rhetoric and the gospel-flavored soundtrack are meant totally earnestly, but to read *The Ladykillers* simply as a parable of good gradually overwhelming evil does it a disservice. Much like Garth's handmade dynamite contraptions, which never detonate exactly when or where they're supposed to, the Coens have rigged their remake with unexpectedly explosive elements—this may be their most expertly booby-trapped screenplay.

Frustrated that the musicians rehearsing in her home have not yet played a note of music in her presence, Marva invites them to perform for her ladies' group. Dorr, who knows that this will expose them once and for all, offers instead to read a verse from the "unquiet mind of Edgar Allan Poe." His chosen poem is "To Helen," a nineteenth-century composition dedicated to Helen of Troy—the proverbial "face that launched a thousand ships." (The connection to *O Brother, Where Art Thou?* is evident: Helen is a pivotal character in *The Odyssey*.) The poem concludes with a tribute to Helen, proclaiming her beauty as a guiding force returning a wandering spirit—perhaps even Ulysses himself—to safe harbor:

> *"On desperate seas long wont to roam*
> *Thy hyacinth hair, thy classic face*
> *Thy Naiad airs have brought me home*
> *To the glory that was Greece*
> *And the grandeur that was Rome."*

Poe will get his revenge at the film's climax in the form of a black bird that dislodges a piece of statuary that falls on Dorr's head, killing him; his last words are "a raven." And the nautical imagery of "To Helen" pays off in the film's most elaborate visual motif: a series of shots depicting a garbage barge, tethered to a tugboat, sailing off toward a shining horizon, used each time one of the "ladykillers" dies, as if they are being ferried into the next life. (In Mackendrick's film, they were shown being dumped in the back of a train.) But at the point when Dorr performs the poem, he's totally in control of his environment. His grandiloquent reading holds Marva and her friends because they've bought into their white visitor's intellectual pretensions; he's sold them on a sense of superiority that's totally unearned and hideously entrenched in context. The Coens cut to Othar's portrait, looking angry and unimpressed at this con job; that Dorr has chosen a poem about "the grandeur that was Rome" also plays up a pre-Christian decadence at odds with the Munson household's piety.

After the reading of "To Helen," Dorr confronts Marva with a half-truth about his intentions. He admits that he is not a musician, but a thief, and excuses himself by saying that he and his men are modern-day Robin Hoods—stealing from bad, profligate men and returning the money to those who need it most. This is him at his craftiest: He refers to the casino as a "riparian Gomorrah," directly appealing to Marva's values, and tells her that if she keeps their secret, he'll make sure the cash goes to a place that she holds dear: Bob Jones University.

Located in Greensboro, South Carolina, BJU is a "biblically faithful, Christian liberal arts university," which until 2000 prohibited interracial dating on campus. Marva's cluelessness about the school's grim history of segregation indicates just how narrow her worldview really is, and while she admirably rejects the professor's offer at first, when the villains are all finally dead and she finds the stolen money stashed away in her basement, she resolves to make a gift to Bob Jones

University. "As long as everybody knows," she says to the local police chief, cheerfully undermining the idea that good Christian charity is supposed to remain anonymous, and pointedly breaking from the script of the original film, in which Mrs. Wilberforce bestowed the cash on "a starving artist."

In *Blood Simple, Fargo,* and *The Big Lebowski,* stolen money goes missing; in *Intolerable Cruelty,* Miles and Marylin's ill-gotten gains go toward funding that rotten, ridiculously cynical reality show. The money is wasted at the end of *The Ladykillers* as well: Instead of lining the pockets of criminals, it goes toward the endowment of a historically racist institution, delivered by a woman who believes sincerely in edifying African-American values. That this ending could be read as a bitter joke about wrongheaded divine intervention—maybe God really does favor BJU after all—is an example of a throwaway joke that's also a boomerang, or maybe one of Norville Barnes's Frisbees, designed to return to sender. When we least expect it, which is to say, at the end of a seemingly innocuous remake of a beloved British comedy, starring Forrest Gump himself, *The Ladykillers* smacks its audience right in the face, and it stings.

HE HAS RISEN
—
The religious undertones of *The Ladykillers* pay off when Marva's Jesus Christ-themed alarm clock startles the General in the middle of an assassination attempt, saving her life.

THE HANGED MAN
—
Professor Dorr's death gives *The Ladykillers* its most morbidly beautiful image, a stark, Tarot-card-like composition that will recur in *True Grit*.

Like many of the Coens' films, *The Ladykillers* revolves around a robbery attempt; here, the theft is successful, but the image of money blowing around the root cellar hints that it will eventually exceed their grasp.

FRIENDS OF THE COENS

"I love these guys. Two heads that seem to share a brilliant and hilariously twisted brain. Their set is always relaxed, low-key, and just plain fun, like the sandbox Ethan referred to at the Oscars a few years back. Between them and Tom Hanks, who was the star of the first movie I got to do with the brothers, the vibe on the set was 100 percent relaxed and collegial. I quickly got over my initial sense of intimidation, and felt totally safe.

And talk about prepared! These guys know how EVERYTHING will be shot before anybody sets foot on set, yet it somehow doesn't feel restrictive. You still feel like a valued collaborator. And since they're way smarter than the actors they work with (which really isn't saying all that much, I guess), you feel like you can trust them absolutely.

Oh. And the days are short. You can actually have a job AND a life. Dinner with your family. I love these guys.

P.S.: In case it needs to be said, they make really, really good movies."

—

J.K. Simmons

FILMS:
The Ladykillers (2004)
Burn After Reading (2008)
True Grit (2010)

Mysterious Ways

2007 — 2009

ACCEPTING THE ACADEMY Award for Best Director from Martin Scorsese—and after waiting respectfully while his brother made a joke about the brevity of the pair's previous acceptance speech after winning Best Adapted Screenplay—Joel Coen told a story that, in the moment, verged perilously close to the sentimental. "Ethan and I have been making stories with movie cameras since we were kids," he began. "In the late sixties, when Ethan was eleven or twelve, he got a suit and a briefcase and a Super 8 camera, and we went to the Minneapolis International Airport and made a movie about shuttle diplomacy called *Henry Kissinger: Man on the Go*. Honestly, what we do now doesn't feel that much different from what we were doing then."

It was a disarmingly sweet anecdote—delivered without a hint of sarcasm—but a few months later, while promoting their follow-up to *No Country for Old Men*, the Coens were back to their usual shrugging public posture. "It's just a weird thing that happened to us and will be forgotten about in a few months," Joel told *Uncut* in October 2008. "It goes straight in the Life Is Strange box," added Ethan in the same interview. "It was never an ambition to grow up and win an Academy Award, so when it happens, you go, 'Weird!'"

To say that the shadow of *No Country for Old Men*—the Coens' most acclaimed, popular, and, arguably, artistically accomplished feature after nearly twenty-five years of filmmaking—hung over *Burn After Reading* would be an understatement. The Washington-set thriller, which premiered to mixed reviews when it opened the 2008 Venice Film Festival and topped out at $60 million at the North American box office (a disappointing number

considering a starry cast including George Clooney, Brad Pitt, and Tilda Swinton), was, like *The Big Lebowski* before it, instantly underrated in proximity to its predecessor. *Variety* called it "arch and ungainly," while *The New Yorker*'s David Denby accused the film of "terminal misanthropy"; in *Time*, Richard Corliss admitted that he didn't even understand what the Coens were trying to achieve.

One way to look at *Burn After Reading* is (as Joel may have been hinting at the Oscar ceremony) as a grown-up version of the brothers' childhood *Henry Kissinger: Man on the Go*—a political comedy dealing with US foreign policy and its discontents. "Imagine a group of dunderheaded Americans who think they would benefit from a covert alliance with the Russian government. They make overtures to that country's ambassador, blithely ignorant that they'll be monitored by US intelligence. A series of cascading mistakes ultimately brings disaster crashing down on their heads." That was the *New Republic*'s senior editor Jeet Heer, reevaluating *Burn After Reading* halfway through the first year of the Trump administration and concluding that the Coens' viciously cynical DC satire looked uncannily prescient in retrospect.

Charges of undue nastiness also arose one year later when the Coens released *A Serious Man*, a comedy about an embattled physics professor who turns to his community's spiritual advisors when a run of bad luck has him contemplating the possibility of divine punishment. Shot, like *Fargo* before it, in the brothers' home state of Minnesota and set in a suburban Jewish community markedly similar to the one that Joel and Ethan had grown up in during the late 1960s (the same period in which the film was set), *A Serious Man* was assumed to be a more "personal" project. But while the Coens admitted that there were some details gleaned from their childhood experiences, they didn't let journalists run too far with such interpretations. "It was not a long-harbored ambition to write something set in 1967 where we grew up," Ethan told *Ain't It Cool News*. Joel was more abstract, citing "the incongruity of Jews in the Midwest" as a creative starting point.

The full-bore Jewishness of *A Serious Man*—following more compartmentalized evocations of Jewish culture in *Miller's Crossing, Barton Fink*, and *The Big Lebowski*—was seized on by critics, including a sizable contingent of dissenters who perceived a strain of ethnic self-hatred à la Woody Allen. "Is *A Serious Man* a work of Jewish self-loathing?" asked Ella Taylor rhetorically in the *Village Voice*. "Hard to tell, if only because . . . just about every character the Coens create is meant to affirm their own superiority." Taylor's scathing critique echoed her *Voice* colleague J. Hoberman's diagnosis, circa *Burn After Reading*, of "Coendescension," and it didn't help matters that the Coens admitted that they enjoyed finding "new ways to torture" their hapless protagonist. (The film ends with a credit claiming "No Jews Were Harmed in the Making of This Motion Picture.")

With its nearly anonymous cast of actors and niche subject matter, *A Serious Man* didn't make a lot of money (just over $30 million in North America), and despite its surprise Oscar nomination for Best Picture, it didn't appear to be headed for enduring status. And yet in a recent poll by the BBC, it was voted one of the hundred best films made since 2000; in 2016, *Vulture*'s Bilge Ebiri called the film "perfectly modulated." More than any of the Coens' films besides *The Big Lebowski*, *A Serious Man* illustrates the process of delayed canonization that often happens with the seemingly minor works of major directors.

In November 2009, two months after the premiere of *A Serious Man* at the Toronto International Film Festival, the Coens were attending open casting sessions in Texas for the leading role in their upcoming adaptation of Charles Portis's 1968 novel *True Grit*. A *New York Times* feature by David Carr revealed that more than fifteen thousand young actresses had either sent in tapes or auditioned for the part of Mattie Ross, a driven girl who

hires a drunken US Marshal to help her apprehend the outlaw who murdered her father. Mattie had previously been played in the 1969 movie of *True Grit* by Kim Darby, whose precociousness had been endearing; the Coens were looking for something different.

"Mattie's a pill," Joel told *Vanity Fair*, explaining that the challenge was to find an actress who could embody an old-maid quality in a preadolescent package. "We saw a tape of Hailee [Steinfeld] a week or so before we met her," said Ethan. "Our reaction to the tape was she was one of the very, very few who could just do the language, which was the washout point for most of the girls. Then, she was totally self-possessed and seemed to understand the character, and possibly too good to be true."

Steinfeld was thirteen years old during the shooting of *True Grit*, and her performance was routinely cited by critics as the film's most outstanding element—even above Jeff Bridges's sturdy work opposite her as Rooster Cogburn. "She nails it," wrote Roger Ebert, who praised Steinfeld for "sidestepping the opportunity to make Mattie adorable"; in the *Hollywood Reporter*, Todd McCarthy, who had carpet-bombed *Burn After Reading* just two years earlier, praised the Coens and their star discovery for "convey[ing] the character's refusal to be deterred, without a trace of gamine-like coyness or girlish cuteness . . . Perhaps Frances McDormand's performance in *Fargo* represented an implicit model."

Like *Fargo, True Grit* enjoyed the kind of mainstream breakthrough that comes with including some warm, palpable emotions amid gunplay and bloodshed. Released during the Christmas holiday season of 2010, it grossed $26.5 million in its opening weekend—by far the biggest number of the Coens' career—and finished with more than $170 million domestically and $250 million worldwide—also clear high-water marks. (The MPAA's decision to give *True Grit* a PG-13 rating, as opposed to the hard R designations affixed to *No Country for Old Men* and *Burn After Reading*, may have factored into its success.) The film's ten Academy Award nominations (including a much-cheered nod for Steinfeld) were the most for any Coens production, but, in another item for Ethan's Life Is Strange box, it failed to win a single one, tying it for the biggest shutout in Oscars history.

No Country for Old Men

RELEASE DATE
November 9, 2007
BUDGET
$25M
DISTRIBUTOR
Miramax
CAST
Tommy Lee Jones
Javier Bardem
Josh Brolin
Woody Harrelson
Kelly Macdonald
Garret Dillahunt
Tess Harper
Barry Corbin

WARNING!

THIS FILM CONTAINS

Bounty hunters	29%
Coin flips	21%
Horizon lines	13%
Loose change	11%
Borrowed shirts	8%
Motel rooms	6%
Amateur surgery	4%
Mariachi music	3%
Dead dogs	3%
Sweating milk	2%
Hope	0%

IN CORMAC McCARTHY'S 2005 novel *No Country for Old Men,* the characters are all trying to get their hands on a suitcase stuffed with two million dollars in cash. However, the most hair-raising scenes involve nothing more valuable than a single quarter.

Toward the end of the book, the psychopathic assassin Anton Chigurh invites a young woman at the business end of his gun barrel to flip a coin for a chance to spare her life. Her name is Carla Jean Moss, and she's the widow of the man he's been hired to kill. At this point in the story, her husband, Llewelyn Moss, is already dead, ironically not even by Chigurh's hand.

Recovering the stolen funds of a transnational drug cartel is not a business that allows for loose ends, and yet Chigurh is willing to risk a living witness on the rise and fall of a quarter. It's the same proposition that he's already offered to the proprietor of a roadside filling station in an earlier scene. The man tentatively calls heads and solemnly watches his would-be killer drive away without any fuss. "Don't put it in your pocket," Chigurh advises the man before leaving. "You won't know which one it is."

The contradiction of a hit man who advocates for a fifty-fifty chance is quintessential Cormac McCarthy. The Pulitzer Prize–winning author specializes in sacred monsters, from the isolated necrophile protagonist of *Child of God* to the monstrous Judge Holden in *Blood Meridian*. Both of those characters cut vivid figures on the page, but Anton Chigurh is a cipher, barely described in the novel beyond a few fleeting impressions: "Blue eyes.

Serene. Dark hair. Something about him faintly exotic. Beyond Moss's experience."

But not beyond the experiences of Joel and Ethan Coen, who had already conjured up several avatars of evil in their work by the time they decided to make a movie out of McCarthy's novel. "Why not start with the best?" was Joel's rationale for why the brothers picked *No Country for Old Men* for their first "official" cinematic adaptation; both directors joked that writing the screenplay was simply a matter of "holding the spine of the open book flat," as if they were just adding stage directions to the author's spartan prose. The idea that *No Country for Old Men* would be an entirely self-effacing exercise dissolves, however, the moment that Javier Bardem appears as Chigurh with that absurd pageboy haircut.

The odd-looking mop-top can be read as a metaphor for the Coens' tactics in adapting *No Country for Old Men*. They're scrupulously faithful to their source material, but they make sure to leave their mark on the story as well. Chigurh is a vision of pure malevolence, just as McCarthy intended, but his haircut is a sight gag on the order of George Clooney's pomade fetish in *O Brother, Where Art Thou?*, an overtly Coen-esque joke in a movie that is otherwise completely stripped down.

Top: "Can't stop what's coming": As Llewelyn hunts antelope, the shadow of an encroaching cloud implies larger, darker forces hovering over the Texas landscape.

Bottom right: In the novel *No Country for Old Men*, Anton Chigurh is barely described physically. In the opening scenes of the film, the Coens honor that vagueness by keeping him out of focus behind the overmatched, oblivious police officer who's arrested him.

At no point in their careers before *No Country for Old Men* had the Coens ever been accused of being minimalists. Their early noirs and comedies alike were all vividly stylized. Even *Fargo*, with its back-to-basics ethos, still featured a plaintive, folky musical score by Carter Burwell to contextualize its Midwestern setting. *No Country* doesn't go even that far: Burwell's contributions to the soundtrack are basically low-level ambient noise. The sound design is muted, as is the color palette, all dusty browns and rusted gunmetal grays; the film's production designer, Jess Gonchor, was inspired by Mark Rothko's abstract canvases, with their horizontal lines and abundance of negative space.

Roger Deakins's camera, which prowled and flew through *The Ladykillers*, remains mostly fixed in place. The filmmakers feature nature as their greatest special effect here—distant shafts of lightning flash in the sky during Llewelyn's escape from some shotgun-toting baddies, and clouds over a valley filled with antelope take the form of a hovering black apparition. The effect of such naturalism is hypnotic; on a strictly technical level, *No Country for Old Men* is possibly the most fully accomplished of the Coens' films.

That it was received as such by the Academy of Motion Picture Arts and Sciences (it won four awards: Best Picture, Best Director, Best Adapted Screenplay, and Best Supporting Actor

for Bardem) was a nod to its brilliant craft as well as a sort of career-achievement citation for its creators. When *Fargo* crashed the Oscars in 1996, it was more a signal that the American indie film had come of age after the calculated juvenilia of Quentin Tarantino and *Pulp Fiction*. The triumph of *No Country for Old Men* was in many ways a vote for the new establishment. Stacked up against its primary award-night competitor, Paul Thomas Anderson's crazed oil-fields epic *There Will Be Blood*, *No Country for Old Men* looked positively classicist. Comparing it to *Blood Simple* and *Raising Arizona*, meanwhile, would locate trace elements of the earlier films— an opening montage of Lone Star landscapes borrowed from *Blood Simple*; Chigurh calmly blowing away a bird in homage to Leonard Smalls, the Lone Biker of the Apocalypse. But the same viewer would probably conclude that the filmmakers' more eccentric edges had been, if not dulled exactly, then refashioned into a hard, gleaming point.

It would be wrong, though, to say that the Coens pull a disappearing act in *No Country for Old Men*, or else that the film is a simple dress-up game in neo-cowboy garb. The script dutifully replicates the dual-track chase structure of McCarthy's novel, with Chigurh trying to retrieve the money from Moss (Josh Brolin), and weathered lawman Sheriff Ed Tom Bell (Tommy Lee Jones) tidying up the trail of corpses behind them. But they also make some

subtle changes that go well beyond what Joel Coen humbly categorized as "compression." If *No Country for Old Men* can be characterized in some ways as the Coens' most self-effacing, least referential work—one that, like *Blood Simple* and *Fargo*, operates primarily on a visceral level—it's equally true that the way they blend their own ideas and interests into the material without overwhelming it evinced a new maturity. The film is a study in how reverence does not preclude self-expression.

McCarthy's novel is hard to pare down, even if it's less epic than predecessors like *All the Pretty Horses* or *Blood Meridian*, the latter of which is steeped in a kind of biblical grandeur. More than any of McCarthy's novels, it's written with a sense of forward thrust. With this in mind, the Coens' first crucial choice in the script was to remove the bulk of Sheriff Bell's first-person reflections on his career in law enforcement, which are essentially digressions from the plot and, as the book goes on, coalesce into a sort of anguished state-of-the-union address. "I think I know where we're headed," says Bell in the book's penultimate chapter. "We're being bought with our own money. And it ain't just the drugs. There is fortunes bein accumulated out there that they don't nobody even know about. What do we think is goin to come of that money?" Sheriff Bell goes on to inventory other social problems (teenagers with "green hair and nosebones"), but the old fogeyish aspects

of his lament are submerged beneath what is unmistakably a strident late-capitalist critique. *No Country for Old Men* is set at the beginning of the 1980s: The quarter that gets flipped by the man at the filling station is from 1958, and Chigurh estimates that "it's been traveling twenty-two years to get here." The story has an allegorical dimension, depicting an American landscape overrun by rapacious, corporate-affiliated villainy. In the roughly contemporaneous *Raising Arizona*, H.I. McDunnough expressed his have-not frustration by referencing that "sumbitch Reagan in the White House," but in keeping with his essentially gentle, humane nature, he quickly adds that the fortieth president may be less of a problem than his advisors.

The criminality in *Raising Arizona* is ineffectual and ultimately harmless—robberies committed with an empty gun. *No Country for Old Men* is more loaded, literally and figuratively. Matched up against a sleek modern monster like Anton Chigurh, armed with a cattle gun that blows a (coin-shaped) hole in people's heads, neither the decent yet ineffectual Sheriff Bell nor the thick-skulled Llewelyn would seem to stand much of a chance, although the latter, a Vietnam vet, puts up an impressive fight. The Coens propose that Llewelyn and Chigurh are at least on the same spectrum of clinical, efficient violence. When Chigurh murders a driver by the side of the road with his can of compressed air, he whispers to the victim, "Hold still," a line taken from McCarthy's text; in short order, the film cuts to Llewelyn crouched at the edge of a cliff with his rifle sight trained on a herd of antelope. "You hold still," he whispers to himself—a repetition not present in the book.

Llewelyn is a hunter in his own right, and Brolin plays him with a sense of steely self-reliance that's somewhere in between square-jawed Old West heroism and the lonely bitterness of the disenfranchised. In the book and the film, Llewelyn takes his discovery of the money as a windfall that serves as a kind of reward for his sacrifices overseas; it's a way out of a dead-end life. But his conscience eats at him in another way, which the Coens convert into an opportunity for witty self-citation. After Llewelyn returns in the middle of the night with the briefcase containing the drug cartel's money, he's framed lying in bed, Carla Jean asleep beside him, in an overhead shot that directly mirrors the image of H.I. when he has his nightmare about the Lone Biker of the Apocalypse.

Both men are racked with guilt over ill-gotten gains, but where H.I. fears that he's unleashed

UNLAWFUL ENTRY

—

Anton Chigurh's habit of blowing out door locks with compressed air evinces his ghostlike stealth.

LOOSE CHANGE

—

Money is a crucial leitmotif throughout *No Country for Old Men*; Chigurh's fixation on coins represents a sociopathic mercenary mindset.

"He saw himself in the cold gray screen": The Coens pick up on Cormac McCarthy's description of Chigurh catching sight of his reflection in a trailer park television and extend it to also include Sheriff Ed Tom Bell. This matched pair of shots alludes to each character's archetypal nature-the killer and the lawman, respectively-while placing them on the same continuum of experience-a sophisticated doubling technique that shows the Coens making subtle but pointed changes to their source material.

No Country For Old Men's stripped-down realism still finds room for spiritual themes and inquiry. The compressed air tank that Anton Chigurh uses to murder his victims is both the instrument and mirror for his methodology: cold, silent, clean, leaving only the barest trace. Here, he approaches his victim with the calm of a faith healer, but he's a death dealer; while his victim stands in the light, Chigurh's hand, which will turn out to have a lethal touch, is cloaked in shadow.

some terrible external force, Llewelyn is preoccupied by the possibility of mercy. At the crime scene, he encountered a mortally wounded man who asked him in Spanish for some water—a dying wish he was in no real position to grant. Llewelyn's choice to return to the desert with a jug of water is foolish: "I'm about to do something dumber than hell," he admits to Carla Jean (Kelly Macdonald) before heading out. Llewelyn's decency is bound up in this small gesture of kindness, which is instantly rendered futile when Llewelyn discovers the intended recipient of the water is dead—as he knew he would be. (Recall the ending of *Blood Simple*, with Visser desperately waiting for a droplet of water to reach his lips—and the hard cut to black that hints he doesn't get his wish.) Llewelyn's misguided empathy is the difference between a clean getaway and being hunted, first by a faceless group of cartel enforcers and then by Anton Chigurh after he's called in to finish the job.

In terms of its narrative progression, *No Country for Old Men* is one of the Coens' most horizontal movies—it's got a linear, cause-and-effect structure free from obvious digressions. But a sense of circularity asserts itself in the connections the Coens forge between their three main characters, beginning with Chigurh and Llewelyn's doubled command to "hold still" and extending through a subtle running motif of repetition and refraction. When Chigurh goes to Moss's abandoned trailer to kill him but finds him gone, he's shown sitting down with a glass of milk and catching sight of his reflection in the television screen, in a stage direction taken from McCarthy: "He looked at himself in the dead gray screen." It's an eerie shot that visually positions Bardem's killer as a monster out of a horror movie rather than a flesh-and-blood person—a two-dimensional bogeyman loose in the free world. Later, when Sheriff Bell arrives at the same trailer, he notices the glass of milk and sits down in the same seat as Chigurh, and sees himself in the television as well—a repetition not present in the book. The Coens' filmmaking deepens McCarthy's themes: The shot suggests that, no less than his quarry, Sheriff Bell is living up to an image—the resolute lawman, the old-fashioned cowboy, an archetype we learn about from going to the movies.

It's an archetype that *No Country for Old Men* works to undermine, tenderly but

also definitively: Jones's worried, mournful expression indicates that Bell knows he's no prime-time hero even as his deputy (Garret Dillahunt) looks up to him with wide, admiring eyes. For most of the story, we are waiting for the sheriff to catch up to the two men he's chasing—to reach Llewelyn and help him, or to reach Chigurh and confront him. And as in *Fargo*, which leveraged Marge's vulnerability as a pregnant woman against her competence as an investigator, we're torn between hope that Sheriff Bell can ride in and play the hero and fear that he's not physically or spiritually up to the task at hand. He's an older man, and he admits that he's never drawn his gun. In a late sequence, he stands in front of two motel room doors, knowing that Chigurh the killing machine may be behind one of them. The Coens stage this moment as Bell's version of the coin flip offered by Chigurh to all his victims: door #1 or door #2, heads or tails. He takes his chance, and the room he picks is empty. All the sheriff sees is his own looming shadow against the back wall, just as he saw himself in the television set in Llewelyn's trailer—a projection at once larger than life and totally insubstantial.

The visual language in this sequence is right out of a horror movie: The Coens cut starkly from Bell to Chigurh, in an almost disfiguring close-up, waiting behind the door in the adjacent room. This is another deviation from the book, where Chigurh waits in the parking lot, so the Coens have heightened the situation—and emphasized the lurking fear of the Chigurh character, which is passed on from Llewelyn to Sheriff Bell. After chasing him for the whole movie, Chigurh eludes Bell, but we get the feeling that Bell is relieved by this fact—because he would not have survived the confrontation.

No Country for Old Men ends with Sheriff Bell, now retired after confiding that he feels "overmatched" by the likes of Anton Chigurh, recounting a dream to his wife in which he is out on the trail with his father, basking in the comfort and security of the older man's presence. No sooner did that feeling of comfort take hold, he says, than he came back to consciousness and with it, the harsh reality that his father is dead and that he will be the next to go: "And then I woke up." The Coens' austerity measures mean that Bell's dream isn't shown like H.I.'s fantasy of home and hearth in *Raising Arizona*, or Ed Crane's reminiscence of domestic stasis in *The*

Man Who Wasn't There; for the first time, they choose not to penetrate their character's inner consciousness, instead allowing Jones's acting to conjure up the requisite image of father and son "out there in all that dark." It's a beautifully acted scene by Jones—the payoff to his reticent, measured performance, with its thick residue of unease. By finally articulating the idea that death, whether in the lurking form of Anton Chigurh or something as inevitable and ephemeral as mortality itself, stalks us all, Sheriff Bell confirms his status as the story's guiding voice. He gets the literal last word on the proceedings, and the rest, as they say, is silence.

He doesn't get to play the hero, however, and it is in ensuring that their modern Western has a hero despite the apparent best candidate's failure that the Coens make their boldest intervention. *No Country for Old Men*'s true climax is the confrontation between Anton Chigurh and Carla Jean Moss, which deviates from the book more than any other scene in the film. McCarthy positions the younger woman (she's all of nineteen years old) as a helpless victim; she briefly protests the coin flip on religious grounds—"God would not want me to do that"—and then heeds Chigurh's order to "call it." She opts for heads, but the coin comes up tails, and after a few more words of explanation from Chigurh, an exhausted Carla Jean ruefully admits that she's come around to her killer's way of thinking. "'Good, [Chigurh] said. 'That's good.' Then he shot her."

The Coens' version of Carla Jean is tougher and more worldly than her literary counterpart: She's played by the Scottish actress Kelly Macdonald, who was thirty when the role was shot and who avoids any teenaged affectations (and rescues the role from child-bride condescension).

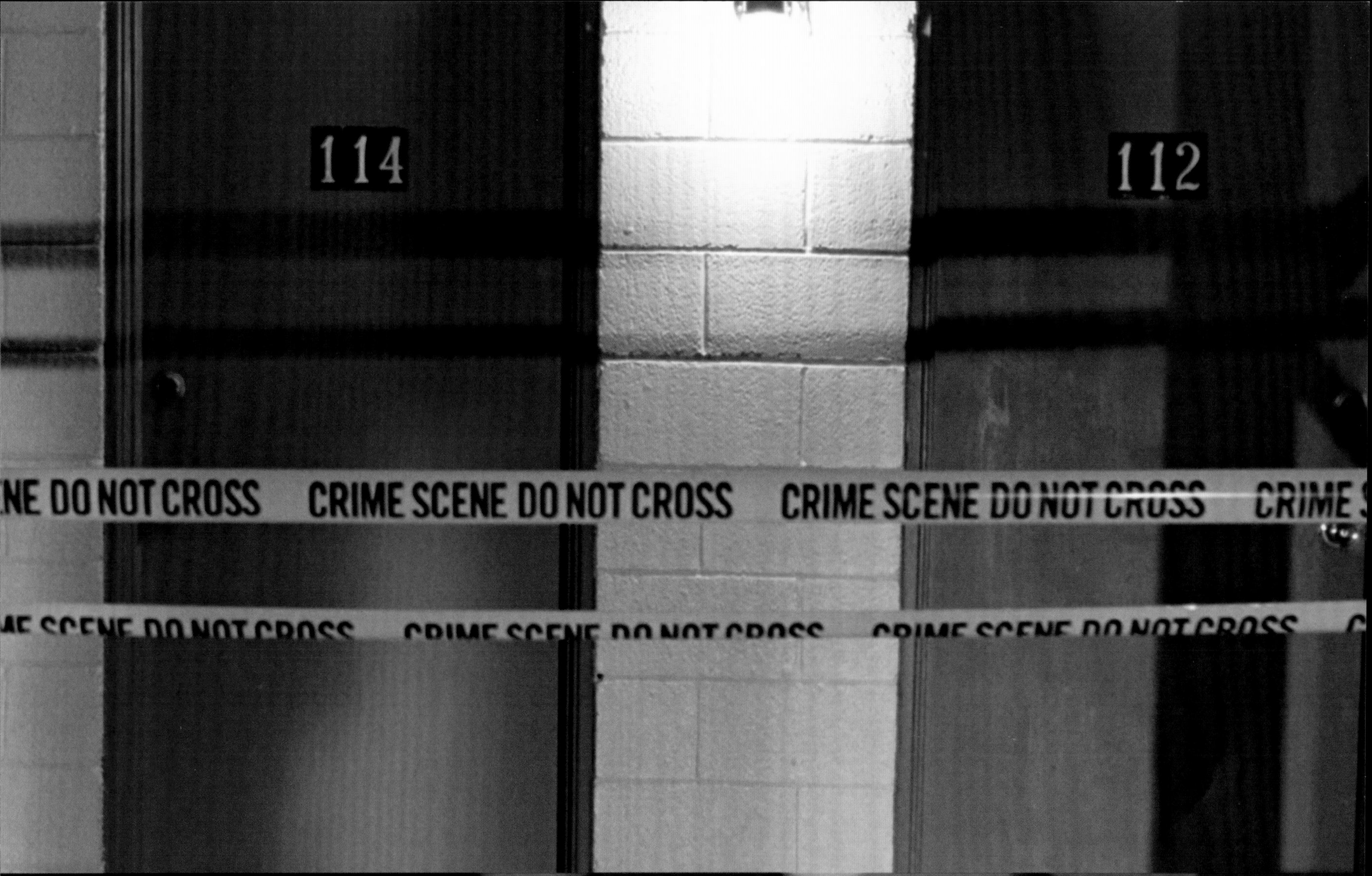
114
112
CRIME SCENE DO NOT CROSS
CRIME SCENE DO NOT CROSS

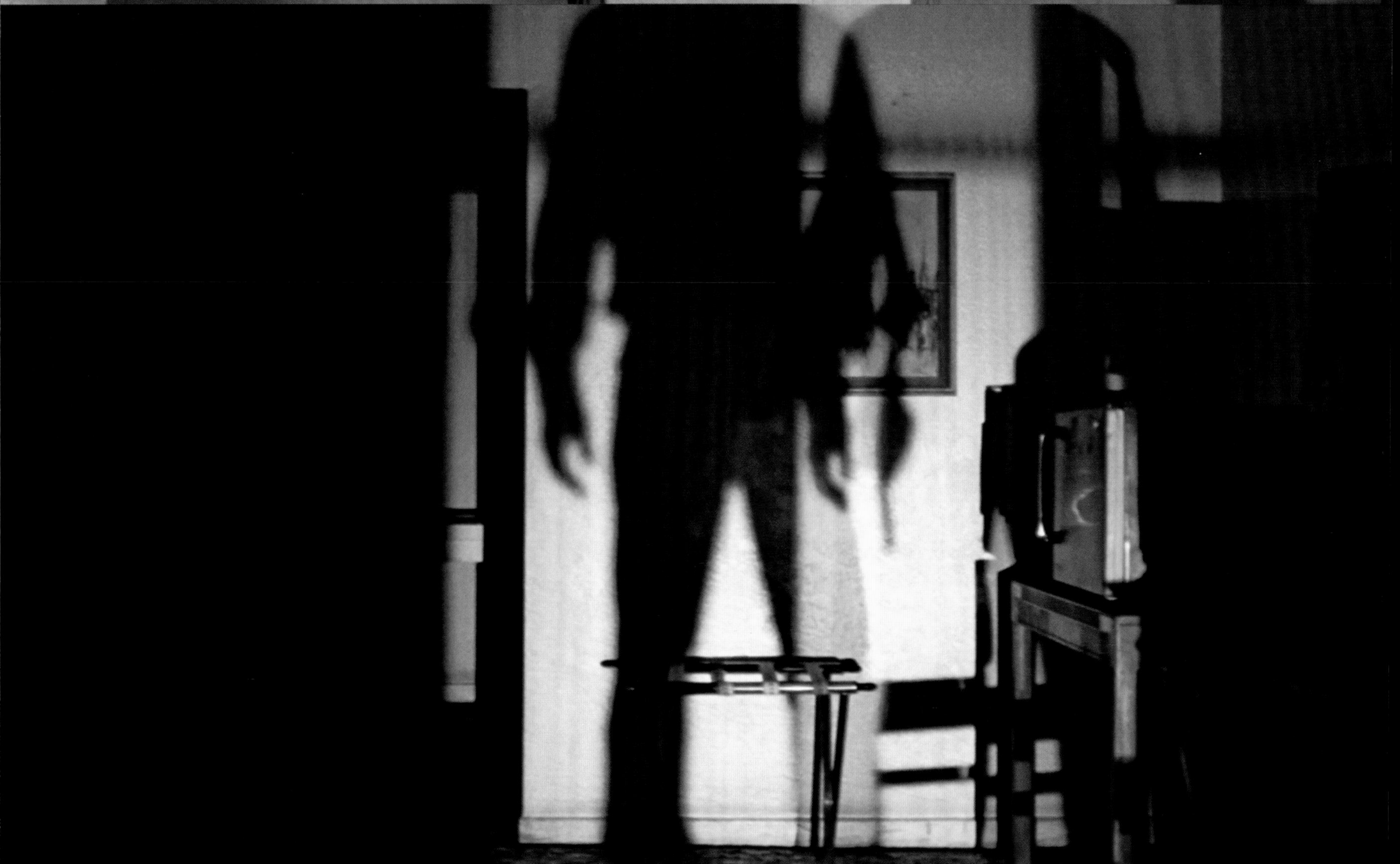

When Chigurh offers her the chance to let the coin decide her fate, she chides him that "the coin don't have no say. It's just you." She doesn't beg for her life. She doesn't come around to Chigurh's way of thinking. She doesn't do what every man in the movie, including even noble Sheriff Bell, via his decision at the motel, ends up doing. Instead, she refuses to "call it." Without getting up out of her seat or even lifting a finger, she stands up to Anton Chigurh and his warped worldview. Bardem acts the character's confusion and consternation accordingly by raising his voice slightly when he orders her to "call it" a second time: She has him worried. And the Coens honor her resistance by cutting discreetly away from her demise. It's the only murder in the movie that is not shown either in the moment or its aftermath; a shot of Chigurh checking his shoes for bloodstains as he leaves the house has an ambiguous distance.

As the lone significant female in a movie whose masculine thrust begins with its title, Macdonald's Carla Jean is not frequently discussed in critical appreciations of *No Country*

for Old Men. The positioning of her last scene as a final reckoning with and rejection of the villain's ethos shows that it should be. In both the film and the book, Chigurh is laid low by a car accident on his way back from Carla Jean's house. McCarthy seems to intend the smashup as proof of his villain's theories of predestination, putting him on the wrong end of a cosmic coin flip. In response, the Coens impose an element of karmic moralism: It's as if Carla Jean's stubbornness is what finally throws her killer off-course.

By privileging Carla Jean's defiance, the Coens slightly reroute McCarthy's themes and also trace a path back to their own work, back to the end of *Fargo*, where Gaear Grimsrud sits caged in a police car behind Marge Gunderson. It's obvious that Ed Tom Bell, a good cop shell-shocked by the violence around him, is a close cousin to Brainerd's chief of police: He echoes her comments about not "understanding" how things have gotten so bad. But Marge's true soul sister in the Coens' filmography is Carla Jean Moss: Their mutual incomprehension of the blunt avarice around them doesn't mean they've given up. Instead, they both try, each

in her way and from very different positions of power, to intervene against what another character in *No Country for Old Men* calls "the dismal tide."

"There's more to life than a little bit of money.... Don't you know that?" Marge plaintively queries her prisoner. It's obvious from Gaear's thousand-yard stare that he doesn't. And neither does Anton Chigurh, whose choice of a quarter as an "instrument" is symbolic in a way that outstrips even his own intentions. All that Chigurh's talk of principles boils down to is the worship of the almighty dollar: "I got here the same way the coin did." And the quarter is also a circle: the latest incarnation, perhaps, of Norville Barnes's Hula-Hoop and its built-in embrace of the profit motive, which gives *The Hudsucker Proxy* its superficially optimistic but inwardly cynical grace note.

In the novel *No Country for Old Men*, Chigurh eventually tracks down the money and brings it to its "rightful" owner—a nameless white-collar thug who is glad to receive it. In the movie, the money disappears, and while it's implied that it's

in Chigurh's possession, we can't know for sure. This is typical: In *Fargo*, Carl Showalter buries a million dollars in the middle of nowhere and the secret of its location dies with him. In *The Big Lebowski*, the ransom money disappears and is barely mentioned for the second half of the movie. In *O Brother, Where Art Thou?*, the "treasure" that sets the whole plot into motion turns out to be nothing but a rumor. And in *The Ladykillers*, the gang's ill-gotten gains are donated to Bob Jones University—which is to say that the money is as good as gone. Marva's ostensible act of charity at the end of *The Ladykillers* exposes her as a sort of holy fool, but she isn't motivated by greed. At the end of *Fargo*, Marge beams when her husband's painting is selected to represent the state's new three-cent stamp—a literal penny-ante honor that she invests with greater worth through her supportive adulation. In just one short but indelible scene, Carla Jean Moss joins the roll call of Coen heroines who refuse to listen when money talks.

Far left: Carla Jean Moss rejects Chigurh's coin flip, an act of moral strength that marks her as the film's secret heroine.

Left: Sheriff Bell's dream of his late father reveals his unconscious fear of his own mortality.

FILMOGRAPHY

```
Hail, Caesar! (2016)
True Grit (2010)
A Serious Man (2009)
No Country for Old Men (2007)
The Ladykillers (2004)
Intolerable Cruelty (2003)
The Man Who Wasn't There (2001)
O Brother, Where Art Thou? (2002)
The Big Lebowski (1998)
Fargo (1996)
The Hudsucker Proxy (1994)
Barton Fink (1991)
```

A fourteen-time Academy Award nominee, Roger Deakins is widely considered one of the greatest cinematographers of all time. He's worked regularly with the Coens since the beginning of the 1990s, creating indelible images in films like *Fargo*, *The Man Who Wasn't There*, and *No Country for Old Men*.

Roger Deakins
CINEMATOGRAPHER

The first three Coen brothers films were shot by Barry Sonnenfeld. Visually, they're very interesting. Were you aware of them before you started working with the Coens?

I knew their films—I'd seen *Blood Simple* and *Raising Arizona*. I didn't see *Miller's Crossing* because they were cutting it—or they'd just finished cutting it—at the same time as when we were doing prep on *Barton Fink*. Those early films were beautifully shot, especially *Miller's Crossing*—but I didn't really take that in hand. They hired me.

In the case of your first collaboration, *Barton Fink,* you're trying to evoke a headspace and there's a certain distortion, exaggeration, and elongation in the image.

The first time I worked with the guys, I remember spending many weeks with them because this is what they wanted. They usually do storyboards of an entire film. But this was especially the case on *Barton Fink*. That whole subjective viewpoint, if you like, came out of the storyboard process and then just gushed into the script.

How did you approach lighting the hotel where the bulk of the film takes place?

They write the script and you talk about it. Then you talk with the production designer about how to shoot it. Then you discuss how you're going to elongate the main corridor, and we did that by putting a photograph at the end of the set to extend it. So an in-camera effect. There were all kinds of these little tricks. You work out problems, you think about the image, and it just develops.

How did you go about filming the actors?

The Coens have a very clear idea of how they want things to look and feel. They send the storyboards to me before the sets are built, so the sets are built with the storyboards in mind. And all the locations are found with the storyboards in mind. If they can't find the exact location, then, you know, the storyboards are adapted to fit the location, and it's a give-and-take process. They will block a scene like most directors do in the morning with the actors, but the actors don't see the storyboards. It's just uncanny with Joel and Ethan how it always ends up that the actors sit where you think they're going to sit. It all ends up being exactly as it was planned. Okay, nine times out of ten.

The Coens are known for their rampaging, stampeding camera movements.

Both *Barton Fink* and *Hudsucker* were very subjective. They were dreamy. Then there was *Fargo*, which was much more observational. It's like a Ken Loach movie. They are actually re-creating something that happened—like a docudrama. They imagined the whole thing as a static camera in the corner of the room capturing everything that was happening, but that's not how it ended up. I think that feeling went all the way through the film. The feel of it being slightly longer lenses, which it was. And being, as I say, more observational. We used quite a bit of handheld in that film.

Would you say films like *Fargo* and *The Hudsucker Proxy* were made more or less the same way as *Barton Fink*, but with more money to work with?

Yeah, totally. But the guys didn't change their way of working. No, no. The script and the idea demanded a bigger budget and demanded bigger sets.

Can you talk about the opening shot of *Fargo*, which I think I've read you weren't even present for?

We were up in Fargo, yeah, and we didn't really get much snow. We had the opening sequence storyboarded, and the plan was that we'd actually go out to this location and to fields with no snow. We put markers down and said, Okay, we'll have the vehicles come up here, and the camera's going to be here, and it's going to be this height, and shot with a fifty-millimeter lens. We mapped it all out so that we could shoot it all very quickly when we got some snow. So we were watching the weather and thinking, "Well, when can we go do this?" And the only time we really got some snowfall, we were on the fourteenth floor of a tower block shooting the scene between Bill Macy and his father-in-law. The shot people talk about, looking down.

Where he goes to scrape the windshield of his car.

We were shooting in there, so we couldn't go out and take advantage of the snow. In fact, it wasn't doing us many favors, because we were up there

trying to get this view, and the snow was more or less blotting it out. I sent my standby operator with a splinter unit to shoot the opening sequence, so he went out in the snow and shot that sequence—none of us were there.

It's an incredibly epic vision that has a lot to do with Carter Burwell's music, too. It feels like something out of *Lawrence of Arabia*, just white instead of beige.

The whole conceptual discussion we had about *Fargo* was the idea of the day and the night. The idea of the day and the snow being white, so you achieved this very graphic, washed-out image. Then when you cut to the night scenes, you would go to this incredible black frame with specks of light.

There's also the incredibly vivid light from the headlights of stopped cars.

Exactly, yeah. You're in the middle of nowhere. You haven't got a load of money. You're wondering what you can practically do in this situation. And the time we had to shoot and everything else . . . Bob Rafelson once said to me, "Necessity is the mother of invention." If you have prescriptions, it forces you to do something that might be more creative than if you had all the possibilities in the world. We not only had to shoot it like that, but it was obvious it was the best way to go.

The Big Lebowski is obviously not like a Ken Loach movie.

It's more like a psychedelic dream. Like a trip. You're deliberately trying to create different looks; you're trying to keep it one film.

Can you talk particularly about how the camera movement in that film was achieved?

Again, it was very carefully storyboarded so you had the time to think about exactly how you were going to create some of those shots. Some of them are blue-screen composites. Some of them are done very simply in-camera. We had to do this shot where the camera is traveling between the legs of the dancing girls as though we were a bowling ball. My grip said, "Oh, just put the camera on a soft pad and I'll push it down with a big pole," and that's basically what we did. We put the camera on a soft pad on the

alley itself, then we just pushed it with a forty-foot pole.

By this point, you'd made four films with the Coens. Was there a point when it became understood that if you were around and they had a script, they wanted you to shoot it?

It was never formalized. For some time I definitely wasn't doing other films because I knew they had something coming up. So it was unspoken. I always thought I was going to be doing their best movie. But then things happen, and I went off to do *Skyfall* and they promised they wouldn't be shooting anything, and then they shot something.

That was when they ended up doing *Inside Llewyn Davis*.

Yeah, so we got out of sync, so maybe I'll work with them again. Maybe I won't. Who knows?

A film like *O Brother, Where Art Thou?*, from a cinematographer's point of view, is interesting to look back on.

Yeah. Nowadays nobody bats an eye when a whole film is digitized and manipulated [and] almost all made in the computer. But, I mean, with *O Brother* there were no digital effects in it.

Yes, we stretched the image, there's maybe one or two shots in there, but basically no digital effects.

How much does postproduction affect how you shoot?

A little bit. If we hadn't been doing that digitization I would have used a lot of filtration to try and shift the greens over. But knowing that was going to happen later, I didn't, and what we needed on the negative in order to facilitate that working in DI—the separation of the colors— we actually needed an image that had the most separation in the colors. So I didn't use filtration. and we would laugh when we were watching film dailies in a theater. We would sit there going, "Yeah, well, it ain't going to look like this, is it?" Because it was all green and lush and exactly not where we wanted to go.

As with *The Hudsucker Proxy*, you're getting right up to the edge of how stylized and how exaggerated you can make a film frame without it becoming a cartoon.

I think with *Hudsucker*, you could push it further because it was so much a fantasy. Reality is stretched. On *O Brother*, reality wasn't really stretched. It was funny, but it was a stylized version of the real world we were creating. I wouldn't say it was fantasy. What we were trying to do with the color was make it look like a picture book. Or a hand-tinted black-and-white film.

***The Man Who Wasn't There* seems like it must have just been so complex with light.**

Joel and Ethan rarely talk about the look of a scene in terms of the light. On *Hudsucker*, which was a very complicated production with big sets and backings and all those technical things, I remember in preproduction Ethan says, "Well, there's one thing we haven't talked about, and that's lighting." And I laughed. I said, "Yeah, well, we've been actually rigging for the last three weeks." So we talked about the lighting. On *The Man Who Wasn't There*, we did reference a few Hitchcock films like *Shadow of a Doubt*. They didn't so much talk about the

lighting, more the feel of the film. That one scene where Tony Shalhoub is in the jail cell and he's going on about Schrödinger's cat—I wanted this strange theatrical look. We talked about the idea of him being in a spotlight.

You achieve this incredible effect where the bars of the actual prison are being shadowed, and it's almost like he's stepping between them.

Again, we talk about the concept, and then you start playing with it. We had the set built and I was playing with the light through the window. I knew the bars were there, but where they were in relation to the lamp and which lamp we used all helped to get the look.

Films like *Intolerable Cruelty* and *The Ladykillers* are not usually discussed in terms of their visuals as much as the films on either side of them. Do you feel that there was something more mainstream or more commercial in how those films were shot?

I didn't think *Intolerable Cruelty* was more or less of a commercial movie than anything else. It was another of their projects and it was something different, and it demanded something a little more glossy. Just the subject—the feeling of Los Angeles. We wanted it to be more glossy so it is more glossy. And *The Ladykillers*, I don't know. *Ladykillers* was an odd one. I actually think it was a much better film than the reactions from the audience.

I do, too.

I thought Tom Hanks was great, and I thought Irma P. Hall was great. It was funny. I quite liked the look of it, too.

You think of the barge, and it starts to become more like a fable.

Well, that's it. Again, it was a bit of a picture-book thing really.

The repeated sequences of each of the bodies dropping off the bridge and the visual quoting of "The Raven" by Edgar Allan Poe. . . .

Sometimes Joel and Ethan want things to look like a picture book. It was very definite in this case. This film wasn't meant to look ultra-realistic—it was meant to be stylized. That idea of, "I'm telling you a story. . . ." Sometimes I feel that people don't quite get that or accept it. In think, in the last twenty years, films have been so naturalistic, and the general style of photography has become a little mundane.

Is this a by-product of the idea that there's more truth in digital?

I think because you pick up a camera and the idea of stylizing a shot is harder to do because it takes more preplanning. So that doesn't seem to be people's strength these days.

Do you think one of the reasons you've continued to work with the Coens is that they're never going to make something that has that pretense to naturalism?

I just think they're very imaginative. All that effort goes up on the screen. I just think they're great to work with because there's no messing around. They're serious filmmakers.

Light is important in *No Country for Old Men*. Lighting in that film, even when it's just the shift from night into early morning during the chase sequence, is incredibly evocative.

Very early on in preproduction, they talked about the fact that there would be no music, and it would all be these little sounds. It's very ambient.

How so?

Just the feel of where the wind's blowing. In lots of shots they'd always want a little wind machine so they just had some feeling of dust blowing through the foreground grass. It would just be moving a bit so they could justify having a little bit of sound. The noise of water is more important than it might be in other films, where people lather music all over it.

There is a long chase sequence that begins in trucks and then becomes a foot chase and then there's a dog, all while you've got the sky changing in the background. How much of that is treated after the fact to give that impression of natural light changing?

You can't really treat something to create that look. You've got to just shoot it. That was a really hard sequence. They spent a lot of time planning that. And that's why I love working with the guys—because they come up with this concept and they go, "We need this," and I go, "That's a really hard thing to do, to get these shots." For this we would storyboard the whole thing and I literally spent weeks going out and looking at the location at different times of the day to figure out exactly where the camera angles should be and when we should shoot each individual shot. Then I sat with the AV technician and we went through all the shots and the schedule and gave a twenty-minute window for each shot in the morning or afternoon. Then I figured in the schedule whether we would be on a night shoot and could shoot something in the morning, or whether we had a night shoot and could shoot in the evening. And after all that, it basically worked. As I say, you can't really re-create it. I mean, you can. You're shooting toward the dying light or the morning light and so you want a reflection on water and you want the landscape to be semi-silhouetted. . . . There's no way you can do that on a computer. Sure, if you spend a

lot of money you can do anything. But then you would really be making an animated movie to achieve that look.

No Country is a film–along with The Man Who Wasn't There–where you cannot find a critic who doesn't think that, visually, it is as well realized as it could possibly be.

I disagree with that one.

You have said in past interviews that you disagreed, and I'm curious to know why.

I don't watch things that don't matter much, but whenever I see *No Country*, I go, "Oh dear."

Why?

Well, you always compromise. You turn the camera on, it's a compromise. You can never get anything exactly as you want. It's just never going to happen, especially on a film like this, where you're running around locations and you're dependent on what the light's doing. In terms of what we were talking about—the scene with the dog and the river—the trouble is shooting in the morning light and the evening light, you're trying to match them together. But the problem is, in the evenings in New Mexico, there are usually more clouds than there are in the morning. There are no clouds. That's just how it is, so it doesn't match.

Are you privy to the editing process?

I barely see anything until it's basically finished. Years ago I would be in New York and I would go into the cutting room on a couple of things. But that was years ago, and certainly not lately. I do think some films get better with age. I think *The Man Who Wasn't There* is the closest for me to realizing what we'd all imagined going into it. I think that's the closest I've got with them of getting . . . something. I can watch that and not be too disturbed.

A lot of cinematographers talk about black and white as like the Platonic ideal of beauty in filmmaking.

I love black and white. I wish everything was black and white. I think the mood of that film, the performances, the cutting, the pacing, the music are near to something totally exceptional. The other thing I should say is that

they had an anniversary screening of *O Brother, Where Art Thou?* in New York a couple of years ago at Lincoln Center. So it's quite a big screen, and it looked great, actually. And I thought it was better than watching it originally. The audience reaction was fantastic. It went down so well. I was thinking that maybe it was ahead of its time. It was quite successful when it came out. It was better than I remembered it, frankly.

What look or feel were you aiming for in *A Serious Man*?

Reacting to the script and what the guys were saying about it and the fact that it was semi-autobiographical. . . . I don't know, you just react to things and that's where it goes. It feels like quite a realistic, less ostentatious film. I did feel that film was a little more personal to them, frankly. I mean, that's where they're from. I think it was a bit more of a personal commentary on their growing up. I'm not saying anything like that happened or it was anything to do with them, but I somehow feel it was more connected to them personally.

The extraordinary opening image of *True Grit* is a flickering light shining through a snowstorm. How did you achieve that?

That was very tricky. Jess Gonchor, the production designer, had basically built this town to make it look like our main location. The guys wanted this shot with the horse riding away and the body in the foreground, and we just couldn't make it work. I couldn't make the atmosphere work. And we were struggling, thinking, "Well, maybe we've got to do it in a couple of different shots." And we were restricted on this one porch for the width of the street I remember, and then I don't know how we got to this idea of just shooting this dead square shot that's the one in the film now and getting back as far as possible. It was like, the shot was ninety degrees to what we were trying to shoot and we did it this way—yeah, we were there just struggling to find, actually, something that actually worked, and we found this shot and they, yeah—they were really happy with it and obviously the track is extended, you know, digitally—the shot is extended so it starts as this out-of-focus start. We weren't physically that far away on the location, but yeah, that was one of the few times where they had this—that's right, there were five shots storyboarded for that little opening sequence and it ended up—we shot this one shot and they said, yeah, that's it, let's just use that shot.

In terms of the nighttime ride toward the end of the film, I wonder if you took a look at *Night of the Hunter*, the Charles Laughton film?

It's a film that's always in their heads, but no, we didn't look at it. I don't remember ever looking at a film with them. I don't even remember talking about that film, but I have that film in my head. There are a lot of films in my head. And they're always there as a reference even if you don't consciously draw them up. That whole sequence was storyboarded, and we just figured it out. We were looking at locations, figuring out how to make it work, and there was one time with the horse running full gallop at night. It was a little nightmarish to do. We were talking about whether we do that on a revolving platform so that we're stationary but the horse is galloping. Eventually I said I wanted to build a road in the forest. So we built a road. I got this little Polaris vehicle to be on the track with this horse, and I did some tests. I

figured out how we could shoot something that was similar to what they wanted. And then we shot the final scene, where the horse dies. We shot that twice. We shot it once against this wonderful mountain backdrop—it was really brilliant—the foreground was grass and there was this mountain behind it and the trees were silhouetted against it. We were watching dailies and they said, "It's too interesting, Roger." I remember Joel saying it. He said, "Yeah, great work but it's too interesting." So we reshot it. The grass field without the mountain in the background.

That's interesting that you have to interpret whether what you've done is too interesting.

I can completely understand it. I remember on *Fargo* when we were looking at locations with designer Rick Heinrichs and we would go into a motel lobby and Rick would say, "Well, how about this?" and they'd go, "Yeah, but it's too interesting." They know what they want and sometimes there's too much clutter in the frame. They're really good at that—getting rid of clutter. Getting rid of that stuff that's actually distracting from what they want the audience to see.

In *Hail, Caesar!* there is the submarine sequence, and when it arrives it feels like the movie has again fully given over to that picture-book quality.

The movie becomes a movie. I thought it was a difficult balance. We were very keen that the submarine looked real but wasn't real. I never got exactly what they wanted, and it's the same with the sequence when George is in the car on the highway at night and coming back from the Malibu house—they wanted it to look real but they also wanted it to look like a fifties movie.

In your experience, is it true that when it comes to a lot of those decisions, they're usually of the same mind?

There are very few disagreements. I mean, I don't know about anything other than just shooting on the set, what the shot is, or what lens we're on. In the past I've found that if we'd have a disagreement, then I'd say, I think we should be on this, with two opinions against one, so sometimes we'd do it two ways. But it's a very, very rare thing.

Tuileries & World Cinema

RELEASE DATE
Tuileries - October 2006
To Each His Own Cinema - October 31,2007

BUDGET
Tuileries - $13M

DISTRIBUTOR
Tuileries - First
Look International

CAST
Julie Bataille
Steve Buscemi
Axel Kiener
Gulliver Hecq
Frankie Pain
-
Josh Brolin
Grant Heslov
Brooke Smith

WARNING!
THIS FILM CONTAINS

French epithets	25%
Leonardo Da Vinci	21%
Ugly Americanism	17%
Slapstick violence	15%
Eye-line matches	12%
Venereal disease	10%
Steve Buscemi's dignity	0%

TUILERIES

Cinephilia	50%
Homosexual innuendo	25%
Llewelleyn Moss	
Cinematic Universe	15%
Nuri Bilge Ceylan Tribute	10%

WITH THE EXCEPTION of the prologue of *A Serious Man*, the six-minute short film *Tuileries*—commissioned for the 2006 omnibus feature *Paris, je t'aime* and named for the first-*arrondissement* metro station where it is set—is the only Coen brothers production that takes place outside the United States. And it takes this geographical dislocation as its subject: Over the course of its six minutes, a US tourist played—wordlessly—by Steve Buscemi is subjected to a series of verbal and physical attacks that complicate and obliterate his romantic preconceptions (and his guidebook's promises) that the City of Lights is a "city for lovers." Spying a local couple making out on the opposite platform, he indulges in a bit of benign voyeurism only to be found out and plunged into the middle of a lovers' quarrel slash psychodrama that gets him kissed (with tongue) and then left battered and bruised on the floor of the train station.

When *Paris, je t'aime* premiered at the Cannes Film Festival, *Tuileries* was shown without subtitles—a formal gag that played up the Buscemi character's confusion and linguistic disadvantage in his new surroundings. The contrast between the boldfaced English-language text in his guidebook, which keeps getting shown in close-up, and the unintelligible French

Qu'est ce que tu regardes, connard?

kehs say kuh too ree-gard, kawn-ard?

invective of the young man who eventually beats him to a pulp crystallizes a subtext of culture clash that, while mostly played for broad slapstick, has a self-reflexive dimension. As its title suggests, *Paris, je t'aime* was conceived as a series of "love letters" to its host city, and the Coens' decision to style their vignette as a nightmare version of transatlantic tourism—about an American in Paris who gets a bag of souvenirs dumped all over him—has a wickedly contrarian quality.

The final shot rests on a postcard depicting the Mona Lisa, whose famously enigmatic smile seems to mock Buscemi as he lies prone on the ground. Da Vinci's muse could be an avatar of sneering European contempt, or a spiritual sister to the girl on the postcard at the end of *Barton Fink*. There are other possible Coen in-jokes in the mix, as when the mother of a small child who keeps hawking spitballs at Buscemi via a homemade peashooter scolds him that it's "not nice to shoot people in the face"—a callback to the actor's fate in both *Miller's Crossing* and *Fargo*. Whatever the level of its sociological satire, *Tuileries* fits into a general pattern of the Coens subjecting Buscemi to undue abuse on-screen, turning his only true leading role in any of their films into a short, percussively edited orgy of humiliation.

One year later at Cannes, the Coens inverted the comic mechanism of *Tuileries* with *World Cinema*, a contribution to the festival's celebratory sixtieth anniversary anthology *To Each His Own Cinema*. It focuses on another American puzzling over a foreign artwork, except this time on his own turf; instead of literally stranding him in another country, it shows him practicing a more vicarious form of tourism. It begins with a sight gag: A cowboy-hatted man walks into the Aero Theatre in Santa Monica, California, looking completely out of place—an Old West dude at the arthouse. He then asks the man at the counter which of the two movies listed on the marquee—Jean Renoir's 1939

classic *La Règle du Jeu* and Nuri Bilge Ceylan's 2006 drama *Climates*—is better. "They're both excellent films" is the theater employee's reply, and his customer ultimately opts for *Climates* on the condition that its Turkic dialogue be subtitled. "You got the words up there to help me follow the story along?" he asks, before leveling an even more crucial follow-up question: "Is there nudity?"

That the world-cinema goer is played by Josh Brolin in character and costume as Llewelyn Moss is a half-sly, half-self-promotional joke: 2007 was the year that *No Country for Old Men* showed at Cannes, and perhaps the Coens couldn't resist a tie-in. The punch line of *World Cinema* is that its brusque, no-nonsense Texan protagonist finds himself moved by Ceylan's story of a decaying relationship—"Hell of a lot of truth in there," he says on his way out of the theater. On one level, the Coens are kidding cultural stereotypes by having Brolin connect unexpectedly with a Turkish art film; they're also evincing their own admiration for Ceylan's cinema, to the point that Brolin opts for it over Renoir's classic (which could be a bit of Yankee revenge on French culture after the pitched battle of *Tuileries*).

World Cinema also packs a significant amount of dramatic ambiguity into its three-minute running time; in a wonderfully acted throwaway moment, Brolin awkwardly tries to pick up the ticket-taker (played by screenwriter Grant Heslov). This strange (and strangely touching) bit of business pays off as he's leaving the cinema and is disappointed to see that a woman has replaced Heslov's cinephile, whom he feels he owes a sincere thank-you, if nothing more. "Just tell him the guy in the hat enjoyed the hell out of *Climates*," he tells her, at which point we might notice him repositioning his own Stetson, a callback to *Miller's Crossing* and its rigorous system of masculinity lost and reclaimed in accordance with the wearing of headgear.

Burn After Reading

RELEASE DATE
September 12, 2008
BUDGET
$37M
DISTRIBUTOR
Focus Features
CAST
George Clooney
Frances McDormand
Brad Pitt
John Malkovich
Tilda Swinton
Richard Jenkins
Elizabeth Marvel
David Rasche

WARNING!

THIS FILM CONTAINS

Morons	28%
Adultery	18%
Mistaken identities	13%
Cold War paranoia	10%
Divorce lawyers	8%
Creative dildo usage	8%
Bad dates	6%
Children's books	4%
Leg lifts	3%
Rotary phones	2%
What have we learned	0%

RELEASED IN SEPTEMBER 2008, *Burn After Reading* was the Coens' first totally original screenplay since *The Man Who Wasn't There* – not work for hire, a remake, or an adaptation. In the press notes, Ethan Coen referred to the script as the brothers' "version of a Tony Scott/Jason Bourne movie, without the explosions," while also citing Otto Preminger's 1962 political thriller *Advise and Consent* as an influence. The latter is a film that the Coens had actually already paid tribute to decades earlier: In *The Coen Brothers: The Story of Two American Filmmakers*, Josh Levine describes the teenaged Joel and Ethan remaking *Advise and Consent* as a Super 8 production with their friends.

Another first: *Burn After Reading* marked the first time since *Miller's Crossing* that the Coens worked with a cinematographer other than Roger Deakins. The pinch-hitter was the brilliant Mexican-born director of photography Emmanuel Lubezki, who had previously worked with directors Michael Mann, Tim Burton, and Terrence Malick, and who went on to win Oscars for his collaborations with Alfonso Cuaron on *Gravity* (2013) and Alejandro González Iñárritu for *Birdman* (2014).

Lubezki's visual signature is a roaming, agile Steadicam, and the opening shot of *Burn After Reading* gives the cinematographer plenty of room to maneuver. It's a bird's-eye view of CIA Headquarters in Langley, Virginia—

a top-down look at the epicenter of American military intelligence. *Village Voice* critic J. Hoberman, no fan of the Coens for what he has long perceived as their glibly skillful sensibility, wrote that this high-angle image hinted at the filmmakers' perennial "Coendescension" toward their characters. Whether or not this visual overture was composed with condescension in mind or Hoberman's own contempt for the directors got the better of him, it vividly and clearly establishes one of the major themes of the movie, which is "The Big Picture." Or, more specifically, it establishes the inability of the people on-screen to see The Big Picture taking shape around them.

There are two main sets of characters in *Burn After Reading*. The first are all either members or satellites of the government-intelligence community in Washington, DC. These are Osborne "Oz" Cox (John Malkovich), a longtime cog in the CIA machine who, as the film opens, is being fired from his post at the "Balkan desk," a designation indicating a certain distance from the action; Harry Pfarrer (George Clooney), an ex–Secret Serviceman now working as a private security consultant; and Katie Cox (Tilda Swinton), Osborn's apparently long-suffering wife, who is carrying on a clandestine affair with Harry. The second set of characters work at a (fictional) downtown Washington gym called Hardbodies: chipper personal trainer Chad Feldheimer (Brad Pitt); middle-aged administrator Linda Litzke (Frances McDormand); and kindly office manager Ted Treffon (Richard Jenkins), who not-so-secretly loves Linda and so tolerates her mediocre job performance.

The division between these groups has been conceived by the Coens as a Cartesian split between people who make their living with their brains, and people who are paid to maintain their bodies and those of their clientele. As *Burn After Reading* goes on, the they begin to mingle in ways that prove increasingly destructive. At the same time, the film slyly implies that the factions actually have a lot in common. Nowhere is this made clearer than in the characters of Oz and Linda, who never meet on-screen but still appear as distorted mirror images of each other.

Oz is a misanthrope with a severe drinking problem, which gets worse after his termination from the Agency. He plans to stick it to his former employers by writing a tell-all about his career—the ultimate violation for a man who has sworn to uphold his country's secrets. In his forced retirement he's a sad, emasculated figure, padding around in a bathrobe. The little bit we hear of Oz's "mémoire" (Malkovich's affected pronunciation of the word is a through-line in his performance) suggests a raging egomaniac bent on revenge rather than revelation, and, like Barton Fink, he suffers from writer's-blocked delusions of literary grandeur—to hear him tell it, he was an architect of twentieth-century American diplomacy.

More specifically, Oz calls himself one of "Kennan's boys," a reference the Coens drop with purpose and precision. A prime mover behind the Truman Doctrine and subsequent expansions of the so-called "containment" strategy in the United States' conflict with the Soviet Union, Kennan was a true paradigm figure. His idea of "strategically limiting" Russia provided the foundation for the Cold War and, trickling down into the 1960s, provided the basis for the country's "police action" in Vietnam.

Oz's identification with Kennan fits with his complaints that "things have changed" since the Cold War—that since the collapse of the Soviet Union, American intelligence seems more a matter of bureaucracy than of a clear-cut mission. (For this Cold Warrior, the United States has suddenly become no country for old men.) Far from simply using politics as window dressing for their comedy, the Coens are staking out a position here, using Oz as a mouthpiece for a commentary on the changing sociopolitical landscape while also suggesting that he's painfully out of touch. The paranoia he lived with— the tension of mutually assured destruction— has faded away.

Given the post–9/11 setting, it would potentially make sense for *Burn After Reading* to stake out a different dialectic, contrasting the now-thawed Cold War with The War on Terror. The Coens are looking in another direction entirely. They're not genuinely concerned with twenty-first-century geopolitics, but instead with the conflation of political and personal paranoia, which becomes the film's true subject, as well as unlocking its hybrid methodology: a romantic comedy combined with a political thriller. Surveillance-style shots of Oz walking around

THE BIG PICTURE
—
The comically exaggerated surveillance-style framing of *Burn After Reading*'s opening shot satirizes twenty-first-century spy movie tropes while preemptively mocking the petty, blinkered perspectives of its characters.

MEMOIR
—
Osborne Cox's proposed memoir represents a betrayal of his principles as a CIA analyst; his bitterness at being demoted prompts him to spill the secrets he spent a lifetime keeping.

Emmanuel Lubezki's camera style is characteristically more ornate and intricate than Roger Deakins's; here the clever use of reflections makes it seem like Katie is single-handedly ganging up on her husband during an argument.

with his wheelchair-bound father, as Carter Burwell's score percussively pastiches the driving momentum of a seventies-style thriller (for instance, Alan J. Pakula's *All the President's Men* [1976]), are justified, but not in the way Oz might think. He fears he's going to ruffle feathers with his memoir, but the person after him is actually just his wife, who is trying to initiate divorce proceedings.

This twist places the film back in the realm of *Intolerable Cruelty*—a comedy of excessive litigiousness. That film applied the classic screwball formula of the remarriage comedy to a plot about serial marriages; its cynical ending examined whether the men and women who serially marry are motivated by true romance, or by the importance of covering one's ass(ets). With only one (tragic) exception, there is no true romance in *Burn After Reading*, only a sick

parody: a movie-within-the-movie titled *Coming Up Daisy*, which appears to be a stilted, insipid romantic comedy. Instead, the characters in *Burn After Reading* hop in and out of bed with one other with the calculated cutthroat velocity we usually associate with spies and double agents.

Katie's hatred for her husband clearly predates his unemployment; Oz resents Katie for resenting him, but what he really comes to realize during his forced retirement is just how much he hates ordinary Americans, so much so that he'd kill one if he ever got the chance. In the case of his temperamental doppelganger, Linda Litzkie, it would seem that his contempt is justified. Vain, brittle, and wildly stupid, she's the nightmare inverse of McDormand's role in *Fargo*. Marge Gunderson's homely grace stands in sharp contrast to Linda's anxious, insatiable narcissism.

Burn After Reading is set in the "intelligence community" of Washington DC; the name of the (fictional) exercise center "Hardbodies" refers to characters who live more through their bodies than their minds. Clad in identical uniforms, the gym's employees could be big-box-retail wage slaves; the cold, sterile environment points to the corporatization of physical fitness, with Brad Pitt's dim-witted trainer Chad at the center of this satirical tableaux.

Like Oz, Linda's worried about becoming a relic, not in terms of her ideology but in terms of her physical appearance: She's desperate for some extra cash to pay for a set of expensive, nonessential cosmetic surgeries. And she finds herself similarly stymied by bureaucracy because Hardbodies' health plan won't pay for elective procedures.

The plot of *Burn After Reading* is kick-started when Linda and Chad find a copy of Cox's "mémoire" on a computer disc that Katie accidentally left behind at the gym. (The blank, unmarked CD appears as a typically circular Coen totem.) After reading over its contents, Chad decides that it is "intelligence shit" and suggests that its owner might pay handsomely for its return, a belief rooted as much in naïveté as greed. As beautifully played by Pitt—who returns to the stoner-beach-bum cadences of his early roles as a serial killer in *Kalifornia* and a couch-surfing stoner in *True Romance* (both 1993)—Chad is an innocent, and thus doomed.

When the pair finally reaches out to Oz, the Coens indulge in a parody of spy movie tropes: a phone call in the middle of the night, with the caller holding the receiver close to his mouth and affecting a low, mysterious, deep-throated voice. After realizing that he's being blackmailed, Oz is doubly furious not only at the theft of his intellectual property, but also at the palpable stupidity of the people on the other end of the phone line. There's a third level to his anger as well: The old spook can't keep a handle on his documents. He's spent most of his life holding things over other people, and now he's at the mercy of nighttime phone callers. Reduced to a civilian, he's battling with other civilians, and he becomes agitated, humiliated, and dangerous. Over and over, he berates Chad and Linda for being "morons," as if more offended by their low IQs than by the fate of his "intelligence shit"; they, in turn, take his tantrum as a sign that they're on to something big and decide to sell the disc to the highest bidder.

Here, the Coens double down on the link between Oz and Linda: His frustration at being out-of-date now that America has moved on from its stalemate with the Soviet Union creates an inverse rhyme with her decision to go to the Russians with what she believes is valuable information. But as a Russian government attaché confides to Linda—in a scene shot against a massive, circular window that riffs on eastern European Brutalist architecture while also alluding visually to the disc's shape—the document is "drivel."

The point of this sequence is that Linda and Chad are not principled dissidents. They just want the money, and if America is harmed in the process, so be it. It won't be, because Cox's supposedly incendiary "mémoire" is ultimately worthless—less "intelligence shit" than "shit intelligence." Its lack of value parallels the fate of other supposedly valuable MacGuffins in the Coens' filmography: the illusory treasure of *O Brother, Where Art Thou?* and the vanished ransoms of *Blood Simple*, *Fargo*, and *The Ladykillers*.

It does end up getting two people killed, however. The first victim is Chad, who, at his friend's urging, breaks into Oz's home to find some other, more valuable "intelligence shit." Harry is already there, waiting for a rendezvous with Katie, and his earlier comment that he's never had to discharge his service revolver pays off here in a brutal sight gag as bloody as anything in *No Country for Old Men*: Hiding in the closet in the manner of a character in a bedroom farce, he blows Chad's head clean off. The Hardbodies contingent suffers another loss at the end of the movie, when Ted makes his own trip to the Cox residence and is cornered by the man of the house, who is armed and extremely intoxicated. "I know you," whispers Oz upon discovering the intruder. "You're the guy from the gym." When Ted tells him that he's "not here representing Hardbodies"—a line that gains resonance in light of Jenkins's slender, frail physique, Oz retorts: "I know very well what you represent. . . . You represent the idiocy of today."

Harry's homemade dildo chair becomes *Burn After Reading*'s emblem of furtive, unchecked sexual desire (and a target for his guilt and frustration when he destroys it with a sledgehammer).

All the former intelligence agent's frustrations—his rage at his employers, his government, his wife, and her lover (and also at himself for having degenerated into such a miserable sad sack)—are channeled in the direction of this hapless, helpless gym manager. "No, I don't represent that, either," stammers Ted, terrified yet somehow firm and forthright in his denial. Like *No Country for Old Men*'s secret heroine, Carla Jean Moss, he's a decent person facing down a monster, and his difference of opinion proves fatal. Oz shoots him in the chest and then finishes him off with an axe on the street outside his house in broad daylight, a horrific act shot identically to Gaear's bludgeoning of Carl in *Fargo*, with the killer creeping up in the background of the frame.

He may not represent idiocy as such, but Ted isn't being very smart by breaking into a stranger's house. It could be argued that both he and Chad get what they deserve, but the Coens draw a subtle distinction between their fates. Chad is a gentle soul, but calling a ransom a "Good Samaritan tax" only rounds off the edges of avarice. When the Russian diplomat theorizes that Linda and Chad are "not ideological," he's not really seeing the big picture. By trying to sell out their own country to the highest bidder, they confirm themselves as good-old-fashioned American capitalists.

Ted, though, has no interest in money. Instead, he's a fool for love. If this deceptively minor character represents anything, it is the futility of pure intentions in a city where the duplicity of the briefing office has migrated into the bedroom. One of the running gags in *Burn After Reading* is that the various romantic couplings are as cloak-and-dagger as the CIA material. "You, too, can be a spy," says Katie's divorce lawyer as she schemes to empty Osborne's bank account from behind his back.

As in *Intolerable Cruelty*, adultery is presented as a contact sport. A serial womanizer who begins a fling with Linda at the same time he's carrying on with Katie (the movie they go see is *Coming Up Daisy*), Clooney's Harry Pfarrer has spent his life evaluating potential threats to his clients, a skill set that makes him an excellent philanderer. At the same time, the accumulated paranoia also has him looking the wrong way when it counts. Terrified of being arrested for Chad's murder, he's caught off guard when the person who's been tailing him turns out to be a divorce lawyer. (Later, he'll also mistake Linda for an operative, never learning that she also sees herself as a character in a real-life spy movie, with regard to Oz's stolen "mémoire.") Harry's response to the humiliation of being served, and of realizing that he's also being cheated on, is to destroy the homemade marital aid he constructed in the basement as a "present" for his wife: a reclining

Top: Chad is one of *Burn After Reading*'s two genuinely innocent characters, and his reward is being killed by a member of the "intelligence community"—the same fate that will later befall Ted.

Bottom: Harry's panicked reaction to finding Chad in the closet shows he's got an unsteady trigger finger; in a film filled with sexual innuendo and subtext, the Coens stage the murder as a lethal kind of premature ejaculation.

DON'T WAIT UP

—

The lime peels provide evidence of Osborne's alcoholism combined with his Ivy League pedigree—hints to the nature of his toxic, volatile personality.

COMING UP DAISY

—

Linda's series of movie dates to see *Coming Up Daisy* lets the Coens place an ordinary, hackneyed Hollywood love story in the middle of their spy-movie-rom-com hybrid.

WINDOW DRESSING

—

The black-and-white surveillance footage and Brutalist architecture of the Russian consulate evoke 1950s Cold War imagery, while the circular window provides a double for the stolen computer disc.

chair jerry-rigged with a mechanical dildo. The sight of Clooney tearfully smashing this monstrosity with a sledgehammer is a direct visual metaphor for a guilty philanderer trying to cut his own balls off. (His orgy of destruction recalls John Goodman as Walter Sobchak, smashing up a Corvette while shouting about it being retribution for what happens when you "fuck a stranger in the ass!")

The only unmarried characters in *Burn After Reading* are Ted and Linda, and in a romantic comedy à la *Coming Up Daisy*, they'd be pushed into each other's arms. But Linda refuses to see her boss as a viable suitor because she doesn't want to admit that he's an age-appropriate partner. Casting around on internet dating sites, she's blind to the nice guy in the next office. Ted's foray into Oz's basement is really an attempt to help Linda out. His reward for this romantic gesture is getting hacked to death in cold blood. (Instead of *Coming Up Daisies*, he's pushing them up.)

The icy veins run all the way to the top. In the film's coda, two CIA overseers (J.K. Simmons and David Rasche) inventory the carnage and conclude that the deaths of two civilians at the hands of their personnel are no big deal, in the grand scheme of things. They're mostly just relieved that a "clusterfuck" whose configuration they'd long since lost track of has tied itself up neatly. Osborne Cox has been rendered brain dead by a sniper's bullet a few moments after killing Ted (the ultimate indignity for a man who got off on being more intelligent than the people around him); Harry has fled to the non-extraditable climes of Venezuela. Chad's body will be burned, and Linda's silence will be bought for the low cost of a few surgical procedures. "Just pay it," bristles Simmons's unnamed commander, relieved that the cost of avoiding an embarrassing public scandal is a paltry (at least to the CIA) $40,000.

More than one critic suggested that this wisecracking pair, who exist at a remove from the action in *Burn After Reading*, are stand-ins for the Coens themselves: bored overlords giggling at the follies of bloodthirsty mortals. This reading would fit but for the fact that these characters are also oblivious to The Bigger Picture. Despite their access to a massive computerized information-gathering apparatus, they're no more clued in to what's going on than anybody else in the movie. They are authority figures without any moral authority, and when they act, it is only out of expediency and self-preservation.

What makes *Burn After Reading* such a bracing movie is not its slapstick nastiness, but the fact that its creators take this contradiction between high-ranking status and bottom-line mentality seriously; like Stanley Kubrick with *Dr. Strangelove* (1964), they have crafted a political satire where the laughs stick in the throat. "What have we learned, Palmer?" queries Simmons's unnamed CIA superior, before answering his own question: "We've learned not to do it again."

He doesn't sound convinced of his own moral. The camera's ascent back into the sky in the final moments suggests that the circle of machinations will remain unbroken. Its vantage reinscribes the puniness of this particular story on a global scale while also suggesting that such pettiness also represents The Bigger Picture. Which leads to the question of whose point of view the first and last shots really represent. Is it the view of a CIA satellite? Or are we seeing through the eyes of an even higher power? It's the same celestial question mark that will hover over *A Serious Man* and *Hail, Caesar!*

COMMUNITY CENTER

THE LEAGUE OF MORONS

FRIENDS OF THE COENS

"Joel and Ethan are pretty transparent about the fact that they
have only ever—in making their phenomenal and phenomenally
sophisticated films over the past thirty years—done what they
first started doing together as children.

Much peaceable playtime, a group of old and newer friends,
a collective hum of amusement and industry: fellowship and fun.
The best of the best technicians with the mellowest of all vibes
working with the most consummate skill.

The script—the pot on the stove—arrives as an already pulsating organ:
no syllable or point of punctuation improvable.
Something you hook your nose onto like a willing fish.

Ethan strumming his guitar behind the camera between setups.
Joel guffawing audibly during takes, maybe in the knowledge that the
audience will drown him out with their own.

This is the atmosphere around them for all of us privileged
enough to have been invited to their particular party.
These are a few of my favorite things."

A Serious Man

RELEASE DATE

October 2, 2009

BUDGET

$7M

DISTRIBUTOR

Focus Features

CAST

Michael Stuhlbarg

Richard Kind

Fred Melamed

Sari Lennick

Aaron Wolff

Jessica McManus

Peter Breitmayer

Brent Braunschweig

WARNING!

THIS FILM CONTAINS

Anxiety	100%
God's wrath	50%
Cold, random indifference	50%
Certainty	0%
Dybbuk	?

I T WAS NOT common practice for American movies to feature end credit reels until the 1970s, yet there is a long history of filmmakers making playful use of that extra screen time. At the end of *Citizen Kane* (1941), Orson Welles placed his own acting credit in small type at the very end of the credit crawl, a hilarious gesture of ersatz self-effacement.

Joel and Ethan Coen have played some similar tricks with their films' credits: Their longtime film editor, "Roderick Jaynes," is an assumed identity, an alias for their own combined efforts in the editing suite. In *A Serious Man*, however, they take this gamesmanship to another level. The film's closing credits contain a joke so subtle that most members of the audience probably missed it, and yet which is also crucial to the overall conception of the work.

In contrast to *Burn After Reading*, which had the starriest cast of any Coen brothers movie to date, *A Serious Man* is populated mostly by relative unknowns plucked from the New York and Los Angeles theater communities. At the time of the film's release in 2009, the biggest name in the cast was probably Fyvush Finkel, an octogenarian stalwart of Manhattan's Yiddish theater scene. Finkel makes a memorable entrance

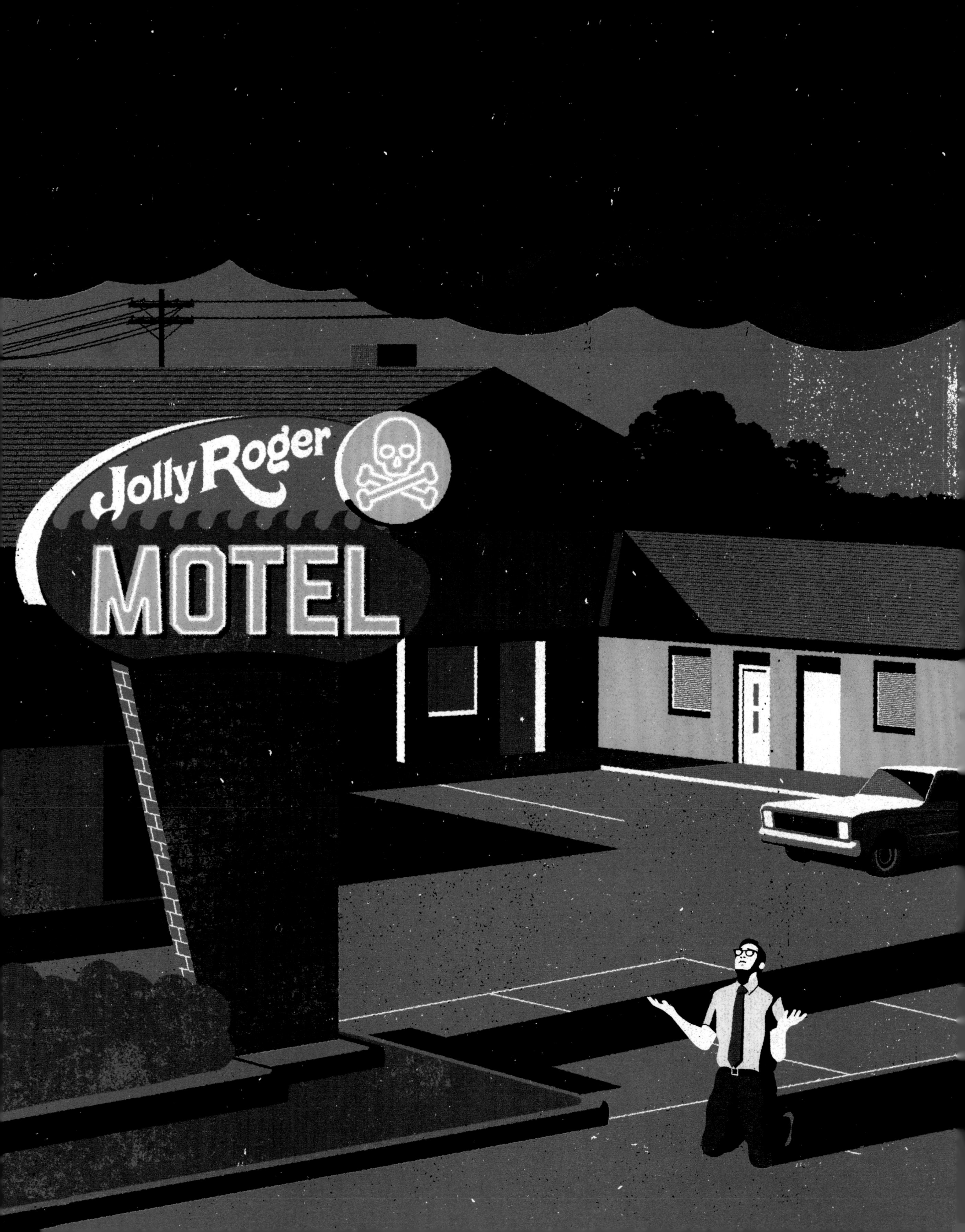
Jolly Roger
MOTEL

about five minutes into the film's prologue, playing a character called Traitle Groshkover, a respected elder in a Polish shtetl circa 1909. Invited in out of the snow one starless night by good-natured Velvel (Allen Lewis Rickman), he's a very gracious houseguest, but Velvel's wife, Dora (Yelena Shmulenson), is horrified by his presence. She believes that Groshkover has been dead for years and that the stooped figure in her kitchen is a "dybbuk"—a malicious possessing spirit of Jewish mythology.

Groshkover laughs off the accusation, but Dora is convinced of his monstrousness and stabs him in the chest with a kitchen knife. At first, Groshkover seems unharmed, but then a spot of blood appears on his shirt and begins to spread. "I know when I'm not wanted," he moans before asking Velvel, "as a rational man," whom he believes is truly possessed in this situation: the angry woman wielding the knife, or the old man at the wrong end of the blade. Groshkover exits into the night, leaving Velvel unsettled

and Dora strangely satisfied. A true believer, she believes that she has acted bravely in expelling an evil force from her home. But Velvel—the "rational man"—is in the throes of an agonizing conundrum. Either his wife has fatally wounded an innocent old man, or else she's invited a terrible curse by incurring the wrath of a demon. *A Serious Man* immediately flashes forward to its main story, which is set in Minnesota in the 1960s, so Velvel never gets an answer. And, as it turns out, neither do we. In the end credits, Finkel is billed as "Dybbuk?" a blink-or-miss-it gag that recalls Welles's citation at the end of *Citizen Kane*. By feigning confusion about their character's true identity, the Coens are actually reaffirming their control over their material. To officially refer to Traitle Groshkover as "Dybbuk?" even after the final cut to black is to insist that *A Serious Man* is a work defined by its ambiguity.

The Coens are not subtle on this point. Proceeding from this distinctly fable-like

The question of whether
Reb Groshkover is or is
not a dybbuk hangs over *A
Serious Man,* beginning with
the unusual staging of his
stabbing: A weirdly bloodless
entry wound gives way to a
spreading crimson stain.

introduction, *A Serious Man* offers itself up as a parable that practically begs for interpretation. And yet the film's epigraph, derived from the teachings of the tenth-century Rabbi Rashi, cautions all of us in the audience against looking too deeply into the matter. It reads, "Receive with simplicity everything that happens to you." Or, as the accidental Korean-American sage Mr. Park (Steve Park) puts it in the film's signature line of dialogue: "Accept the mystery."

Contrary to its own advice, *A Serious Man* is a dauntingly sophisticated movie, starting with its brilliant, precise use of location and period detail. Many journalists suggested that it was the Coens' "most personal" work to date due to it being set in their home state of Minnesota in the same era when they grew up, but the tone is not straightforwardly fond nor nostalgic—less a roman à clef than an act of knowing, detached anthropology. Where *The Big Lebowski* and *The Ladykillers* feature characters who are still suffering from the hangover of the 1960s (The Dude, Walter Sobchak, and Garth Pancake), *A Serious Man* takes place on the eve of the big blowout bacchanal. The dateline is 1967 during the Summer of Love, but university physics professor Larry Gopnik (Michael Stuhlbarg) and his buttoned-down brood feel about as far removed from sunny, sexy San Francisco as Dora and Velvel.

One of the underlying jokes in *A Serious Man* is that the superstition of the shtetl has since crossed an ocean and settled in the suburbs (our knowledge of the grim historical reality of twentieth-century Jewry shrouds this ellipsis, as well as Dora's belief that she's protected her household from harm). There is continuity here, and community, but the times, they are a-changin'. Like so many films about the 1960s, *A Serious Man* is set along the fault line of a generational divide. Larry, a university physics professor trying to secure tenure, rejects the encroaching counterculture, while his son, Danny (Aaron Wolff), is an eager convert to the church of drugs and rock 'n' roll (sex still being a foreign concept to a twelve-year-old boy). At home, Larry plays old forty-five rpm records of Jewish folk songs, while Danny smokes up and rocks out to his transistor radio, which seems perpetually tuned to the spacey sounds of Jefferson Airplane, including at school, where he listens to "Somebody to Love" in lieu of his droning instructors.

The confiscation of Danny's radio by his Hebrew school principal is the first instance of cultural clash in *A Serious Man*, which draws much of its comic tension from the collision of old-world and new-world mentalities. When Larry's wife, Judith (Sari Lennick), shrilly declares that she wants a divorce, it means that Larry needs to procure a "gett," a specialized religious document that will allow her to marry another man within the Jewish faith and without any charge of adulterous behavior; every time he mentions it to another Jew in his orbit, they react with confusion at such an archaic term. Danny spends the film preparing for his bar mitzvah even though he'd rather be watching *F Troop*—another example of his immersion in pop culture. And despite being a man of science who lectures undergrads about physics and mathematics, Larry frantically visits a series of rabbis for spiritual guidance.

Larry's work is itself slightly rabbinical: As a physics professor, he's charged with explaining huge, complicated concepts, and uses narratives to bring the ideas to life in a way that makes them more dramatic and comprehensible. "The stories I give you in class are just illustrative—they're like fables, say, to help give you a picture," he tells Clive Park (David Kang), a student who's come to his office in some distress over a failed midterm. "I mean—even I don't understand the dead cat. The math is how it really works."

The cat in Larry's example is Schrödinger's cat, the subject of a famous thought experiment by the Austrian physicist Erwin Schrödinger in which the animal, a flask of poison, and a radioactive source are placed together in a sealed box. If an internal monitor detects radioactivity—i.e., a single atom decaying—the flask is shattered, releasing the poison that kills the cat. Schrödinger's experiment implies that after a while, the cat is, simultaneously, alive and dead. Yet, when one looks in the box, one sees the cat either alive or dead, not both alive and dead. The idea is that in the outside universe, the cat is alive and dead at the same time—which is impossible, but also a paradox. You can't know until you look inside.

"I understand the physics," replies Clive, whose cryptic diffidence instantly undermines Larry's authority. "I understand the dead cat." The irony of a student who fails a test yet claims perfect understanding is paralleled with how the Coens

THE LORD TAKETH AWAY
—
The confiscation of Danny's radio is the first instance of culture clash in *A Serious Man*; he's being punished for using it to listen to rock music instead of taking in his Hebrew lesson.

LESSONS LEARNED
—
Danny's disinterest in his school's curriculum is a sign of adolescent distraction, but also of a younger generation rejecting the traditions that their parents cling to for solace.

"In this office, actions have consequences!" Larry's cluttered office space suggests his frantic state of mind when he suspects a student is trying to bribe him for a better grad; he's buried under a tangle of pressures and obligations. Later, he ends up taking the money and changing his student's failing grade—an action shown to have possibly apocalyptic consequences in the film's final shot.

integrate Schrödinger's riddle into the film's plot. The reason Clive is in Larry's office is because the professor has found an envelope containing $3,000, placed there by parties unknown. He assumes that it is a bribe from Clive—who won't confirm or deny his suspicion—but he doesn't know for sure: Their debate over the envelope is itself an "illustration" of an uncertainty principle. Larry doesn't accept the money, but, crucially, he doesn't return it, because he can't prove that Clive is the rightful owner. And as long as the money is in his possession, as "evidence," bad things happen to Larry: His wife begins an affair; his job status is threatened; he begins an affair of his own with a neighbor.

The last of these developments is Larry's own choice, his version of enjoying the "new freedoms," as his new sexual partner, Mrs. Samsky (Amy Landecker), puts it during their pot-stoked first encounter. (High on marijuana, Larry regresses to adolescence—and becomes a mirror for his son.) Still, he has a hardwired inclination to look past his own behavior and blame his problems on external culprits, like Clive and his father, or else his friend turned romantic rival Sy Ableman (Fred Melamed), Judith's new lover.

Sy is a more plausible antagonist: He's hideously manipulative, but perceived within the community as "a serious man" of the sort Larry so desperately

wishes to be. ("Let's have a good talk," Sy tells Larry, leading the latter to begin a conversation with one of his students in the same way; as in *The Big Lebowski*, words and phrases migrate from character to character.)

Because Larry lacks Sy's self-assurance, he seeks advice from a series of rabbis—religious figureheads whom he hopes can satisfactorily "illustrate" the reasons he's suffering while giving him a solution to the "math"—a way to fix it. The junior rabbi (Simon Helberg) is a wet-eared go-getter who tries to convince Larry he's having a crisis of perception. He advises him to try to look at his situation with fresh eyes, using the synagogue's layout as a metaphor for how Hashem is present in all things: "God is in the parking lot," he says with a practiced, smiling smugness. A few links up the scholarly food chain sits Rabbi Nachtner (George Wyner), who bamboozles Larry with a shaggy-dog story about a dentist who discovers a Hebraic message carved into a client's molars—and whose all-consuming curiosity about the meaning of this find nearly destroys his life.

"The story of the goy's teeth" is the comic high point of *A Serious Man*, a percussively edited, stylistically bravura short film with the same self-contained quality as the shtetl-set prologue. The similarity is intentional: Both vignettes serve as "illustrations"

Larry's neighbor regards him as an outsider in a suburban community that hasn't fully integrated its Jewish residents—another variation on what Mr. Park calls "culture clash."

The junior rabbi's contention that God can be seen in the parking lot is an unconvincing "illustration" that is nevertheless given a kind of sinister credence at the end of the film.

of the film's larger ideas, with the latter constructed as a parody of Larry's own quest. The Coens use Jefferson Airplane's psychedelic track "Bear Melt" as a soundtrack here, another link between Larry and Danny, whose love for the band has been made plain from the first scene; the song's grinding rhythm propels the story of Dr. Lee Sussman (Michael Tezla), as he obsesses over whether or not the inexplicable appearance of the phrase "save me" in one of his patients' mouths is a message from God. Nachtner's story is really about Larry, not Sussman: He's trying to tell the professor that any attempt to interpret God's plan is beside the point. "These questions that are bothering you—maybe they're like a toothache. We feel them for a while, and then they go away."

For Larry, whose marital problems are amplified by intersecting crises at work, these platitudes ring hollow. The screenplay for *A Serious Man* is a veritable inventory of quotidian torments: Not only can Larry not prove that Clive and his father have tried to bribe him, but his tenure is being threatened by a series of anonymous letters criticizing his credentials (the sender is eventually revealed to be Sy Ableman, a soft-spoken villain whose punishment is to die in an automobile accident). Larry's marital problems have forced him to move into a cheap motel called the Jolly Roger with his mewling, unemployed brother, Arthur (Richard Kind), a sad sack afflicted by an enormous sebaceous cyst on his neck that requires constant mechanical draining.

A Serious Man is a cold, gleaming narrative contraption, and yet it locates pathos in family dynamics: not only Larry and Danny's carefully developed bond but also the relationship between Arthur and Larry. In keeping with the film's biblical subtext, which positions Larry as a Job figure—a hapless innocent tested by God—he is also, from his brother's point of view, reminiscent of Abel: a successful, envied sibling. Like Larry, Arthur is a "bighead," crafting an obsessively detailed, book-length diagram he calls "the Mentaculus—a probability map" that is his own attempt to illustrate the workings of the universe (the Mentaculus is visually doubled by Larry's final, outsize classroom chalkboard scribble, which hovers over him like an ominous galaxy).

Instead of the respectability of academia, Arthur applies his genius to gambling, which, combined with his barely closeted homosexuality, marks him as an outsider and a screwup—the black sheep of the Gopnik clan. He doesn't act out murderously like Cain—he complains. "Look at everything Hashem has given you," he rages at Larry. "You've got a family. You've got a job. Hashem hasn't given me bupkes." "It's not fair to blame Hashem," Larry responds. "Sometimes you have to help yourself." This well-meaning, condescending brotherly advice is the height of hypocrisy, because Larry is himself obsessed with the idea that God should be answerable to him. Not heeding Nachtner's advice to relent in his quest (nor Mr. Park's koan-like advice to "accept the mystery," referring to the bribe), he angles for a meeting with his synagogue's senior rabbi, the legendary thinker Marshak (Alan Mandell). In order to build himself up, Larry tells Marshak's secretary that he is "a serious man"—that his problems are important enough to warrant the great man's consideration.

Marshak's door gets closed in Larry's face (echoing Dora closing the door on the dybbuk in the prologue), but the old man does avail himself to bar-mitzvah-boy Danny in a scene that wrings an intriguing variation on a Coens staple: the hero's confrontation with a wizened avatar of power. Unlike Sidney Mussburger in *The Hudsucker Proxy* or Herb Myerson in *Intolerable Cruelty* (or the Big Lebowski himself), Rabbi Marshak is not a nasty grotesque. Rather, he treats Danny very sweetly, returning his radio and dispensing some Top 40–style wisdom: "When the truth is found to be lies . . . and all the joy within you dies . . . then what?" It doesn't occur to Danny to ask what Marshak means, or to question whether the rabbi's quotation of Grace Slick points to the profundity of pop music or the great sage's senility. Instead, he accepts Marshak's benediction with simplicity (it helps, maybe, that he's stoned out of his mind at the time) and smiles obediently when the old man tells him plainly to "be a good boy."

This moment of communion between an ancient and an adolescent pointedly excludes middle-aged Larry, whose own personalized, Jefferson Airplane–scored parable flew over his head. Always wry musicologists, the Coens also include a scene where Larry takes a call from the Columbia Record Club demanding payment for a copy of Santana's album *Abraxas*. "I didn't ask for Santana *Abraxas*! I didn't listen to Santana *Abraxas*!" he rages impotently, cluing in to the fact that it was Danny who ordered the record but not to the significance of its title; "Abraxas" is a word rooted in Gnostic philosophy (derived from the Torah and Jewish mythology) that has been used in different periods to denote the presence of God or a Supreme Being. So when Larry rails against *Abraxas*, it's also a rejection of the divinity he seeks in a more literal-minded way—an indication that, like Lee Sussman, he's focused on the wrong messages and symbols.

Nachtner's metaphor of the toothache that gradually goes away proves apt: Larry's apparent delivery from his misery emanates not from receiving answers from God but the simple passage of time, which ends up healing some of his wounds. He receives tenure and ends up back on good terms with Judith, which means that he's no longer hemorrhaging money on lawyers and motel rooms. (As in *Intolerable Cruelty* and *Burn After Reading*, divorce is an expensive proposition.) He doesn't return the $3,000 sitting in the envelope on his desk, however; he's incurred just enough debt during his run of bad luck that the extra money will come in very handy. And since he's keeping the money, he needs to comply with the unspoken implication that it's been offered in exchange for a passing grade.

By changing the grade, Larry is not only threatening his oft-stated credentials as a

Left: "Do you take advantage of the new freedoms?" Mrs. Samsky appears to Larry as a color-coded temptress—a chance to take revenge on his own cheating wife in the midst of their separation.

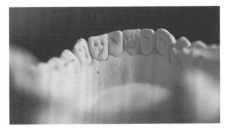

THE GOY'S TEETH

Rabbi Nachtner's strange, metaphorical parable is directed specifically at Larry, who misses the cue to reflect on his own quest for meaning and instead asks impatiently what the message in the teeth meant.

COMING OF AGE

Danny's disinterest in Judaism is counterbalanced by his choice to get high before his bar mitzvah, which gives the ritual the very air of mysticism and wonder it's meant to contain as a rite of passage.

serious man, but he's also not being a good boy. He erases the F on Clive's transcript and replaces it with a C, contemptuously adding a minus sign, as if to minimize the scope of his transgression (he's like Jerry Lundegaard in *Fargo* fudging the serial numbers on the stolen cars). In the same moment, his telephone rings. It's his doctor, asking if he can come in to discuss some disturbing test results. Across town, Danny's class is being evacuated from their Hebrew school because of an approaching tornado. The Coens cut from Larry's stunned, mortified expression to Danny trying to pay his own debt of twenty dollars to a pot-dealing classmate. "Fagle, I've got your—" he begins before swallowing the final two words—"your money"—upon sighting the massive twister in the distance.

Recall that in the book of Job, God appears in the form of a tornado as proof of his absolute power. That the storm poses a threat to Danny and his classmates as they wait in the school parking lot for the teacher to unlock the door to the basement is clear. The question is: What is the tornado doing there in the first place?

In effect, the Coens are taking us back here to the beginning of the film—to Velvel and Dora trying to make sense of the sinister mystery on their doorstep. This great whirling vortex could just as easily be a by-product of typical Midwestern weather patterns as a manifestation of divine wrath against Larry and his family, just as the seemingly terminal diagnosis Larry receives over the telephone could just be bad biology rather than a heavenly corrective of his avarice. Like Finkel's dybbuk, the tornado comes wrapped in enigma—it's its own swirling, corkscrewing meteorological question mark.

"That fucking flag is going to rip right off the flagpole!" shouts one of Danny's classmates, an aside that opens up the possibility of a national-allegorical dimension. If the tornado isn't the end of the world, it's at least a vision of a terrifyingly uncertain future: The 1960s as exemplified by Jefferson Airplane are over. Now the wind howls over Grace Slick's vocals, drowning them out.

The Coens pin this complex, polyvalent parting shot to Danny's point of view, gazing over his shoulder. The image of a young man staring down a gathering storm is no less striking in a secular context than in a religious one; it could even be a rewrite of Sheriff Bell's dream at the end of *No Country for Old Men*, with the son suddenly forced onto life's front lines in the place of his father. But scan the precise composition of the frame, with cars and pavement in the foreground, and the ending is also a pretty good joke. The junior rabbi was right all along: God is in the parking lot.

FILMOGRAPHY

```
Hail, Caesar! (2016)
Inside Llewyn Davis (2013)
True Grit (2010)
A Serious Man (2009)
Burn After Reading (2008)
No Country for Old Men (2007)
Paris, je t'aime (2006)
The Ladykillers (2004)
Intolerable Cruelty (2003)
The Man Who Wasn't There (2001)
O Brother, Where Art Thou? (2000)
The Big Lebowski (1998)
Fargo (1996)
The Hudsucker Proxy (1994)
Barton Fink (1991)
Miller's Crossing (1990)
Raising Arizona (1987)
```

J. Todd Anderson
STORYBOARD ARTIST

J. Todd Anderson has been drawing the Coens' storyboards for thirty years, helping them to pre-visualize their characters and camera movements and providing a reference point for every other stage of production.

You're the first guy who sees the Coens' work after they've completed their scripts, correct?

I can tell you this: I'm the first guy who sees the movie. If I do what they ask me to do, and I get it right, that follows suit from there on, in that it's pretty much locked in place. The way these guys do things—and I've been around the block a few times myself, as far as working with other directors goes—I can tell you that it's like we shoot the movie first on paper. It's very existential in that, from that moment on, the movie has been shot and they just build on top of that.

When you started working on *Raising Arizona*, you couldn't have perceived the level of

importance that your work would have to this gigantic body of films.

I can't see into the future, but I can tell you that I knew they were going to be great filmmakers; I was fortunate enough to get one thing in my life right. I knew they were going to be some of the greatest filmmakers we have in this country, and I wanted to be a part of it. I had seen *Blood Simple* in college, and I remember thinking a couple of times, "These guys are speaking my language, this is what I understand." When I met them, I wasn't too far off that mark. We got along very well and I haven't really looked back since—I really haven't. That's how it worked back then and that's how it works now. We're just older.

What in *Blood Simple* specifically appealed to your illustrator's sensibility?

By that time I had seen a lot of movies, and I'd made a couple of films in college, one of which did really well for me in that I actually made some money from it. And the way that I made that movie was by storyboarding it. I'd read up on storyboarding and pursued it, and I'd done several experiments in college, largely from what I'd learned from books about Hitchcock and this lovely book that's still on my shelf, the illustrated screenplay of *Raiders of the Lost Ark*. It was filled with work by these incredible artists who weren't comic-book artists: They were storyboard artists. So when I saw *Blood Simple,* I knew there was something going on there because I could tell that the Coens had storyboarded it. I applied everything I knew from watching *Blood Simple* and doing my own movies to the work I did on *Raising Arizona*. When we collaborated, there was a lot of talk about continuing along from Hitchcock, the way he did things. As an example, one of the first things Joel Coen told me when we were working on *Raising Arizona* was that there would be no "regular" angles in the movie. He said, "It's either a little high or a little low." And I was really able to understand what he was saying because, once Joel had established that, there was more to just being "a little high or a little low." It was like, where exactly is it a little high or a little low? That's what we were into very early; getting shot-specific things done early, before we'd even put the camera down. And then of course they had Barry Sonnenfeld, who is one of the greatest cinematographers, so those were some marvelous sessions, and I was very fortunate to get invited back. Because that film, when I saw it, was one of the greatest experiences of my life. Watching that movie after it was done, when I saw it in New York, I had never seen anything like that, where the things that we drew all of a sudden became real.

Films like *Raising Arizona* and *Hudsucker Proxy*, both of which are very graphic and shape-based and, in some ways, almost cartoonish, seem to me to lend themselves to storyboarding. It seems to me that for *A Serious Man* or *Inside Llewyn Davis*, those concepts could be harder to realize visually. Did you find that was the case?

With every movie that they do, they'll come up with a few films they really like and we'll talk about them. Way back when we did *Barton Fink*, Joel and Ethan would say, "Think Kubrick!" A couple of Kubrick's movies were good references for me because I'd seen all those pictures. That's kind of how we'd smoke out what we were doing because we were trying to find a tone, and I was lucky enough to be able to translate that tone into my drawings. I might add, one of the only ways you can see tone in their movies is by going through the whole storyboard. To this day I don't know how that happens. They sit down and they go through everything that we've drawn, and as they step through it, I can almost see the tone and pacing of the picture coming out.

Is camera movement itself built into the storyboards?

Generally, yes, and when we draw, Roger [Deakins] or Bruno [Delbonnel] is usually very close by. Both generally do not go very far; they sit in on a lot of sessions. On *Hail Caesar!*, Roger would be in the room when we were rehearsing a drawing, and if the guys were trying to come up with a camera move, they'd question Roger, and then they'd shape it up, and I'd eventually draw it and hopefully get it right. I'd have to do a few sketches sometimes, but if you get Joel

and Ethan and Roger happy and together in one room, you're home. You really are. Because after that it's usually a week or two weeks after that they start shooting. The whole crew has the storyboard for the whole movie. So when Betsy [Magruder, AD] gets a hold of them, she does the schedule from the drawings. She's able to look over those cryptic drawings before we finish them up and she builds the schedule from that. That's the advantage these guys have; the movies are already shot before we shoot them.

So do you think that there is a relationship between that process and the tightness with which the films are edited?

Absolutely. One hundred percent. The "rough cuts" are not usually much longer than the final cut, and it's because they shoot only what they need. I read about Hitchcock when he did *Rebecca*, and about how the studio was so upset because he would only shoot what he wanted to and they couldn't cut it together. Through the years, I've watched them turn this into an absolute black art. I don't know if there's anybody in the business who can replicate that. I'm pretty happy to just sit back and be mystified now.

I'd be curious as to the specifics of how some of their movies were drawn. For example, in some ways *Fargo* is a very simple movie visually, especially after something like *The Hudsucker Proxy*.

If I could be at liberty to correct you, I'd say that it's deceptively simple.

I wondered if you could talk about drawing that, because it's one of my favorite movies of theirs in terms of how it looks.

First of all, *Fargo* was a little contaminated for me because I got to act in it.

Yeah, you're the corpse in the field when Marge shows up at the scene of the roadside murder. And it's doubly funny because it's a cameo for you that is this kind of thankless cameo in that you're a corpse, but you're also part of this weird urban legend involving Prince.

Here's how it happened. Ethan and I went to a movie. And Prince was in that movie, and they put his little symbol on the credits. Then Ethan, on the way out of the theater, said, "We should do something like that for you, J. Todd. I'm serious!" We made a phony-baloney symbol that resembled his, except that we put it on its side and I put a smiley face on it. We were just joking about it; we put it in there as a joke. Everybody believed it; it was a very weird time. It was fun, it really was, but everybody believed it. Rumor has it that Prince was there, and he was not. Prince had nothing to do with it. It was a joke that Ethan, Joel, and I came up with that we thought was funny, so they did it.

Can either of the Coens draw themselves?

Yeah, Ethan draws a little bit. He draws thumbnails. He happens to be a pretty *darn* good artist, and I follow his work. He and Joel have a meeting before their meeting with me once they've written everything, and Ethan brings a little notebook full of loose thumbnails. Joel writes the shot list. They get it in their mind what's going to happen, what has to move, and Ethan will do a really simple drawing. I used to kid him a lot because they had these pig noses on them, and he'd say, "That's because it's a low angle." So there's a language there that Ethan gives to me when he draws. Both brothers give me great descriptions of how they see the shot, and I start sketching until I ring the bell. Once I'm in there, I can figure out what to do, because I've read the script. I don't read too deeply into their scripts incidentally, because if I start assuming things and coming up with my own ideas, they are almost always wrong. The first session I do with them, before we do anything else, is so fast and so loose you can't believe it. You see the drawings and you can't really understand what they are, but I take those drawings back and then I work them up a little bit, and then I bring them back and they give me a critique on them. "Yeah, that's it" or "Nope, that's not it. We're going to change this, we're going to do that." And then I make my corrections and just continue on down the stream. We do it in this kind of linear stance, where I work very much off Ethan's little drawings when I need a hint. We have a way of doing things now, and when we're finished with that process, they're ready to shoot.

SCENE
SET UP 2

22. TWO SHOT –Dora and Velvel watching him go.

22. TWO SHOT –Dora and Velvel watching him go.

. Wide looking through the doorway into the house as Dora walks into the for
uts the door into the lens.

1. MED WIDE PULLING AUTOLOCHUS as he marches up the column of slaves to the well. The PULL BACK reveals Jesus as Baird pushes the last slave away and grabs the dipper from The Christ staggers back in wonderment.

2. POP IN on AUTOLOCHUS as he enters a close-up. PAN off variations.

I've read that you often take six to eight weeks to do what you do.

Yeah, and I've got to tell you, another thing that mystifies me is it takes them roughly the same amount of time to shoot these movies as it takes me to draw them. One of the things to keep in mind about this process, and what you're talking about, is the aspect of taking a really solid idea and making it better. And one of the ways they do that is that they are pretty confident in what they want to do because it makes them happy, and when they do it they find the people who can take their ideas and their direction further than they ever thought, like Jess and Mary and Roger, Nancy Hague, Peter Kurland, Betsy, Bruno, and Bob. These are people who, once they know their set direction, they're off. Muhammad Ali used to say, "It ain't bragging if you can do it," and what they're doing is they're taking that idea and turning it into something much greater than the brothers could ever get with their imagination. The Coens surround themselves with great people. I'm not talking about myself; I'm talking about all these other people they surround themselves with. Those people are able to understand what the Coens want, so they're in the process of taking this idea and honing it. And they know when to stop. They know when that process is done. Years ago I was working with Frank Oz, and he said that one of the tricks in this business is being able to watch your work over and over and over again and make these subtle changes. And I watch these guys and they're able to do

that; they can watch it and they can do it with just incredible focus.

Do you think that the director credit being shared made it become more of an even split between them in terms of directing on set?

They've always been the directors, both of them. They're just one guy, man. I've read about people in history who have been able to do things like this, like the Wright brothers.

So you would say at no point was Joel any more interested in the camera or the composition of shots than Ethan?

It depends on what day it is; one day it'll be like that, and the next it'll be flipped. There's no hard and fast rule there except that "they both direct." That's how I see it. One sees it from one direction, the other sees it from the other direction, but it's the same shot. When I met them, one of the things I learned how to do was have them both in front of me. Because if I would talk to one, when the other one came up, he would say, "Tell him what you just said." So I said, "From now on it's got to be both of you in front of me." That's the way it works best. And that's the way we've done it ever since; I don't really listen to anything they have to say unless they're both in front of me. They're the yin and yang, man. One of them is the yin one day, then he's the yang on another. They complement each other in scale, and it's very hard to explain that to people. Most brothers don't get along. In most businesses, they don't get along. But these guys are always so complementary

of each other in so many respects, they have so many ways of doing things.

I know that when I saw *Inside Llewyn Davis* I found it very moving, in that it's about a guy who is trying to create music by himself after losing his partner. It just seems like the saddest thing. In the movie he's a stubborn asshole and he wants to be a solo artist; he doesn't want to play with others because he can't imagine collaborating with anyone else.

Don't get me wrong—they are different people. I know them on a separate level, who they are when they're not working together. I know Ethan a little better than Joel, but when they're not with each other they're different people, and I deal with them like different people. Occasionally when we're out somewhere and we're not working, it can be hard to separate that, but if there's one thing I know how to do it's shift gears and work with both of them, and I enjoy that a lot. They don't finish each other's sentences; they don't do any of that. When I talk to them, and when we're not working, they talk to me differently. It's the way it works. There's a point where we pull the rope and walk. That's when it starts happening, when I turn on a different set of senses and abilities and try to get my priorities straight on what they want. I'm part of a team here, and I just do my best to give them what they want. It's all about the next and best Coen picture, and that's why I'm here. I'm very lucky to be here.

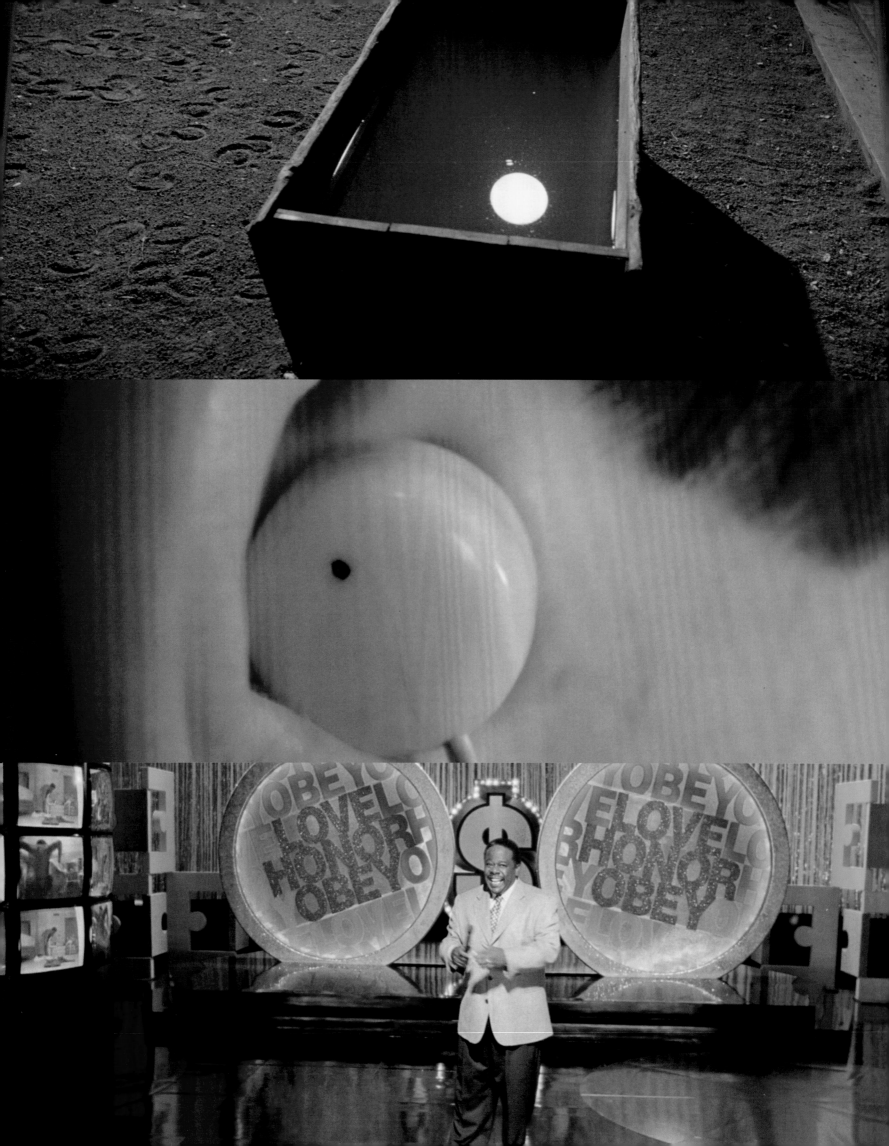

That's Entertainment!

2010 — 2016

N 2005, DAVE Van Ronk's memoir, *The Mayor of MacDougal Street,* was published posthumously, a niche item snapped up mostly by folk music aficionados familiar with the late singer-songwriter's modest output and legend. A self-taught guitar player who shifted from jazz to folk styles in between stints with the Merchant Marine, Van Ronk became a fixture of the Greenwich Village coffeehouse scene of the early 1960s; in the book, Van Ronk's account of the period and his own misadventures on the way to, from, and at gigs (as well as cameos by more famous names like Bob Dylan) makes for enjoyably picaresque reading. "His acid voice is part of what draws you into the book," Joel Coen said in conversation with the *New York Times* in 2013. "It's the best thing I know of in giving a sense of what it was like to be a working musician at that time."

'Is the Coen Brothers' Next Film About Iconic Folk Artist Dave Van Ronk?" asked a *Collider* headline in June 2011, referring to comments the Coens had made during an onstage interview in New York with Noah Baumbach. But in interviews leading up to the premiere of *Inside Llewyn Davis* at the 2013 Cannes Film Festival, the filmmakers were careful to point out the new film (their first in three years after *True Grit,* the longest lag time between projects since the gap separating *The Ladykillers* from *No Country for Old Men*) was not a biopic or a straight adaptation of *The Mayor of MacDougal Street* so much as an imaginative leap into its milieu. "In our minds, [Van Ronk] was 'the generic folk singer' until we kind of figured out who

the main character of the movie actually was," Ethan told NPR. The film was shot on location in New York City, the first of the Coens' films to be explicitly set in their base of operations, and financed largely by the French distributor Studiocanal with a final budget of $11 million.

Just as they did for the character of Mattie in *True Grit,* the Coens undertook a broad search for an actor who could play Llewyn Davis: One of their criteria was that whoever they cast would be able to sing and play guitar (a different approach than in *O Brother, Where Art Thou?,* where George Clooney lip-synched "Man of Constant Sorrow"). The casting of the relatively unknown thirty-three-year-old Oscar Isaac, a former ska band vocalist who told every publication that would listen that he grew up with a poster for *Miller's Crossing* on his bedroom wall, turned out to be a masterstroke. When the film bowed at Cannes to superlative reviews, his tough, unsentimental, and musically convincing performance was singled out as the most outstanding element. ("The success or failure of the film resides on Oscar Isaac, and he absolutely wears the Coens' precise dialogue and tone like a glove," wrote Kevin Jaggernauth for *IndieWire.*)

The Coens didn't stick around Cannes to pick up their Grand Prix (runner-up) prize from the Steven Spielberg–headed jury, a detail that was noted by a few journalists (and seen as being in keeping with their typically media-averse personas). But just as *Barton Fink* triumphed at Cannes and then floundered in its North American release, *Inside Llewyn Davis* failed—to quote the music club owner played in the film by F. Murray Abraham—to "really connect with people." (The film's final haul of $32 million in the US was enough to recoup its budget.)

Some of *Inside Llewyn Davis*'s most vocal detractors were Greenwich Village veterans who felt, in the words of musician Suzanne Vega, that the Coens had taken a "vibrant, crackling, competitive, romantic, communal, crazy, drunken, brawling scene and crumpled it into a slow brown sad movie." (Vega was quoted in a January 2014 *Chicago Reader* article entitled "The Folk-Song Army's Attack on *Inside Llewyn Davis*," an image out of *Lord of the Rings*.) More generally, though, the problem was that the film's stark, unforgiving tone was exactly as advertised; the raves of newspaper and magazine critics weren't enough to entice audiences to see a movie about an unlikable character in a relatively obscure pop-cultural context. The T-Bone Burnett–produced soundtrack of folk standards (mostly performed by cast members Isaac, Carey Mulligan, and Justin Timberlake, with a couple of original Van Ronk and Dylan chestnuts thrown in for good measure) didn't come close to approaching *O Brother, Where Art Thou?*'s chart dominance. (A concert film entitled *Another Day, Another Time*, was recorded at New York City's Town Hall and broadcast on Showtime.)

After *Inside Llewyn Davis*, the Coens returned to a premise that had been rattling around since 1999, when they'd talked with George Clooney on the set of *O Brother, Where Art Thou?* about their idea for a comedy set in the silent-film era, centered on a matinee idol playing a Roman centurion. "It's about the movie business and life and religion and faith," Ethan told Anne Thompson during the press tour for *Inside Llewyn Davis*. "There's a good chance that would be next." In 2014, the Coens confirmed that the film, entitled *Hail, Caesar!*, would feature Clooney (who supposedly pushed them for years to make it happen) but be set instead in the 1950s, focused equally on a vainglorious movie star and a hardworking studio "fixer" overseeing several troubled productions.

Compared to the intimate and stripped-down *Llewyn Davis, Hail, Caesar!* was a massive studio production, budgeted at $20 million by Universal Pictures and shot in Los Angeles. Instead of looking for an unknown actor to play an unknown singer, the Coens larded their cast with movie stars including Josh Brolin, Channing Tatum, Tilda Swinton, Jonah Hill, Scarlett Johansson, and Ralph Fiennes, whose presence gave the story's Old Hollywood setting a layer of self-reflexive credibility. The cleverness of the conceit was heightened by the decision to set the action at Capitol Pictures Studios, the same fictional backlot that figured into *Barton Fink*, although the Coens downplayed the idea that the film was a big in-joke. "Many of the reviews of *Hail, Caesar!*—good and bad—say it's

spoofing or parodying or satirizing," Ethan said to *Time Out*. "What the fuck? I don't understand that. Look at the Channing Tatum dance number. We're not spoofing. We're trying to do a good dance number!"

The critical split suggested by his comments was real. *Hail, Caesar!* opened the 2016 Berlin Film Festival around the same time it opened across the United States—a strange release strategy for filmmakers used to launching during the fourth quarter of the calendar, in awards season. In *Variety*, Justin Chang praised the film's "poker-faced exuberance" while noting that "its more thoughtful, elusive undertones could stand in the way of broader public acceptance." He was correct: The film's CinemaScore—derived from audience polling—was a dismal C–, suggesting that for all its familiar faces and bright, boisterous energy, *Hail, Caesar!* had mostly confused a mainstream constituency.

The real fallout from *Hail, Caesar!*, though, came in the aftermath of an interview the Coens did with the *Daily Beast* in which the brothers responded to criticisms that their work was not particularly "diverse," especially with regard to the new film's all-white cast. "Why would they single out a particular movie and say, 'Why aren't there black or Chinese or Martians in this movie? What's going on?' That's the question I don't understand. The person who asks that question has to come in the room and explain it to me." "It's important to tell the story that you're telling in the right way," added Ethan. "Which might involve black people or people of whatever heritage or ethnicity—or it might not." Some commentators seized on these comments (and Joel's claim that the whole discussion was "idiotic") as ammunition to try to take a pair of Oscar-winning filmmakers down a peg. Others expressed regret that a pair of beloved, influential artists weren't being more proactive or politically correct in a polarized climate increasingly conducive to culture warrior posturing. (Considering *Hail, Caesar!*'s subtext about whether or not mass entertainment can [or should] serve as a Trojan horse for ideology, the controversy was at least somewhat appropriate to the film at hand.)

In August 2017, Netflix announced that the Coens would write and direct a six-part miniseries entitled *The Ballad of Buster Scruggs*, making them the latest in a series of major filmmakers (including Bong Joon-ho, David O. Russell, Woody Allen, and Martin Scorsese) to work directly with the streaming giant. The project was described as a Western comprising six separate stories, which would make it the Coens' first true foray into episodic storytelling. The Coens' joint statement about the deal was even more succinct than their awards-show acceptance speeches: "We are streaming motherfuckers!"

True Grit

RELEASE DATE
December 22, 2010
BUDGET
$38M
DISTRIBUTOR
Paramount Pictures
CAST
Jeff Bridges
Hailee Steinfeld
Matt Damon
Josh Brolin
Barry Pepper
Dakin Matthews
Jarlath Conroy
Paul Rae

WARNING!
THIS FILM CONTAINS

Charles Portis	30%
Charles Laughton	20%
Henry Hathaway	15%
John Ford	15%
John Wayne	10%
Whiskey	7%
Snake venom	3%

THE CASE CAN be made that *A Serious Man* concludes with a cameo from the Almighty, so it is appropriate that *True Grit* begins with a religious overture. Underneath a piano melody borrowed by composer Carter Burwell from Anthony J. Showalter's nineteenth-century hymn "Leaning on the Everlasting Arms," the camera slowly zooms in on a house illuminated by firelight. Seen through a four-paneled window, the blaze looks like nothing so much as a burning cross. The holy trinity of Christian references is cinched with an opening title plucked from the Old Testament: "The wicked flee where none pursueth." A Bible verse provides an apt epigram for a film centered on a posse of bounty hunters tracking a wanted man through post–Civil War Texas, a landscape where the Good Book still holds sway.

True Grit was a big-tent movie for the Coens: Its massive box-office success and string of Oscar nominations—ten in all, the most of any Coens film—suggested that the brothers had, for the first time since *O Brother, Where Art Thou?*, stirred up the sort of big, crowd-pleasing emotions generally antithetical to their brand. Juxtaposed against the cold-blooded screwball moves of *Burn After Reading* and the barbed subcultural satire of *A Serious Man*, *True Grit*'s deluxe production values and big, clean narrative lines—as long and linear as the horizon itself—seemed to point toward shifting creative impulses. "It's cornier," admitted Joel Coen to *Vanity Fair*. "Well, corny's not a dirty word for us either. When you're talking about a young-adult adventure story, there's something very simple and elemental about those kinds of stories. You don't want to change that. It's what's compelling about them as stories. It's where they get their power."

The young-adult story in question was Charles Portis's 1968 novel *True Grit*, previously filmed in 1969 by Henry Hathaway. That movie, a commercial hit in its own right, was famous mostly for winning John Wayne his only Academy Award for Best Actor in the part of the one-eyed US Marshal Rooster Cogburn; in interviews the Coens said they were not remaking *True Grit* the movie but adapting the book. As in *The Ladykillers* and *No Country for Old Men*, however, the Coens' fidelity to their source material is a complex proposition. Their *True Grit* is indeed much closer to Portis's novel than Hathaway's film, but the few alterations they do make push the story into the same anxious, ambivalent realm as their previous work. Even that seemingly broad, declarative Bible verse—a parallel to *A Serious Man*'s opening invocation of the tenth-century Rabbi Rashi—reveals itself as sleight-of-hand. "The wicked flee where none pursueth," is only half the story; the Coens carefully omit the second half of Proverbs 28:1, which goes on to say that the "righteous are as bold as a lion." Mattie Ross (Hailee Steinfeld), the film's teenaged heroine, will display a lion's share of boldness as she tries to avenge her father's murder, and yet *True Grit* is finally a treatise on the ugly futility of vengeance, rousing in places but suffused with the same aching, existential melancholy that cloaked *No Country for Old Men*.

This reticence to celebrate the settling of accounts marks *True Grit* as a movie somewhat out of step with its early-twenty-first-century moment. When Quentin Tarantino opened *Kill Bill* (2003) with a secular proverb—"Revenge is a dish best served cold," a sentiment authored by Shakespeare but credited by QT to *Star Trek*—he was stating his personal preference for deliciously chilly violence. Over the next decade, this fetish would become industry standard as Hollywood experienced a renaissance of revenge thrillers, from spiritual remakes of seventies exploitation pictures like *Death Wish* (1974) to the baroque cruelties of torture-porn standards like *Hostel* (2005) and both versions

of *The Girl with the Dragon Tattoo* (2009 and 2011), with their rape-revenge narratives. *True Grit* is violent but not sensationally so; it's less gory than *No Country for Old Men* even as it takes life and death seriously, and grants the latter its sting. Whatever comedy there is in the Coens' approach is front-loaded: A scene set at a public hanging features memorable speeches from two condemned killers before a third convict's last words are suddenly muffled under his hood. There's also something funny about the undertaker who greets Mattie upon her arrival in Carson City, where she's come to retrieve the body of her father, who was killed by one of his hired hands during a dispute at a card game. Played by the wizened character actor Jarlath Conroy, this mortician has an stilted, formal way of speaking, which makes even friendly statements sound oddly ominous, as when he offers Mattie a place to stay in his funeral parlor. "If you would like to sleep in a coffin, it would be all right," he assures her, as he has plenty of those on hand in a city where the mortality rate seems alarmingly high. On the eve of a journey that will see her set out in the wilderness to avenge her father, Mattie is being invited to experience a sort of sneak preview of her own demise.

The line, which Conroy repeats with pathological flatness in the style of so many Coens characters stuck in their own personal loops, is not in Portis's novel: It's an addition. It serves, like "accept the mystery" in *A Serious Man*, as a skeleton key for unlocking the major themes of the movie around it. It's a way into the material for Mattie and the viewer alike. By juxtaposing their heroine's desire for retribution with the imagery of the funeral parlor, the Coens imply that revenge isn't just cold—it's positively clammy. Mattie begins the film by bunking down next to death, and just keeps getting closer and closer until, in an eerie echo of the undertaker's invitation, she finds herself literally six feet under during the climax.

True Grit is filled with corpses in various states of decay: criminals dropped neck-first from the gallows; a body hanging from a tree in the middle of the woods with its eyes pecked out; a skeleton gleaming in the darkness of an underground cave. The eccentricities of Jeff Bridges's Rooster Cogburn and Matt Damon's Texas ranger LaBoeuf (and the comic skill of the

NEW IN TOWN
—
As Mattie Ross rides into Fort Smith, the town is subsumed by her reflection in a train compartment window; the film will re-create the myth of the Old West in its heroine's image.

HAVE GUN, WILL TRAVEL
—
Mattie prizes her late father's Civil War-era Colt handgun and intends to use it to avenge his death; its symbolic weight far exceeds its actual size.

The sequence where Rooster and Mattie come across a corpse dangling from a tree in the forest does not derive from Charles Portis's source novel; the stark, Tarot card-like composition of the Hanged Man is a Coen original, working on both a graphic and thematic level. Mattie's elevated position suggests she is momentarily above matters of life and death; later in the film, when she falls into the cave, she'll be on the other end of that arrangement.

Rooster Cogburn's inebriated stasis
recalls Bridges's role as The Dude in
The Big Lebowski; as the film goes
on, the alcoholic marshal shakes
off his torpor and shows his mettle
protecting Mattie out on the trail.

MY AIM IS TRUE
—
Mattie shoots Tom Chaney, but her moment of triumph is short-lived; the courage it takes to pull the trigger fails her after she falls into a cave and is bitten by a snake—a poisonous consequence of vengeance.

EVERLASTING ARMS
—
The final shot of Mattie as an adult framed by gravestones and scored to a nineteenth-century hymn is elegaic and wickedly ironic; now an amputee, she leans on "the everlasting arms."

actors playing them) are very nearly swallowed up by the severity of the presentation. As in *No Country for Old Men*, with its tamped-down, even-keel style, there is a sense that the Coens are forcibly holstering their ironic tendencies in *True Grit*, with scenes like the public hanging as evidence of itchy trigger fingers. But if the sincerity of the filmmaking was indeed hard-won, that only makes it all the more impressive.

One commonality between *No Country for Old Men*, *Burn After Reading*, *A Serious Man*, and *True Grit* as "late" Coen films is a general paucity of cinematic allusions. Compared to their frenetic pre-*Fargo* output, or the wildly postmodern gestures of *The Big Lebowski* or *O Brother, Where Art Thou?*, these films are relatively self-contained: They're less of an inter-textual workout. There are references to other Westerns in *True Grit*, and they're obvious to the point of being perfunctory: Picking up on one unsubtle visual cue, film critic Armond White noted that "when Rooster looks into an abandoned mineshaft, his silhouette recalls *The Searchers'* final image of John Wayne's Ethan Edwards." John Ford's 1956 classic, itself a critique of righteous vengeance, has been quoted visually (and otherwise) by dozens of directors from Martin Scorsese and Steven Spielberg to S. Craig Zahler in *Bone Tomahawk* (2015), but there is a little more juice in the Coens' homage than most. The pilfered image links Bridges to his predecessor in the role of Rooster Cogburn, and then ups the symbolic ante by having him unload his revolver drunkenly through the open archway—an

archaic figure firing impotently and pointlessly into the void.

Rooster is to be Mattie's instrument against Tom Chaney (Josh Brolin), the mad-dog gambler who murdered her father. Over the course of their travels together, Rooster becomes a sort of surrogate father even as his past serves as a cautionary tale: His wrecked body and heavy drinking are the by-products of a lifetime spent as a professional killer. It's a running joke in all the versions of this story (the book and both movies) that Mattie is generally more determined and competent than the veteran trail hound she's hired on account of his "true grit," but Steinfeld's performance transcends the plucky cuteness of Kim Darby's interpretation in Hathaway's film and even Portis's depiction of the character. Her Mattie is so poised and relentless that she's almost scary, while Bridges shows great generosity in ceding the movie and turning Rooster more or less into a supporting character.

His humility owes in part to the fact that the actor carries far less iconic baggage in the part than Wayne did: In 1969, the role of Rooster Cogburn was a way for Duke to simultaneously send up and honor his many Western heroes—a prematurely valedictory victory lap for a career that, for the most part, always stayed in its lane. Bridges has appeared in his share of Westerns but is a more versatile actor (and like Wayne, he ultimately won his Oscar for a wizened, sentimental performance, in 2009's *Crazy Heart*). Bridges's Rooster is thus less immediately iconic than Wayne's, although his

introduction on the stand at a trial, framed by the American flag, shows the Coens straining a bit for symbolic significance. Thankfully, Bridges's acting is agile and funny: he acts Rooster's drunkenness with the same heavy-bodied grace as The Dude's pot-addled trawl through Los Angeles in *The Big Lebowski*.

Even through his alcoholic fog, Rooster is experienced enough to try to warn Mattie of what lies ahead, telling her that pursuing Tom Chaney is more than a "coon hunt." "It is the same idea," Mattie replies, an equivocation that's both practical and naive. Mattie truly has no idea of what lies in front of her; she sees through Rooster's "braggadocio" but is oblivious to her own. As it goes along, *True Grit* keeps poetically disabusing her of her illusions about life and death. When Mattie and Rooster come across a corpse hanging out in the woods—shot in a manner identical to Professor Dorr dangling from the bridge at the climax of *The Ladykillers*—it's an image with the stark, ominous clarity of a tarot card.

This scene is not in the original film or the novel; it's a Coen original, and its visionary grotesqueness demands to be reckoned with. When Rooster moves to cut the body down, explaining that he can probably get some money for it, it cinches a link between death and the material and psychological economy of a time and place where bounty hunters like Rooster have been granted special dispensation to operate. Rooster's marching orders typically end with "dead or alive," so his indifference to the hanged body in his midst makes sense; it's

all the same to him. But there is still a palpable and moving humanity in the way the Coens have him instruct Mattie, who has climbed the tree to cut the body down, to stay hidden when he's actually selling the body to a group that rides up afterward. From where she's sitting in the branches, Mattie still occupies the moral high ground.

Her elevated status doesn't last; *True Grit* brings her down to Rooster's level, and also to Chaney's. Her first meeting with her father's killer is beautifully staged with each character standing ankle-deep in a mountain stream—a boundary

physically separating her from the beginning of her quest and its ending. The stream also doubles as a portal into Chaney's debased world: It's an American vision of the Styx. Holding her ground in the water, Mattie succeeds in winging him with a shot from her father's Colt, and is then dragged across the stream, away from Rooster and LaBoeuf. Without fully meaning to, she's crossed over to a different realm. She needs to be rescued, and she will be, which is not the same as saying that she's saved.

The most famous moment in Hathaway's *True Grit* is when Wayne's Rooster, emboldened by

his paternal responsibility and also relishing the opportunity for one last gunfight, snarls "Fill your hands, you son of a bitch" at "Lucky" Ned Pepper (Robert Duvall) and his gang of outlaws and rides at them, bridle between his teeth and guns blazing. It's a scene that the Coens replicate dutifully, right down to the distanced, wide-angled camera perspective. The differences are more important than the similarities, however. In Hathaway's *True Grit*, Rooster also kills Tom Chaney shortly after his triumph over Ned Pepper, sparing Mattie from having to get her hands dirty. In the Coens' film, Mattie shoots Chaney dead, just as she

does in Portis's novel. In the same instant, she falls down into a cave crawling with poisonous snakes: The two moments are synced as tightly as Larry changing Clive's grade and the arrival of the tornado in *A Serious Man*. Actions have consequences: By pulling the trigger, she's brought this upon herself.

Mattie's experiences in the cave are nightmarish in the Coens' *True Grit*—darker and more disturbing than the same scene in Hathaway's movie, which lets her escape with little more than a broken arm. The Coens pay off earlier choices beautifully here: Whereas earlier Mattie had been placed above the fray by Rooster during the episode with the hanged man, he must now descend into the cavern to save her; standing at the mouth of the cave, he aims his guns at the snakes crawling around her and blasts away in a redux of the *Searchers* homage, framed now not as a fool but a savior. The religious inflections of the movie's opening scene return and deepen: Rooster carves a miniature cross into Mattie's hand before sucking out the venom, and when the pair gallops back to civilization on Mattie's horse, the soundtrack swells once again to the strains of "Leaning on the Everlasting Arms."

Burwell's interpolation of the hymn may be the most ecstatically emotional use of music in the Coens' entire filmography: The arrangement is spare, but laid on top of darkly glittering, moonlit shots of the riders moving steadily across the landscape; it transports *True Grit* into a magic-realist realm that abandons the audiovisual language of the Western altogether. Instead, the Coens boldly evoke Charles Laughton's visionary 1954 thriller *The Night of the Hunter*, which used "Leaning on the Everlasting Arms" as a theme. In that film, beneath a starry sky, young John Harper (Billy Chapin) drifts downriver with his sister, Pearl

Jess and me — my daughter, Jess, was my assistant on this one, man, she was good.

(Sally Jane Bruce); they are innocents, pursued by wickedness in the form of Reverend Harry Powell (Robert Mitchum), a conman who has the words "love" and "hate" tattooed on his hands. Those tattoos, probably the most famous in film history, are the character's psychotic nod to the duality of everyman; in *True Grit*, Harry's contradiction is transferred to Rooster Cogburn, the guardian angel who is also a contract killer.

Rooster's harder side emerges when he's forced to shoot Mattie's ailing mustang pony, Little Blackie, which he does with a cold efficiency that belies the act's intention as a mercy killing. From inside her snakebit delirium, Mattie is guiltily furious; she feels responsible for an innocent creature's death, even if Rooster pulled the trigger. But it's not just Little Blackie who she's grieving, or even her father. Rather, it's their opposite number Tom Chaney, whose murder, however righteously orchestrated, has compromised her purity: There's no going back for Mattie. In this brilliant, hallucinatory sequence, the Coens distill every element of *True Grit*: the rugged beauty of the Western; the fragility of human feeling; and the consequences that come with, to paraphrase Sheriff Bell in *No Country for Old Men*, becoming a "part of this world." Mattie's "true grit" in killing Chaney

binds her to Rooster once and for all—the old killer and his apprentice—but it also takes her far away from the girl she was when she first rode into Carson City. And, as the Coens show so elegantly but viscerally in the film's coda, it causes her to literally lose a part of herself as well.

Kim Darby's Mattie barely seems fazed by her trials; it's strongly implied that she'll heal before long, and the original *True Grit* ends with a last hurrah for Rooster (really for John Wayne). Steinfeld's incarnation loses her snakebitten limb even despite Rooster's best efforts: The poison has spread too deeply. When the Coens flash forward twenty-five years to the character's middle age (where she is played by Elizabeth Marvel), the effect is startling beyond the eerie sight of her stump barely disguised beneath formal attire. The woman on-screen is so pious and uptight that she can scarcely seem to breathe; her earlier precocity has hardened into something far less endearing. Having been contacted by Rooster for a reunion, she returns to Texas only to learn from the owner of a Wild West show that the old gunfighter died a few days earlier.

Everything about this final sequence of *True Grit* is informed by a feeling of loss, starting with us

in the audience: We feel as if Steinfeld's Mattie has been stolen from us and replaced with this unpleasant stand-in. We recognize something of the younger woman's determination in her demeanor, but note that neither the death of Tom Chaney nor the passage of time has healed the wounds that set her off on what turned out to be a largely self-destructive errand. If anything, the injury has only grown more painful.

In the last shots, Mattie stands by her father's gravesite, a visit that has as much to do with Rooster Cogburn as Frank Ross. She then walks away against a gray horizon: Like her former mentor and protector, she has become a silhouette. As she fades into the distance, we see that she is a lopsided icon, and the song on the soundtrack reveals itself as a sort of perverse joke: "Leaning on the Everlasting Arms" as a send-off for an amputee. Nobody follows her as she goes—not even the camera—and while the lack of a pursuer may not mean that Mattie Ross is wicked, her isolation begs the question of the cost of her righteousness. At the end of *True Grit*, everything seems to have been spent. "Time just gets away from us," Mattie says in voice-over on the soundtrack, her once-promising future now and forever behind her.

1. Nathanael West's tale of 1930s Hollywood creeps is central to *Barton Fink*'s web of literary allusions.

2. Producer Scott Rudin sent the Coens advance galleys of Cormac McCarthy's lean, violent thriller - the first popular novel they ever adapted.

3. Rather than copying Henry Hathaway's 1969 film version of *True Grit*, the Coens stayed faithful to Charles Portis's source novel.

4. Edgar Allan Poe's Gothic short story is quoted late in *The Ladykillers*; a sinister-looking raven appears in the climax to help dispatch Tom Hanks's villain.

5. The Coens claimed to have not read Homer's epic before making *O Brother, Where Art Thou?* but the film is filled with specific allusions nonetheless.

6. Dashiell Hammett was a major influence on *Blood Simple*; the film's title comes from a phrase in his 1929 detective novel.

7. Old Testament themes pervade the Coens' late films, particularly *A Serious Man* and *Hail, Caesar!* both of which deal with crises of faith.

8. The plot of *Miller's Crossing* integrates numerous details from Hammett's 1932 novel, including the running symbolic motif of hats.

FILMOGRAPHY

Hail, Caesar! (2016)
Inside Llewyn Davis (2013)
True Grit (2010)
A Serious Man (2009)
Burn After Reading (2008)
No Country for Old Men (2007)
The Ladykillers (2004)
Intolerable Cruelty (2003)
The Man Who Wasn't There (2001)
O Brother, Where Art Thou? (2000)
The Big Lebowski (1998)
Fargo (1996)

After apprenticing on *The Hudsucker Proxy*, Mary Zophres has designed and provided the costumes for each of the Coens' successive films, dressing iconic characters such as Marge Gunderson, the Dude, and Anton Chigurh.

You worked as a PA on *Barton Fink* and assisted on the costume design for *The Hudsucker Proxy*. What were your first impressions of working on a Coen brothers set?

Richard Hornung was the costume designer on *The Hudsucker Proxy*. I learned so much from him. He had an ease with the Coens and was very attentive to their script and to the development of the characters. That is a lesson that I've always kept with me as a designer. To serve the script, and the director first, and to fully carry out the cinematic world that they have envisioned. When I was the assistant costume designer on *The Hudsucker Proxy*, I never thought I'd be designing costumes for the Coens.

I'm very interested in the superficial simplicity of costume-designing *Fargo*, which is one of the Coens' only really contemporary movies, and seemingly less stylized than their other early work.

In its simplicity, the costume design is, in fact, very stylized. It has a very controlled palette and very specific silhouette. The landscape of Minnesota in the wintertime is bleak and devoid of color. Joel and Ethan and I discussed how the palette of the film should be the same. Gray, tan, and brown were the main colors that I used to mimic the winter Minnesota landscape. When there was a garment of color, I processed it by fading it down and overdying it with a gray-tan wash. We wanted to emphasize the freezing temperature so a bundle-up silhouette was very important. The two characters who don't "belong" to this environment, Steve Buscemi and Peter Stormare, have different silhouettes; they're less prepared for the elements. I also don't consider this movie "contemporary." I intentionally backdated the clothes by at least ten years and gave it a Midwestern look. I shopped exclusively in Minnesota. Only there could I find the clothes that I needed for the look of the film and for the climate. I combed through thrift stores (such as Savers) to find the right clothes and dressed cast and extras accordingly.

Marge's coat is quite iconic, and I like that it makes noise when she walks in it: It really helps to define the character.

Yes, I loved that coat. It's a uniform parka. It's practical, brown, has the right amount of bundled-up bulk. It worked perfectly for the character and for the look of the film, but it was noisy, something one usually avoids because it interferes with the sound and dialogue of the film. Joel and Ethan liked the sound the coat made when Fran swung her arms while walking. Peter Kurland, our sound mixer, had to figure out ways to wire Fran for sound so that they could still hear her dialogue. In postproduction, they even brought the coat out of storage to use in the Foley mix.

I'm also fascinated by the ensemble that Marge wears when she goes to see Mike Yanagita in Minneapolis; it's the only time in the film that she's dressed in a stereotypically feminine way, and it stands out.

Yes, I wanted that outfit to feel different than what Marge wears in her everyday life. I built the blouse specifically to look like she had dressed in something nice for her meeting with Mike. I wanted her wearing something a bit uncomfortable like the meeting with Mike turned out to be.

Is it wrong to assume that after the success of _Fargo_, the budgets the Coens had for things like costume design went way up? Was there a feeling moving forward that there would be more resources to work with?

Yes, that is wrong to assume. We usually don't have enough money to accomplish what is in the script. Our appetite is usually bigger than our budget. And once Joel and Ethan agree to a budget, they never go back to the studio and ask for more money. That has been ingrained in me since my very first film with them. And, even when we had more money, like on _Hail, Caesar!_, we had enormous tasks to accomplish with the movies within the movie. More than five hundred Roman soldiers were built and molded; the "water picture" required the manufacture of a several hand-beaded mermaid costumes and synchronized swimmers. The parlor drama required the build of ballroom gowns, the Western was a build, the Tilda Swinton twin reporters were all made to order, and there were thousands of period costumes to rent. So we had to count every penny on that film. What's great about Joel and Ethan is that they don't ask for options. They make their decisions early on, and 99 percent of the time, they stick with them.

Does the extent to which the Coens pre-visualize their films limit you as a costume designer? Is there something constraining about working to a very specific template?

No. It's very helpful. I've never found it to be constraining. It gives you very strong footing, and a direction to head in. There's plenty of room for your own input, your own thoughts and creativity, but you're not just swimming in this bottomless pool of "What direction am I supposed to go in?"

Can you talk about your process and how you find inspiration for specific characters' costumes once you've read the script?

I read their scripts many times and break it down by scenes and character. I make notes during the read of what topics I'd like to research. And I do a lot of preliminary research to find the visual inspiration for the look of the film. We always have a preliminary meeting where I've gathered all my research, and I usually have divided it by character. I go over this research with Joel and Ethan, and we find a visual path for that particular film. Then I sketch and assemble research boards to show them at the next meeting

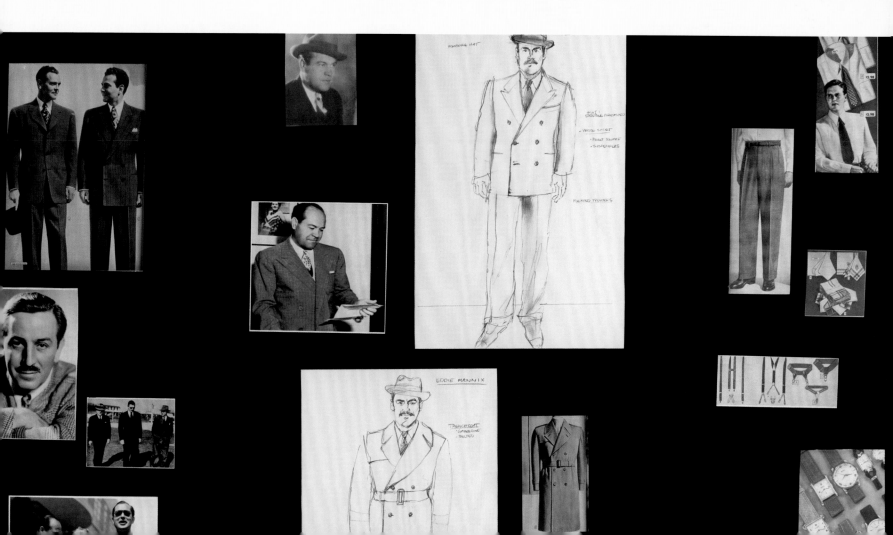

AUTOLOCHUS / BAIRD
BREASTPLATE

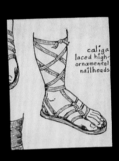

caliga
laced high-
ornamental
nailheads

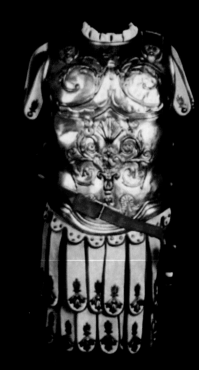

"CARLA JEAN"

Kelly MacDonald

BUS STATION & TO S
LEWELYN

KLACE
ERFLY ON A
CHAIN

ES
LT
ON
E
ORAL

SHOES & BAG - AGED SOME

where we fine-tune the look. And then it's time to gather clothes, fabrics, etc. to begin the prep for the film. Some specific character ideas come from the research process. For instance, for [Tom Hanks's character in] *The Ladykillers*, the first person I thought of when I read the script was Mark Twain, and that's where I got the detail of the bow tie. For Josh Brolin in *Hail, Caesar!*, the mustache came from a photo of Walt Disney. I'm always pulling these inspirations from different places, and I land on things that I like and then that they like as well.

What kind of input did you have into Javier Bardem's haircut in *No Country for Old Men*?

I usually start before hair and makeup. I was researching ideas for Chigurh's character, and I was looking through a file at the research library labeled "criminals 1970s" because it seemed like a good place to start. I came across a photo of a man sitting at the counter of a restaurant with his elbow on the counter. The man in the photo resembled Javier Bardem. He had a side part with bangs sweeping over his forehead, and length to his ears. The hair was specific and it seemed right for that character. I showed the photo to Joel and Ethan and they liked it, so I sent it to our hair designer, Paul LeBlanc, who is one of the greats. Paul took inspiration from the photo and made it more calculating. Javier joked about having to live his life that summer with that haircut.

The film is unthinkable without that haircut. . . .

Yes, it ended up defining his character. I decided that Chigurh was an outsider who was trying to blend into the surroundings. He wears cowboy boots and a denim jacket but even in his attempt to blend in I still wanted him to look awkward and menacing. His boots are pointy and look like they could injure someone. His jacket is stiff like armor and his palette is the darkest end of the palette of the film.

It's interesting though, because in *No Country for Old Men*, there's actually a lot of focus on Llewelyn's wardrobe, how he goes and buys those nice new cowboy duds with the money.

He makes the decision to steal the money; he doesn't seem to have any qualms about taking what isn't his. I wanted the shirt he buys with the money to give him a different look–to be noticeably different from the shirts he's worn throughout the film. I saw a shirt in the research. It was in a book of photographs by Richard Avedon about the West. There was a photograph of a roping cowboy who was wearing a cowboy shirt with a vertical pattern. I found the shirt in a thrift store but I needed a duplicate because it is what Llewelyn dies in. So, I had fabric printed to match the shirt I had found in the thrift store to make the second shirt.

What about Llewyn Davis's coat? That's such an integral part of his character.

It was always scripted that he'd be ill-prepared for the weather. So then I knew that I wouldn't give him a winter coat; I'd give him a blazer. And we tried on some plaid wool blazers that were very popular in the sixties, and we found this one corduroy jacket that we all liked. He doesn't change in the movie, either. He doesn't have a suitcase. He wears the same pair of pants the whole time, and changes his shirt once.

He sleeps in his clothes, too.

No, he sleeps in his boxers and a T-shirt. But choosing a look that an actor will wear for the entire film is important and can be difficult. You have to love what you're going to put that character in, because he's going to wear it for the whole film. And that's even more intimidating than having someone who has a hundred costume changes. So there was a lot of care taken with that costume, but I'm really happy with how it turned out. And it was a good silhouette on him. The reference that Joel and Ethan gave me was Dave Van Ronk, this musician who was under the shadow of Bob Dylan, but Oscar Isaac is a very different physical specimen. We felt like the shape of his pant leg was integral to the character. We went with something that would have been popular in those days—this skinny peg leg. But it's well-worn, so it looks like he's owned it for at least five years. It's not threadbare, exactly, but it's worn.

Well, he has a very worn, kind of agile silhouette because he keeps being doubled with the cat throughout the movie. And the cat almost becomes part of the costume when he's on the subway, too.

We picked the color of the coat before they landed on the cat, but I remember us talking about how the cat kind of blends in with the coat and how it's a good thing.

What about the things in their scripts that are direct references to other movies? In *The Big Lebowski*, David Huddleston is in a wheelchair with a blanket on his lap just like General Sternwood in *The Big Sleep*; in terms of the costume design, is there a deliberate attempt to replicate that character?

Well . . . you know, that very well might have been in their brains, and there have been other times where we have referenced that movie, but in that case it wasn't. I mean, it was in the script that he was in a wheelchair, with a blanket on his lap, but it didn't seem to be a deliberate reference to *The Big Sleep*.

Is there a difference between the way the Coens have cultivated their public persona and how you interact with them on a film set? Or do you not really think about these things after twenty years of collaboration?

I don't really think about "their persona." I've known them for more than twenty years now and I love them. We have an ease between us that is very comfortable. They communicate their vision clearly. People often ask me what the Coen brothers are like. I tell them they are very smart and totally normal. I think they prefer to stay out of the spotlight, which is why they shy away from press and interviews. It's kind of the opposite of what others in this business are like, so I think it seems unconventional for the film business.

Inside
Llewyn Davis

RELEASE DATE
December 6, 2013
BUDGET
$11M
DISTRIBUTOR
CBS Films
CAST
Oscar Isaac
Carey Mulligan
Justin Timberlake
Ethan Phillips
Robin Bartlett
Max Casella
Jerry Grayson
Jeanine Serralles

WARNING!
THIS FILM CONTAINS

The Mayor of	
MacDougal Street	23%
Harry and Tonto	20%
Bob Dylan trivia	17%
Highway driving	13%
Paying of dues	9%
Moussaka	7%
Santeria	6%
Harpsichord accompaniment	5%

"THE FILM DOESN'T really have a plot. That concerned us at one point; that's why we threw the cat in." So said Joel Coen at the 2013 Cannes Film Festival press conference for *Inside Llewyn Davis*, which went on to win the festival's Grand Prix—the best Croisette result for the brothers since their Palme d'Or for *Barton Fink*. Even for those long since accustomed to the Coens' downplaying of their own films' intricacy, Joel's comments were hard to take with a straight face.

The red mackerel tabby in question (portrayed by three different cats) is considerably more than a supporting player in *Inside Llewyn Davis*, and a very different sort of four-legged metaphor than the one in *A Serious Man*, where Schrödinger's cat was used as an abstract illustration of the Uncertainty Principle. In *Inside Llewyn Davis*, the cat is a doppelganger for the title character, a luckless folk singer in early sixties New York who slinks through the city with self-sufficient agility. When Llewyn (Oscar Isaac) takes the subway from the Upper West Side back to Greenwich Village the morning after crashing at the apartment of some friends—and accidentally letting their cat out after locking the door behind him—we watch the stations flash by from the animal's wide, peering eyes, which are reflected in the train car's glass as it sits on its new custodian's shoulder.

Desperately calling his host's office from a subway station platform, Llewyn gets drawn into a literal game of broken telephone. "Tell him Llewyn has the

"Llewyn is the cat":
The Coens humanize their
protagonist by forcing him
to care for a cat whose
rambling, elusive nature
mirrors his own.

cat," our hero pleads into the receiver. "Llewyn is the cat," replies the receptionist brightly as his face crumples in frustration. She's got it all wrong, except, of course, that she hasn't. "Llewyn is the cat" is as succinct and accurate a way as any to describe a film about a feckless stray who goes off on an adventure and eventually finds his way home, and the Coens keep finding ways to cinch the link between man and beast. Bruised, cold, and looking for a place where he can stow his furry little problem for a few hours, Llewyn makes a beeline for the apartment of fellow singer (and ex-lover) Jean (Carey Mulligan), clambering up her fire escape and slinking in through an open window with feline grace.

If Llewyn is a cat, then he's a tom who probably needs to be neutered. Upon Llewyn's arrival, Jean furiously reports that she's pregnant, demanding money that she knows her ex-lover doesn't have

for an abortion. Moving on from Jean, Llewyn—who has recently started working as a solo artist after the suicide of his recording partner, Mikey Timlin, and isn't dealing well with the grief—proceeds to methodically alienate his remaining allies in New York. His manager, Mel (Jerry Grayson), is irritated by his client's demands to see royalties on an album that isn't selling. The prosperous Upper West Side academics Mitch and Lillian Gorfein (Ethan Phillips and Robin Bartlett), previously always happy to open their door to Llewyn after he's had a rough night, are horrified when he brings their precious missing pet home and they discover that it's been accidentally switched out for a female look-alike.

Dejected, he hitches a ride to Illinois with a heroin-addicted New Orleans jazzman (John Goodman) and his valet (Garrett Hedlund), and is forced to abandon the second cat by the side of the highway just outside Chicago, only to (maybe) encounter it again on the drive home. Finally, an insert shot near the film's end shows an advertisement for Fletcher Markle's live-action Walt Disney drama *The Incredible Journey*, in which a cat survives by its wits on a trek across "200 perilous miles of Canadian wilderness!" Walking past the movie theater, Llewyn stops and studies the poster with an expression of recognition.

With all this in mind, Joel Coen's joke about the cat being an afterthought to the story of *Inside Llewyn Davis* reveals itself as such an untrustworthy assessment that it loops all the way back around to being an interpretive key. In lieu of a plot, the Coens use the cat(s) in *Inside Llewyn Davis* to sketch a pattern of loss, pursuit, deception, detour, and retrieval that doubles the main character's impulsive physical trajectory with that of the animal constantly eluding his grasp, as well as to forge cultural connections beyond the narrative. For instance, it may seem to be a mistake for the Coens to include *The Incredible Journey*, a film that came out in 1963, in a movie whose climax depends on the action taking place in 1961. It's worth noting, though, that 1963 was also the year that the French government placed an unusual animal into orbit 130 miles above the earth: a heroic cat named Felicette, who replaced a different cat who went missing minutes before blast-off and whose own incredible journey was overshadowed by Laika, the more famously anthropomorphized cosmonaut from the Soviet Union.

It is on this more ephemeral level of hints, allusions, and things left unsaid—the ingredients its creators just happened to "throw" into the mix—that *Inside Llewyn Davis* ranks among the Coens' richest and most rewarding films. Its deep casualness mirrors that of *The Big Lebowski*, with important symbols passed off as incongruous non sequiturs and complex observations about ambition, artistry, and aloneness—the three major themes developed via Llewyn's character and his various failures as a friend, a lover, and a performer—brocaded into its finely stitched audiovisual fabric. Like *O Brother, Where Art Thou?*, *Inside Llewyn Davis* is a stylized musical that layers its soundscape on top of an exquisitely desaturated cinematographic palette. With Roger Deakins otherwise occupied shooting the James Bond film *Skyfall*, the Coens hired French DP Bruno Delbonnel, who used vintage

album covers (including 1963's *The Freewheelin' Bob Dylan*) as a visual inspiration. In contrast to Deakins's characteristically vivid, sharp-edged images, *Inside Llewyn Davis* is draped in a veil of soft, pale light. The camera also travels less—or at least, less conspicuously—than in the majority of the Coens' other films, and the presence of so many unobtrusive compositions indicates a commitment to realism distinct not only from *O Brother*'s enchanted-backwoods-Americana but also the psychedelicized textures of the similarly sixties-set *A Serious Man*.

The carefully muted color scheme means that any vibrancy has to come from the soundtrack, which was personally curated by the Coens with their old *O Brother* collaborator T-Bone Burnett. These selections end up doing the heavy lifting in a film that gives off an impression of airiness. Beyond their common denominator as being period-appropriate—"If it's not new and it never gets old, it's a folk song," jokes Llewyn before beginning his rendition of the ageless lament "Hang Me, Oh Hang Me"—the songs in *Inside Llewyn Davis* have been chosen for their capacity to signify in several different directions at once. When Llewyn sings "Hang Me, Oh Hang Me," he steps into the character of a man compelled to welcome death as an escape from a cruel world, a self-pitying persona that seems prefab until the rest of the film fills it in. Sitting in the audience at the Gaslight Café, Llewyn watches and listens to Jean, her new beau, Jim (Justin Timberlake), and their honey-voiced friend Troy (Stark Sands) do a three-part harmony on the perennial "Five Hundred Miles," whose rambling-man narrative anticipates his upcoming arduous trip out of town. The oddball protest anthem "Please Mr. Kennedy," recorded by Llewyn and Jim alongside freelance sideman Al Cody (Adam Driver) during a low-paying studio session, does the same thing, from a decidedly more oblique angle. It hyperbolizes the plight of the freelance traveler, with Llewyn giving voice to a nervous astronaut's plea to not be shot into outer space, a cowardly voyager rejecting his incredible journey in advance.

This absurd scenario ties in nicely to the scene where a frustrated Jean asks him if he ever thinks about the future: "You mean, like flying cars and stuff?" he responds, echoing the fear of "things to come" that lurked in the sci-fi digression of *The Man Who Wasn't There*'s surreal flying saucer (and will resurface in the collective name

A SORRY MESS
—
This short, sincere apology note is the only thing Llewyn writes himself in the film; unlike his friend Jim—or Bob Dylan—he is a singer, not a composer.

A LITTLE PROBLEM
—
Jean's unwanted pregnancy places *Inside Llewyn Davis* alongside other Coens films exploring paternal anxiety.

Jim, Troy and Jean—a folk trio patterned after (and given the film's setting, predictive of) Peter, Paul and Mary. Bathed in ethereal light at a Greenwich village folk club, they project a softer, more beatific image than Llewyn Davis, whose music is more directed towards hard truths. The group's beautifully harmonized performance of "Five Hundred Miles" does what Llewyn cannot; they "connect with people" while he sits silent amidst the audience's sing-along.

chosen by the group of blacklisted screenwriters in *Hail, Caesar!*). In addition to mocking the fad for cheesy novelty songs that split the folk music movement down the middle between political commitment and goofy pastiche, "Please Mr. Kennedy" channels the larger anxieties of an era where the disappearance and replacement of preexisting orthodoxies was simultaneously cause for celebration and alarm within different subcultures; instead of the political protest typically associated with folk music, however, the song's subtext is self-serving. Llewyn's contempt for "Please Mr. Kennedy" (which Jim wrote) comes out of his respect for the form, while also painting him as a bit of a reactionary. It's significant that Llewyn decides to be paid for his work as an independent contractor rather than a session musician, as it means he won't receive any royalties. By the end of the film, Llewyn's stubborn aversion to fashion—and with it, to change of any kind—will be recast as a trap.

O Brother, Where Art Thou? unfolded in a fantastic version of thirties-era America where virtually every character had the gift of song regardless of their vocation. *Inside Llewyn Davis* is set in a world of professional musicians, and the atmosphere is thick with tension between the Platonic idealism of music as a "joyous expression of the soul" and the bottom-line rejoinder that its main function, for the musician, is to pay the rent. The former point of view is expressed by Lillian, the gracious cultivator of a living-room folkie social scene. The latter comes courtesy of Llewyn himself, whose determination to succeed without compromising his craft—"This is what I do for a living!" he thunders—recalls *Barton Fink*, who was similarly humorless about his occupation. But where Hollywood came calling for Barton with its siren song, Llewyn isn't necessarily in a position to sell out. The Soggy Bottom Boys had a hit without really trying; Llewyn, whose solo album isn't selling, has to go knocking on the doors of power brokers like Bud Grossman (F. Murray Abraham), proprietor of the legendary (real-life) Chicago jazz club, the Gate of Horn.

It's a matter of record that the Coens based the character of Llewyn on the late American folk singer Dave Van Ronk, a fixture of the Greenwich Village music scene of the early 1960s. Not only did they take the film's title from his 1964 album *Inside Dave Van Ronk*, but the cover of Llewyn's own solo record replicates its design and layout almost identically, with one major difference. Van Ronk was photographed with a cat, while Llewyn is shot solo, perhaps because he already is the cat and doesn't need to share the frame with his twin. On his car trip to Chicago, Llewyn sings Van Ronk's 1963 song "Green, Green Rocky Road" to annoy Goodman's folk-averse New Orleans jazzman Roland Turner, and several anecdotes from the musician's posthumously released 2005 memoir, *The Mayor of MacDougal Street,* are woven into screenplay—including the author's own pilgrimage to the Gate of Horn to audition for Albert Grossman (the clear inspiration for Abraham's character).

No scene in *Inside Llewyn Davis* demonstrates the Coens' bold yet controlled mix of fact and fiction—and of music-industry gossip and mythology—than Llewyn's encounter with Bud, which is accordingly positioned at the story's exact midpoint. Everything in the film either leads up to or away from this fateful moment. The real Albert Grossman was instrumental in the commercial mainstreaming of folk music, described by music critic Michael Gray as "a breadhead, seen to move serenely and with deadly purpose like a barracuda circling shoals of fish." Abraham duly lends his avatar a watchful skepticism, sizing Llewyn up as a potential commodity from the moment he walks in the door. The audition is thus framed as a test of the singer's mettle, which makes sense insofar as the Gate of Horn takes its name from a passage in *The Odyssey*: "For two are the gates of shadowy dreams, and one is fashioned of horn and one of ivory. Those dreams that pass through the gate of sawn ivory deceive men, bringing words that find no fulfillment. But those that come forth through the gate of polished horn bring true issues to pass, when any mortal sees them."

Real heroes, in other words, are those who can pass through the Gate of Horn unscathed; lest we doubt that "Llewyn is the cat," consider that when the animal's name, which is strategically withheld in the early scenes, is finally revealed, it is Ulysses, just like George Clooney's treasure-seeker in *O Brother, Where Art Thou?* That iteration of Homer's hero recorded a hit song by accident. Bud is looking for a surefire bet that he can take to market. He asks his guest to play something "from inside Llewyn Davis," a double entendre referencing the name of his solo record and also Mrs. Gorfein's earlier comment

Cinematographer Bruno Delbonnel turns the Gate of Horn into a lonely space haunted by the ghosts of gigs past.

The cameo in the film's final moments by the silhouette of Bob Dylan recasts Llewyn's life as the reopening act to a greater singer's career: a punchline that's less hilarious than melancholy.

about singing being a "joyous expression of the soul." Llewyn chooses the medieval ballad "The Death of Queen Jane," about the death in childbirth of Jane Seymour, the third wife of Henry VIII. The barely restrained anguish with which Llewyn performs the song seems to be about his professional desperation, or maybe his dead partner, until we clue into lyrics referencing a troubled birth and the possible death of an heir ("If I lose the flower of England, I shall lose the branch, too"). It seems that Jean and her upcoming procedure—to say nothing of the illegitimate son that Llewyn has recently learned is alive and well in Akron, Ohio, after the child's mother chose to skip her own abortion—are very much on his mind.

The deeply felt performance fails to impress the hit-maker, who informs Llewyn, in the film's most flatly devastating line: "I don't see a lot of money here." The Coens' ambivalence about the actual value of financial reward is well established, and there is an aspect of music-biz satire at work here as well. Albert Grossman was responsible for putting together the singers

known as Peter, Paul and Mary, and the Coens circle back to history by having him nudge Llewyn to become part of a trio. His refusal could be the arrogance of a man who wants to be a star on his own terms; like his spirit animal, Llewyn is defined by solitariness. Whether this reluctance to work with others (shown also in the "Please Mr. Kennedy" scene) is directly related to Mikey's suicide is unclear, but then so too is whether or not Bud's middling assessment of Llewyn's potential is to be trusted.

There are two movies inside *Inside Llewyn Davis*, and although they look and sound identical—like the two cats—they are very different creatures. In the first, a good-but-not-great musician keeps sabotaging his prospects because he believes success is an all-or-nothing proposition—the attitude that leads him to perform something as archaic and alienating as "The Death of Queen Jane" for a man who might otherwise make him into a star. In the second, parallel version of the story, a generational talent is unfortunately mistaken for an also-ran. In a 2013 interview with the

Grid, Oscar Isaac revealed that Llewyn's performance of "The Death of Queen Jane" was designed to look forward even as it reaches back: "He's actually ahead [of his time] musically: when he sings 'The Death of Queen Jane.' In the opening chords you can hear [The Who's] 'Baba O'Riley.' So it's not that he isn't good—it's that in his situation, being good doesn't matter enough. There are countless stories of people who died penniless and years later, it was understood that they were actually amazing."

Bud is one of several characters in *Inside Llewyn Davis* who stands in for the fears of disapproval that drive Llewyn's perfectionism. The shooting and editing in the scene at the Gate of Horn is closely mirrored in the later sequence where Llewyn goes to visit his catatonic father, Hugh (Stan Carp), in a nursing home and plays him a traditional Welsh song, "The Shoals of Herring." Hoping to elicit an emotional response from the person who first nurtured his musical gifts, Llewyn discovers that the old man has been moved in a different, more visceral way: He soils himself. Both Bud's and Hugh's responses serve as figurative blows to Llewyn's ego, whereas the nameless, faceless man who confronts him in the alleyway outside the Gaslight Café in the film's first and final scenes quite literally brutalizes him with his bare hands.

Ostensibly, this is punishment for Llewyn's nasty heckling of another folk singer on the bill, a woman with a harp who looks and sounds uncannily like Lillian Gorfein, and similarly catalyzes a spasm of self-loathing: "I fucking hate folk music," Llewyn exclaims when confronted with her rendition of "The Storms Are on the Ocean." The man who meets him in the alleyway is her protective, vengeful husband, although he comes off less like a character within the narrative than a blunt instrument being wielded by some higher power, sent to Greenwich Village to kick Llewyn when he's down.

The near-identical staging of Llewyn's two encounters with this stranger structure the film as a circle, or maybe a Möbius strip, with Llewyn prevented from either learning from his mistakes or easing his suffering. Our last glimpse of the character is of a battered man smiling to himself as his assailant hails a cab out of town— an escape route that Llewyn himself can never take. His final line is defiant, even as it's being muttered out of earshot of its intended recipient: "Au revoir."

This kiss-off is steeped in ironies so dark that they have no bottom. For one thing, Llewyn is defending the same home turf that keeps crumbling under his feet, as if he's cozily at home in his little rut. The only way he's ever going to get to say "good-bye" is to somebody on their way out of town, because for him, all roads lead back to the Gaslight Café—and to his status as the opening act for somebody better. That somebody is Bob Dylan, whose silhouetted appearance in the background as Llewyn heads out to take his pummeling provides the inevitable conceptual punch line,

TOUGH CROWD
—
Like Bud Grossman at the Gate of Horn, Llewyn's invalid father passes a negative, devastating judgment on his son's performance: Without saying a word, he soils himself.

SOLO ARTIST
—
The title of Llewyn's first, unsuccessful solo album rhymes with Mrs. Gorfein's claim that music is "a joyous expression of the soul."

and helps to tie up all the script's musical-historical loose ends. In a film populated by thinly veiled stand-ins for Albert Grossman, Dave Van Ronk, and Peter, Paul and Mary, the arrival of the real Robert Zimmerman—who is a Minnesotan Jew just like the Coens—tips things finally in the direction of authenticity.

The song that Dylan sings, "Farewell," is written from the point of view of a man expressing bittersweet regrets about moving on, and the title refrain rhymes perfectly with Llewyn's own "au revoir." But "Farewell" is also an original composition, and the contrast between the man who can only perform traditional songs and the one who spins them out of whole cloth—between the dogged interpreter and the visionary songwriter—registers as a gut-punch. As a singer, Llewyn is drawn so strongly to the archetype of the lonely guitar-slinger that he becomes him: a man of constant sorrow, forever singing the same old song. But from the beginning, Dylan's work fused a respect for his forebears with the desire to push things forward, and to create characters as well as inhabit them. Who else but the man who wrote "The Times They Are A-Changin'" should appear here as an emissary of the future that a traditionalist like Llewyn Davis can't quite imagine, and which the Coens' purgatorial structure won't permit him to experience? Playing over the end credits, Dylan's "Farewell" becomes a long good-bye to a film whose protagonist remains trapped in the loop.

THE CAT CAME BACK
—
Llewyn's reunion with the Gorfeins' cat brings the story full circle, completing the script's Möbius strip structure and setting it in motion for another spin.

"AU REVOIR"
—
Nearly every song on the film's soundtrack uses the word "farewell"; Llewyn's final words translate the sentiment into French.

A Map of Coen Brothers' Road Trips

CANADA

MINNESOTA

NEW YORK

AKRON
OHIO

CAESARS PALACE

LAS VEGAS

CHICAGO

LOS ANGELES

MISSISSIPPI

NORTH
PACIFIC
OCEAN

TEXAS

MEXICO

N
NE
NW
3
E
MS
SE
S

•••••• INSIDE LLEWYN DAVIS
——— FARGO
➤➤➤ NO COUNTRY FOR OLD MEN
♪♫ O BROTHER, WHERE ART THOU?
------ BARTON FINK
✕✕✕ INTOLERABLE CRUELTY

Hail, Caesar!

RELEASE DATE
February 5, 2016
BUDGET
$22M
DISTRIBUTOR
Universal Pictures
CAST
Josh Brolin
George Clooney
Tilda Swinton
Alden Ehrenreich
Ralph Fiennes
Scarlett Johansson
Channing Tatum
Frances McDormand
Jonah Hill

WARNING!
THIS FILM CONTAINS

Dialectical materialism	26%
Elocution lessons	19%
Hedda Hopper	12%
Esther Williams	11%
Red Scare	10%
Singing and dancing	9%
Lasso tricks	7%
Swords	3%
Sandals	2%
Grapes	1%

"WHY THE OBSESSION with tail-consuming circularity?" That was film critic Kent Jones in the year 2000, probing the Coen brothers on the occasion of *O Brother, Where Art Thou?* Despite that film's Homer-derived linearity, Jones noticed that aspects of it were indicative of its makers' more reiterative tendencies. The script's neat trick of having the "old-timey" music of the Soggy Bottom Boys speak to their cash-strapped, Depression-era moment—the "man of constant sorrow" as an eternally recursive figure—was an ouroboros to go with "the demonic loop of *Miller's Crossing, Barton Fink*'s unconscious cannibalization of his own masterpiece . . . *Hudsucker*'s circles within circles?"

Jones's inventory missed the rotating ceiling fans that whir through *Blood Simple* and the tumbling tumbleweed rolling behind the opening credits of *The Big Lebowski*. Had he waited a few years, he could have included the spinning hubcap that morphs into a flying saucer near the end of *The Man Who Wasn't There*, or the fateful quarter that serves as a synecdoche of *No Country for Old Men*'s coin-flip worldview.

The 1950s-set *Hail, Caesar!*, about the troubled production of a Hollywood Bible spectacular à la *Ben-Hur*, doesn't answer Jones's query about why the Coens' films are so filled with circles. But it's a good opportunity to ponder it. Like *Inside Llewyn Davis*, it's a film that has been structured carefully

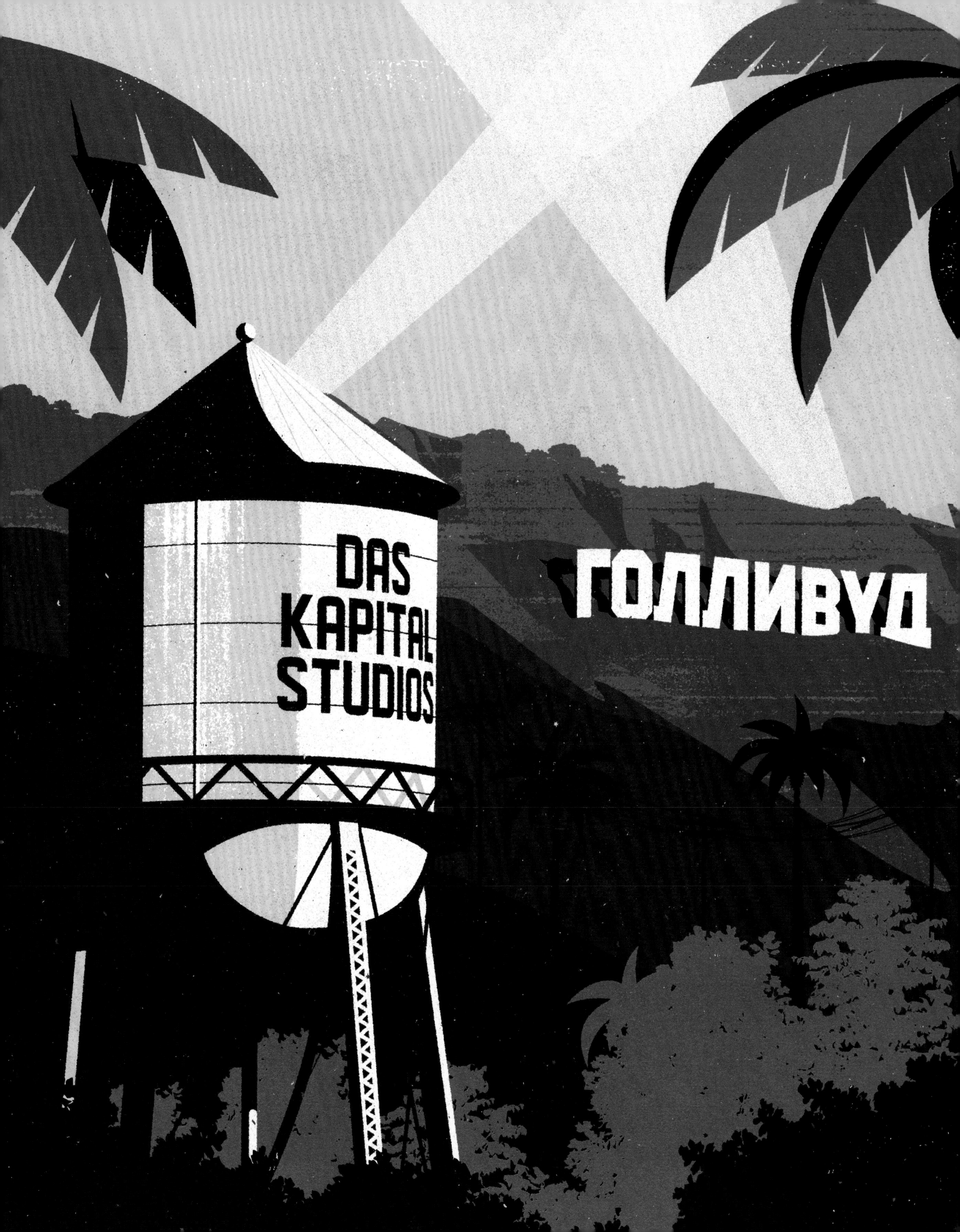
DAS
KAPITAL
STUDIOS
ГОЛЛИВУД

so that its first and (basically) final scenes are exactly alike, and its most potent visual symbol is again a sphere, the titular celestial object of *Lazy Old Moon*, a fictional Western excerpted in a scene where several of the film's characters—all of whom work at the fictional Capitol Pictures Studios—go to the movies.

Seated in the theater next to the starlet he's been set up with by the studio's publicity department, up-and-coming movie cowboy Hobie Doyle (Alden Ehrenreich) watches his character sing a tribute to the eternal, reassuring indifference of the heavens. The song accompanies a bit of old-fashioned burlesque, as a burly drunk nearly drowns himself trying to grab the glowing full moon reflected in the water of a wooden still. The lyrics and philosophical thrust of Hobie's tune are reminiscent of *The Hudsucker Proxy* and its reassurance that the planet will keep turning despite our best efforts: "Lazy old moon, keep shining." The implication is that it's better to just go along for the ride, to "accept the mystery," as Mr. Park puts it in *A Serious Man*.

The Coens love their koans, and deliberately quote one here. "Enlightenment," wrote the thirteenth-century Buddhist poet Dōgen Zenji, "is like the moon reflected on water." For the bearded fool in *Lazy Old Moon*, everything isn't Zen. The image is one of earthbound folly; yearning for the ephemeral ends with the seeker all wet. The audience's raucous laughter at his pratfall drowns out Hobie's sweet-voiced singing, but instead of being disappointed, he joins in.

This vision of an audience getting off on an image of misfortune is not a throwaway moment in the seemingly unwieldy, but actually hard-cut, glittering, multifaceted object that is *Hail, Caesar!* The namesake of Lazy Old Moon represents an expression of the Coens' fondness for and knowledge about old Hollywood genres, something that can also be said for *Hail, Caesar!* as a whole. But just as the film's affectionate pastiche is laced with sarcasm, Hobie and the audience's reaction to the drunk's plummet into the water still cuts to something at the core of these filmmakers'

Besides evoking the sword-
and-sandal epics of the
1950s, the titular film-
within-the-film of *Hail,
Caesar!* satirically equates
Roman splendor with
Hollywood decadence.

sensibility: the question of whether or not they are "mean" to their characters.

There is no shortage of intolerable cruelty in the Coens' films, and while some of that is inherent to the sorts of stories they tell—to their predilection for crime thrillers and noirs—the most wounding examples derive from specific filmmaking choices more than narrative necessities. At the end of *Blood Simple*, the dying Visser is denied a drop of water by a hard cut to black and a soundtrack selection that mocks the end of his life by implying that mortality is just business as usual. In *Fargo*, the camera maintains a pitiless distance as Jean Lundegaard runs, hooded and screaming, outside the cabin in the woods, prompting giggles from her kidnappers, who regard her as a living piece of slapstick entertainment. Llewyn Davis's existential humiliation for being the opening act for Bob Dylan is reinforced with a series of brutal body blows in a back alley; the tragedy of Ted's murder in *Burn After Reading* is dismissed as meaningless collateral damage moments later by a pair of CIA spooks.

Most of these moments are played at least partially for comedy: The circle turns back to J. Hoberman and his term "Coendescension" applied to the high-angled Google Earth views that bookend *Burn After Reading*. That film's end credits display the words "Written and directed by Joel and Ethan Coen" just as the camera starts shooting into the sky, which could be taken as the brothers giving us "the high hat." Or: Who died and made them God, anyway?

Watching the dailies for Capitol Pictures Studio's new biblical spectacular *Hail, Caesar!* (the title kids 1953's *Quo Vadis?*), in-house fixer Eddie Mannix (Josh Brolin) encounters a title card reading "Divine Presence to Be Shot"—a double-barreled double entendre suggestive both of holy imminence and a contract that's been taken out on the Almighty's life. This duality of portent is perfect for a movie that takes a time-out to define the meaning of "dialectics." In its most basic outline, *Hail, Caesar!* is about a plot hatched by blacklisted Communist screenwriters to hold Hollywood hostage in the surrogate form of a movie star, all the better to honor the party line about snatching back the means of production from their masters (while using the ransom money to bankroll Muscovite operations).

The irony of matinee idol Baird Whitlock (George Clooney) getting a lecture on the merits of *Das Kapital* from men recently exiled by Capitol (Pictures) is rather thick, updating (but not refining) the hypercritical projection of Clifford Odets in *Barton Fink*, which gets referenced in a recurring shot of waves crashing against the surf outside the kidnappers' palatial, steel-and-glass beachfront hideout.

Of all the Coens' films, *Hail, Caesar!* is at once the most explicitly political and the hardest to gauge, even more than the mournfully reactionary *No Country for Old Men* or the viciously cynical *Burn After Reading*. The near-climactic image of a silenced Russian submarine surfacing off the coast of California to the sounds of a massed choir while Communist stooges paddle toward it in a visual parody of *Washington Crossing the Delaware* is as deliriously paranoid as anything in *The Manchurian Candidate* (1962).

The Coens do not specifically reference John Frankenheimer's classic, but they honor its anything-goes spirit—its spiteful, terrified dialectic—by playing both sides of the Red Scare for laughs. As in *The Manchurian Candidate*, which parodied Senator Joe McCarthy and prophesied the Kennedy assassination through motifs of mind-control and Freud-meets-Mrs.-Bates mommy issues, the joke in *Hail, Caesar!* is not that the Communist threat to America is overstated, but rather that it's already on our shores. The revelation that one of Capitol's biggest stars, the handsome hoofer Burt Gurney (Channing Tatum), is the leader of the Russian plot destabilizes the story's reality. It's a ridiculous twist, topped off with Tatum's solemnly Soviet bearing and diction after his secret identity surfaces alongside the Soviet submarine. But it also gets at something true and resonant about the period, which is the intersection of celebrity and ideology. Not only the endless media speculation about the political affiliations of movie stars, but also the contemporaneous cult of personality represented by the Church of Scientology and its habit of trying to bring marquee names into the fold.

The Manchurian Candidate's plot device of brainwashing an American hero also figures into Baird's hasty indoctrination. Instead of getting angry with his captors for drugging and abducting him, he's swayed to the cause, plied with compliments and finger sandwiches and finally all but hypnotized by the philosopher Herbert Marcuse (John Bluthal) and his soothing, Marx-inflected rhetoric that "history and economics [are] the same thing." The casting of Clooney, an avowed and outspoken liberal whose 2005 film *Good Night, and Good Luck* dramatized journalist Edward R. Murrow's battles with McCarthy, as a psychologically malleable moron is wickedly satirical. Clooney refines his overtly moronic performance style from *O Brother* and *Burn After Reading* to emphasize arrogance more than idiocy, turning his own stardom into a joke. Or else, perhaps, the butt of one: In the conservative publication the *National Review*, Armond White wrote that the actor has "the air of an out-of-district politician. . . . Can't he see what the Coens are up to?"

Near the end of the film, Baird is retrieved from his cozy peril by Hobie, who brings him back to Eddie's office. Putting his sandaled feet up on the desk, Baird begins preaching the virtues of the good little red book. "We're in this factory serving up these lollipops, what used to be called 'bread and circuses,'" Baird says brightly, his faux-Roman garb from the set of *Hail, Caesar!* literalizing the analogy. (This confusion of screen personas and private selves runs throughout *Hail, Caesar!*, as in the contrast between Hobie's discomfort in the fancy clothes given to him on the set of *Merrily We Dance* and the cowboy costume that fits him like a second skin.)

All of a sudden, the matinee idol is pontificating about the need to upend the "status quo." Eddie, whose respect for the top-down mentality represented by Capitol Pictures is also a form of slavish, religious devotion, quickly slaps some good old-fashioned Capitol-ist sense back into his wayward movie star. "You're going to do it because you're an actor and that's what you do. Just like the director does what he does and the writer and the script girl and the guy who claps the slate. You're gonna do it because the picture has worth! And you have worth if you serve the picture and you're never gonna forget that again."

Leaving aside the embedded irony that what Eddie is describing actually sounds an awful lot like a utopian form of socialism, his angry rant also recalls the climax of *Barton Fink*, but with the sympathies slightly redistributed. (That both films take place at Capitol Pictures cinches the connection even more snugly than the similarities in staging.) Barton's studio-mandated sentence to labor forever in well-compensated anonymity—to never get to put his name to even the derivative scripts he'll be pounding out for eternity—is arguably a case of the punishment fitting the crime. For the sins of being a pretentious effigy of Clifford Odets, he's condemned to one of the Coens' custom-made Catherine wheels. However, it's not as if Lipnick's worldview is redeemed by *Barton Fink*, either: His vulgar descriptions of the mass audience that his star writer can't lower himself to please, plus his militaristic costume, make him into as much of a grotesque caricature as Barton.

The real-life Eddie Mannix, who worked for MGM from the studio's inception until his death in 1963, was not a noble figure: The things he did to keep actors' names out of the tabloids and maintain the appearance of equilibrium—the Hollywood equivalent of "status quo"—were morally and ethically questionable. Mannix

STUDIO NOTES

—

The impossibility of representing God on-screen is kidded during an in-house rough-cut screening of *Hail, Caesar!*; the same mystery of divine presence figures prominently in *A Serious Man*.

RELIGIOUS STUDIES

—

Eddie Mannix's invitation to spiritual leaders to parse the content of his studio's new production incites a nuanced theological debate that's far loftier than his employer's bottom-line motivations.

27

The high walls of the Capitol Pictures backlot cast ominous shadows over its biggest star, Baird Whitlock, whose fame does not preclude marginalization within a massive system.

"The Future": The blacklisted
screenwriters who kidnap
Baird Whitlock believe
they are on the right side
of history—and of "the
dialectic"—but their greed
and vanity (pointed up by
the gilded seaside luxury of
their surroundings, with its
mixture of antiquity and Art
Deco) undermines their left-
wing ideological position.
It's the same hypocrisy as
their fellow Capitol Pictures
scribe *Barton Fink,* and *Hail,
Caesar!* plays as a sequel to
the earlier film's scabrous
classic Hollywood satire.

was accused of consorting with gangsters and helping to ruin the reputations of actors who didn't fall into line. The Coens' version of Eddie is hard-boiled only on the outside. When he's bad-mouthing Baird, it seems to come from a place of belief in his own mission more than as a Lipnick-esque show of power. If Eddie closely resembles any of the Coens' characters, it's not Lipnick or either of Brolin's previous roles as Llewelyn Moss in *No Country for Old Men* and Tom Chaney in *True Grit*. Those men were hard, Western types who didn't ask questions; Eddie stalks around like a film-noir detective, but he's a spiritual seeker, like Larry Gopnik in *A Serious Man*. They've made their version of Mannix into a maddeningly devout Catholic who attends confession daily and

seeks absolution and spiritual clarity, possibly to compensate for the fact that he knows he's in a dirty business.

Not that the Coens make it that dirty. The backlot setting would suggest subversion similar to Kenneth Anger's bawdy tattletale opus *Hollywood Babylon*, but *Hail, Caesar!* doesn't go for the showbiz jugular. Eddie's schedule is filled with annoyances rather than matters of life and death. He must stage-manage a modern virgin birth for the glamorous, unmarried-but-pregnant starlet DeeAnna Moran (Scarlett Johansson) to help maintain her public image; not surprisingly for these Preston Sturges fanatics, the solution inverts the director's 1944 immaculate conception *The Miracle of Morgan's*

LAZY OLD MOON

—

Singing cowboy Hobie Doyle is modeled on B movie star Kirby Grant, with a nod to Ricky Nelson's role in *Rio Bravo* as well.

LET THERE BE LIGHT

—

Throughout *Hail, Caesar!* the Coens juxtapose images of the Old Hollywood studio machine with religious iconography.

Left: Revealed as a Soviet agent, Burt Gurney offers a salute to his comrades while clutching his beloved dog, Engels. When his pet falls into the ocean, Burt saves him instead of recovering a briefcase of ransom money—symbolically choosing a Socialist namesake over capital.

Creek. Along the same lines, he's got to fend off identical-twin gossip columnists Thora Thacker and Thessaly Thacker (both played by Tilda Swinton as outrageously costumed avatars for Hedda Hopper and Louella Parsons) and keep them from reporting on Baird's disappearance, or releasing information alluding to a gay love affair in his past. And, lower down on his priority list, there's the pitched battle between Hobie and his new, supercilious director, Laurence Laurentz (Ralph Fiennes), whose attempts to get his (studio-imposed) cowpoke leading man to deliver Noël Coward–ly bon mots in the drawing-room comedy *Merrily We Dance* evoke Lina Lamont's pitched battles with diction in *Singin' in the Rain*—a film that, as in *The Hudsucker Proxy*, seems to serve as a guiding influence.

These myriad subplots, and the movies-within-the-movie that serve as backdrops for each, give *Hail, Caesar!* an atomized feeling. It's a busy, digressive movie, and at times it feels like the Coens are working overtime to cram in references. Hobie's date to *Lazy Old Moon* is an up-and-coming young actress named Carlotta Valdez (Veronica Osorio), a nod to Kim Novak's character in *Vertigo* (1958). A director spied on the set of a Western resembles John Ford, while Frances McDormand appears as a secluded film editor named C.C. Calhoun, modeled on Alfred Hitchcock's wife/editor Alma Reville. There's also a degree of stylistic indulgence: The scenes on the set of *Hail, Caesar!* feature all sorts of ersatz splendor, while Eddie's rounds also take him through the filming of an *Anchors Aweigh*-style musical number called "No Dames," featuring Burt Gurney doing an extended Gene Kelly vamp. The nautical theme of the number sets up the closet Communist's appearance on the submarine at the end, when the Navy blues he wears for his movie role are swapped out for enemy colors.

What holds *Hail, Caesar!* together—very tightly, in fact—is a third dialectic. Not the one between belief and doubt, which manifests most obviously (and comically) in the scene where Eddie and his chosen religious advisors bicker about the nature of divinity: "These men are screwballs," moans the rabbi of the differently denominated Christians in the room. Nor is it the divide between Capitol and Kapital, which resolves when Baird's ransom disappears (like all the Coens' briefcases) beneath the waves in Malibu, lost to Burt's impulsive choice to hold on to his

lapdog instead of the money. (That dog's name is Engels, which shows that the ideologically motivated Burt is, at least, a man of his principles.) The thematic glue in *Hail, Caesar!* is the strange, irreconcilable relationship between the reassuring "make-believe" represented by the movie industry—in the form of crowd-pleasers like *Lazy Old Moon* or faux-profound biblical spectaculars like Baird Whitlock's star vehicle—and the unmanageable, complex contingencies lurking both on and outside its well-manicured grounds.

At the same time that Eddie is trying to babysit Capitol's overpaid, oversexed, overexposed talent roster, he's also having secret meetings with a recruiter from Lockheed, who wants him to change vocations. The man, who has set their meetings in a Chinese restaurant, says that his company's investment in aeronautical manufacturing represents "the future," and produces a photograph from the Bikini Atoll to back up his claim. But "The Future" also happens to be the forwarding address left by Baird Whitlock's kidnappers, reflecting their belief that they are not only on the right side of the class struggle but also the architects of some impending proletariat revolution: Tomorrow belongs to them. The decision facing Brolin's efficiency expert is thus between two industrial complexes: one devoted to the creation of fake worlds, and one whose endgame is the possible destruction of this one. The Coens have selected Lockheed carefully, given their legacy of pioneering the first ICBMs.

Fear or uncertainty about the future informs nearly all the Coens' films, from H.I.'s paternal anxiety in *Raising Arizona* to Everett's optimistic prognostications of an "age of reason" at the end of *O Brother, Where Art Thou?*, to Llewyn Davis's inability to get past his arrested, extended adolescence. In *The Man Who Wasn't There*, Billy Bob Thornton's Ed Crane tried to invest in a technologically progressive "future"—a dry-cleaning start-up—and paid with his life. This iteration of Ed(die) makes a different choice, consigning himself to the cozily insane stasis of assembly-line movie production rather than working for the architects of the apocalypse. This decision is framed by the Coens as the payoff to the character's Catholic fidelity and integrity, both to his professional superior (the unseen Mr. Skank, a doppelganger for the former MGM head Nick Schenck) and his God. But *Hail, Caesar!* is also filled with images and dialogue that speak to the character's shameful self-division. He's filmed several times walking beneath a massive prop of disembodied, classically sculpted legs adorned with a fig leaf. The Cartesian conundrum between his intuition and gut instincts, meanwhile, is distilled into his job title as Capitol's "head of physical production." As conceptual gags go, this one's a whopper: We might say the Coens joke, therefore, they are.

Circularity and dialectics have been the guiding motifs for the Coens for a long time, back to when the opening voice-over of *Blood Simple* colloquially contrasted American and Soviet systems of belief. Their turn toward parables of faith tested and reinforced is relatively new. The tortured Christianity of *Hail, Caesar!* complements the Talmudic agony of *A Serious Man*; in both cases, the Coens are working through what seems to be a genuine ambivalence toward the opposed (and thus dialectical) institutional edifices of dogma and doubt.

And, for all the claims that the directors always hide within their massive clockwork contraptions—back to Jones, and his description of "defiantly impersonal movies"—their decision to make a film that functions simultaneously, and pretty much equally, as a critique and a celebration of the machinery of moviemaking suggests that they're leaving it all on-screen. Like *Lazy Old Moon, Hail, Caesar!* is another shimmering bauble for us to grasp at futilely even as we suspect that somebody—the Coens, or maybe an even higher power—laughs at us for trying.

Eddie Mannix's problems as
Capitol Pictures' fixer
are matched by a more
existential dilemma: The
disembodied legs of a
classical statue mock his
sense of incompleteness.

Jess Gonchor
PRODUCTION DESIGNER

FILMOGRAPHY

```
Inside Llewyn Davis (2013)
True Grit (2010)
A Serious Man (2009)
Burn After Reading (2008)
No Country for Old Men (2007)
```

Jess Gonchor began working with the Coens in 2006 on *No Country for Old Men*, and he's designed each of their productions since, equally adept at evoking a tactile, lived-in realism as well as wildly stylized cinematic backdrops.

How did the Coens approach you to work on *No Country for Old Men*?

They had seen *Capote,* and there was something in it that they liked, whether it was the style or the simplicity of it, the understatement, or the color palette. We met in New York and had an interview about me doing *No Country for Old Men*, and afterward they contacted Bennett Miller and asked him to tell them about me. Bennett wrote them an email, which I still have, about what a great person I was to work with, and it sealed me getting the job. And Joel wrote back to Bennett and said "This is a great review of Jess—now can you write a letter for my co-op board?"

I read that you were influenced by Mark Rothko when you were figuring out how *No Country for Old Men* should look.

Yes. I created a Rothko-style painting of the colors that I thought would be in the movie. I thought the film would be horizontal: There are a lot of landscape shots, very grounded on the bottom, and then a few colors in between the earth and the sky. I thought that there should be a lot of negative space—in a way it was a modern-day Western. So I had muted colors, and a blue sky above, and then in the middle I spattered blood red all over the image. Then I shrunk this Rothko down to index card size, laminated all the cards, and wrote my phone number on the back of them and told everybody that if they saw any other colors on the set that weren't in the chart, they should call me, so I could yell at them to yank it out.

I thought of Jackson Pollock as well when the deputy's shoes scuff up the police station floor near the beginning of the movie; the aftermath of the murder scene is like an action painting.

That was a set, and I had an idea for this white floor. We were going to make it look a little dingy and dirty, and then I was going to put a seal over it so it wouldn't get any marks on it. It looked great, and everybody loved it, and then we were shooting on a Saturday night and while Javier Bardem was choking the guy,

I saw how their boots were marking up the floor. I spent the rest of the weekend trying to get the scuffing off the floor with whatever I had. I went to Joel on Monday morning to apologize and he said, "Are you crazy? I love those marks."

How did you approach designing *Burn After Reading*?

I think in a movie like that if you notice production design, then I've done something wrong. I had to approach that movie for what it is, which is a farce. It's a very clean movie, without any clutter to slow your eyes down. We needed spaces that the characters could move through quickly, because there's a lot of walk and talk. The Russian embassy is a little bit stylized, though. You see these embassy buildings in American cities and they're a bit over-the-top, they have this Brutalist architectural style. I wanted to create that sort of environment. And the characters think they have these important state secrets on a DVD, so I made a bit of a joke with this big circular window in the embassy.

It's funny that you mention that since I feel like I see circles all over the place in the Coens' movies. . . .

In *Burn After Reading*, you have this bunch of nitwits and nincompoops, so it's a rat wheel. It's the mouse on the wheel going round and round. It's a statement that none of this is ever going to be resolved.

You said you didn't want *Burn After Reading* to have a lot of clutter, and I thought of Rabbi Marshak's office in *A Serious Man*, which is where that film sort of takes a turn into the surreal; it's got all these bizarre specimens in jars and artifacts. It's much more heightened and Gothic than the rest of the movie, which has this totally suburban texture.

We were originally going to shoot *A Serious Man* in Conservative synagogues, which look more like churches than temples—they're very stark and cold environments. But it wasn't the right vibe for the movie, which is about suburbia in the 1960s; you can't go from that to Mrs. Samsky's house next door,

you know? So we decided to go the Reform route, which is all lush red carpet and shellac walls. And I think we turned a corner there. I don't think the shots of Danny being high at his bar mitzvah would have worked so well in another environment. But to get back to Rabbi Marshak's office, my favorite line in this movie is when his secretary opens the door and Larry sees Marshak for a second before she closes it again. She says, "The rabbi is busy now," and he yells, "He didn't look busy!" So every time I go to see Joel and Ethan at the office in New York, they'll be sitting on opposite sides of the room, writing, and I'll pull the door open and say—I have to do it—"You don't look busy!"

Can you talk about the cave that Mattie falls into near the end of *True Grit*? It's such a severe and frightening space, and very different from how it looks in the original Henry Hathaway movie.

That's the darkest. That cave was something that we had to create; it was about thirty feet deep and had to be tailored to a stunt woman who was going to fall down to the bottom.

Roger had to have a light at the top, and we had to tie it visually to the environment that we were shooting in in New Mexico. I'd never done anything like it before: It had to feel like this void that Mattie couldn't climb out of. There's a lot of visual drama there. We mocked it up with sticks first. A lot of the work I do with Joel and Ethan is very low-tech. We don't do pre-visualizations on a computer; if we have to build a facade, I go out to the location and figure out how wide and tall the building is going to be and look at it with a viewfinder. We'd rather do it the way it was done before too much technology came into it.

Where did the look of *Inside Llewyn Davis* come from?

I think the look of that movie came from *The Freewheelin' Bob Dylan*; that was the visual reference. If you walk through Greenwich Village now, it's an explosion of colors, there are Starbucks everywhere. We had to re-create the West Village in the East Village, which has less visual noise and is less congested.

Was there any attempt to model the Gate of Horn set in the movie on the real Chicago nightclub?

There were two Gate of Horns, and they're both closed now. The first one was a walk-down, underground. The other one, you couldn't even tell it was a club. We wanted the Gate of Horn to be the pinnacle of the film, when Llewyn goes to see Bud Grossman, because he's finally going to get his shot at doing what he really wants to do.

The exterior is the only really vertical space in the whole movie.

Yes. It's very vertical, and there's also more color in there than there is in the rest of the film. It feels like there are possibilities there, maybe, and then he plays a song and Bud says, "I don't see a lot of money here." And then the rest of the places in the movie all have lower ceilings and feel like tighter spaces, except for the rest stop bathroom. . . . We wanted to make something a little crazy there.

That's a Kubrick bathroom; it looks like *The Shining*.

Yeah, exactly. There's a lot of fluorescent lighting. I try to pick my points about where to heighten reality in all these movies.

With *Hail, Caesar!*, you're not just re-creating Old Hollywood; you're re-creating the sets of Old Hollywood movies: You've got the Noël Coward drawing-room comedy, the musical, the Western. But what I want to ask you about is that giant pair of legs that's standing on the Capitol Pictures lot—it's such a strange and suggestive image.

It wasn't in the script, actually. Back in the days of movies like *Ben-Hur* the studios wouldn't build full sets; they'd do a big structure like a temple using a glass matte painting. In *Hail, Caesar!*, I wanted people to see what filmmaking was all about, so I came up with this giant set of legs, which could have multiple meanings. Either it's just a half a statue because the studio in the movie couldn't afford a full build, or half of the statue has been taken down . . . but I was also trying to mirror how Eddie Mannix is always constantly walking around, putting out all these fires on every soundstage at Capitol Pictures. It had a few meanings, and I thought it had a nice presence throughout the whole movie.

I should also say that set decorator Nancy Haigh has been a huge part of bringing these movies to life. It's important to tell a story with the sets that helps move the film along and develops the characters without complicating them. Nancy's the queen of that.

An Outroduction

by Adam Nayman

Forced to choose between two possible "futures" at the end of *Hail, Caesar!*–one cozily predictable at Capitol Pictures, the other unknown and possibly apocalyptic working for the nuke-mongers at Lockheed-Martin–Eddie Mannix opts for the only reality he's ever known: a world of make-believe. His decision to stay on as Nick Schenk's number-one fixer provides the movie with its happy ending, even as it points toward a perpetual motion beyond the boundaries of narrative closure. With Eddie prowling the grounds, Capitol Pictures will continue to run like a clockwork operation; the last thing we see him do is check his watch. It's an image of a man who is in complete control of his little corner of space and time . . . at least until the camera drifts in the sky and the credit "Written, Directed, and Produced by Joel and Ethan Coen" soars into view, bathed in a halo of heavenly light. It's a reminder, as if we needed one, of who's really in charge.

In Eddie's own words, he and the rest of Capitol's employees have worth because they "serve the picture"—they're cogs in the machine. The Coens are fond of such self-effacing caretaker types: Eddie joins Moses in *The Hudsucker Proxy* and the omniscient Narrators of *The Big Lebowski* and *O Brother, Where Art Thou?* as characters whose role is to maintain the status quo, or else to assure us that it will remain unshaken down through the generations. (The portrait of Othar in *The Ladykillers* exerts its own form of godlike influence over the action.) This idea can

be expressed brightly, as in *Lebowski's* closing voice-over, with its promise of a "little Lebowski on the way," or with bracing harshness: Sheriff Bell's dream in *No Country for Old Men* makes the same point about the child being the father of the man but in a more sober, morbid vein. "Can't stop what's coming," says another old man in the same movie, and the notion of deference as the only truly workable posture is as much a feature of the Coens' work as their play with archetypes and allusion or their smart-alecky sense of humor.

The gradual taming of hellcat H.I. in *Raising Arizona* is an early iteration; he grows out of one set of worries and into another, mollified by the understanding that this transference is the way of the world. The benign acceptance represented in different ways by Marge and The Dude—the cop and the radical as soft-bellied homebodies—keeps the theme in play into their middle period. Meanwhile, the Coens' most overtly ambitious protagonists, whether driven artists like Barton Fink or Llewyn Davis, or immoral shysters like Visser or Jerry Lundegaard, all ultimately fail to impose their will on their respective situations; each ends up a "loser" of kind, or else, like Tom in *Miller's Crossing*, achieves a Pyrrhic victory (Tom's tip of the hat anticipates Eddie's glance at his watch; both are gestures indicating a desire for control of the self). All that "idea man" Norville Barnes really does is go with the flow (and swivel) of the world around him. And if one of their characters does stray—or gets pushed—out of his or her lane, they take a severe hit in

the process. Think of Anton Chigurh at the close of *No Country for Old Men* or Mattie Ross in the final shot of *True Grit*, matching, his-and-her shots describing not walks into the sunset, but damaged figures limping away from the fray.

Whether or not the Coens' cinema anxiously thematizes a fear of change or else powerfully inscribes it is a question worth asking, though probably not of the filmmakers themselves; one imagines them quoting Jefferson Airplane lyrics à la Rabbi Marshak, a serious man who recognizes the importance of being cryptic. Consistency, whether defined in terms of artistic and technical quality or dramatic and philosophical interest, is the hallmark of the Coens' cinema, and, for most critics and viewers, it's far from being the proverbial hobgoblin of little minds. On the contrary, Joel and Ethan are bigheads; even dissenters concede to their conceptual cleverness, and ever-resourceful means of realizing it on-screen. Their ability to wring variations on a few evident, recurring tropes and obsessions—most present as far back as *Blood Simple* and then developed, rerouted, and multiplied over time—is undeniable, and there's no reason to expect it will wane.

The tension between characters who are prone to repeat themselves, whether literally through reiterative dialogue or behaviorally as "recidivists" of all stripes, and the terror of what just lies beyond their respective, circumscribed loops is what keeps the Coens' consistency from feeling complacent. If it seems to some like they're always addressing the same thing–the contingencies of existence in a world where something can and almost surely will go wrong– this can be taken as an acknowledgment of responsibility to reality, even if it's more often refracted through the glittering prisms of genre. If Homer's *Odyssey* and Hammett's and Cain's morality tales can be analyzed as genuine reckonings with their historical moments, are the Coens' appropriations necessarily ersatz, or does their very existence speak to an increasingly post-modern condition—one where a deep, sustained, and even decadent engagement with the past shapes our understanding of the present and anticipation of the future?

Between Eddie's dilemma and the collective nom de plume chosen by blacklisted screenwriters, *Hail, Caesar!* evokes the frightening, uncertain specter of "the future" more explicitly than any of the Coens' other period pieces, with the possible exception of *The Man Who Wasn't There*. I began this book by describing the image of the Mentaculus in *A Serious Man*, an equation so long and daunting that it heads off any attempt at completion, even as its size and complexity holds the promise of genuine revelation. But at the end, I'm haunted even more by Ed Crane's dream of sitting on the couch with Doris near the end of *The Man Who Wasn't There,* a scene whose simplicity inspires its own sort of interpretive madness. Here, the status quo is cozy and terrifying; it's also past and present; dream and reality; grim comedy and deadly serious. Because Ed has no future—in dry-cleaning, Birdy, or anything else—he idealizes a past that he and we know to have been soul-destroying. And then, to once again paraphrase Sheriff Bell, he wakes up, to a foreshortened future racing up to meet him. He can't go home again.

The individual reaches his end; the world keeps on turning all the same. The Coens' acceptance of these eternal verities evinces true humility, even if their technique–and its attendant, elevated authorial self-regard, from jukebox Greek choruses in *Blood Simple* to the real thing in *O Brother, Where Art Thou?*—can be (and often is) taken for a bit of the old high-hat. They evoke the real and cinematic past with the skill of authentic conjurers, yet steadfastly refuse to forecast beyond the present moment (it would be surprising to see them attempt a science-fiction epic or postapocalyptic fable à la *The Road*). The Coens' journeys into the past are not retreats: they always add something to the genres they take on rather than leaving them the way they found them. That mixture of reverence and boldness is what makes their work so rewatchable. The only thing that I know for certain about the future is that I'm planning to spend it with these movies all over again.

Image Credits

Photography

Illustration

Bibliography

Adams, Jeffrey. *The Cinema of the Coen Brothers: Hard Boiled Entertainments.* London: Wallflower Press, 2015.

Andrew, Geoff. *Stranger Than Paradise: Maverick Filmmakers in Recent American Cinema.* New York: Proscenium Publishers, 1999.

Barker, Andrew. "Coen Brothers Script Hunter's Career." *Variety.* May 2008.

Bergan, Ronald. *The Coen Brothers.* London: Orion, 2000.

Bradshaw, Peter. Rev. of *The Man Who Wasn't There. The Guardian,* Oct 2001.

Calhoun, Dave. "The Coen Brothers Talk '50s-Style Filmmaking For Latest Release *Hail, Caesar!" Time Out London.* March 2016.

Chang, Justin. Rev. of *Hail, Caesar! Variety.* February 2016.

Cieply, Michael. "MacDougal Street Homesick Blues." *The New York Times.* January 2013.

Ciment, Michel, and Hubert Niogret. "Interview With Joel and Ethan Coen." *Positif.* July/August 1987.

Ciment, Michel, and Hubert Niogret. "A Rock on the Beach: Interview with Joel and Ethan Coen." *Positif.* Sept 1991.

Coen, Joel and Ethan. *The Hudsucker Proxy.* London: Faber and Faber, 1994.

Coen, Joel and Ethan. *The Ladykillers.* London: Faber and Faber, 2004.

Corliss, Richard. Rev. of *Blood Simple. Time.* Sept 1984.

The Coen Brothers: Interviews. Ed. William Rodney Allen. Jackson: University Press of Mississippi, 2006.

The Coen Brothers' Fargo. Ed. William G. Luhr. Cambridge: Cambridge University Press, 2004.

Coursdon, Jean-Pierre. "A Hat Blown by the Wind." *Positif.* Feb 1991.

Ebert, Roger. Rev. of *True Grit. Chicago Sun-Times.* Dec 2010.

Edelstein, David. "Invasion of the Baby Snatchers." *American Film.* April 1987.

Hinson, Hal. "Bloodlines." *Film Comment.* March/April 1985.

Hoberman, Jim. "The Coen Brothers Make Another Mockery with *Burn After Reading." Village Voice.* Sept 2008.

Jameson, Richard T. "Chasing the Hat." *Film Comment.* Sept/Oct 1990.

Joel & Ethan Coen. Ed. Peter Korte, Georg Seesslen. New York: Limelight Editions, 2001.

*Joel & Ethan Coen: Blood Sibling*s. Ed. Paul A. Woods. London: Plexus Publishing, 2003.

Levine, Josh. *The Coen Brothers: The Story of Two American Filmmakers.* Toronto: ECW Press, 2000.

Lopez, John. "The Coen Brothers Talk *True Grit." Vanity Fair.* December 2010.

Lowe, Andy. "The Brothers Grim." *Total Film.* May 1998.

McCarthy, Todd. Rev of *True Grit. The Hollywood Reporter.* December 2010.

Mottram, James. *The Coen Brothers*: *The Life of the Mind.* London: Batsford, 2000.

Orr, Christopher. "30 years of Coens: *Miller's Crossing." The Atlantic.* Sept 2014.

Palmer, R. Barton. *Contemporary Film Directors: Joel and Ethan Coen.* Chicago: University of Illinois Press, 2004.

The Philosophy of the Coen Brothers. Ed. Mark T. Conrad. Kentucky: University Press of Kentucky, 2012.

Ridley, Jim. "Brothers in Arms." *Nashville Scene,* May 2000.

Romney, Jonathan. "Double Vision." *The Guardian.* May 2000.

Russell, Carolyn R. *The Films of Joel and Ethan Coen.* Jefferson, North Carolina: McFarland & Company, Inc, 2001.

Taylor, Charles. Rev. *The Ladykillers. Salon.* May 2004.

Taylor, Ella. "A Serious Man: Seriously Bad For the Jews." *Village Voice.* October 2009.

Tyree, J.M. & Ben Walters. *BFI Film Classics: The Big Lebowski.* London: Palgrave MacMillan, 2007.

Weintraub, Steve. "Joel and Ethan Coen Interview—*No Country for Old Men." Collider.* Nov 2007.

Yamato, Jen. "The Coen Brothers: The Oscars are Not That Important." *The Daily Beast.* Jan 2016.

Acknowledgments

The Author would like to thank . . .

HAVE TO begin by thanking David Jenkins, who initiated this project two years ago over coffee at the Toronto International Film Festival, and guided its myriad whirling, moving parts into place, whether we were communicating by phone, email, Google Doc, WhatsApp, Skype, mental telepathy (or even in person during my trip to London in the home stretch of production). He is a fine editor and a serious man, and he really tied the book together.

Over at Abrams, Eric Klopfer was the big-picture/bottom-line guy—the Man Behind the Desk—but always seemed happy to be in the trenches with the rest of us. Thanks also to the New York team of John Gall, Mary O'Mara, and Denise LaCongo.

Back in London, Clive Wilson was the second person after David to talk to me about writing a book on the Coens, and made sure I knew exactly what I was doing before I started doing it. Helen Jackson wrangled most of our interviews and photo permissions and was instrumental in the push to the finish line. If this book looks good, it's entirely due to the clever, gorgeous illustrations and graphics by Oliver Stafford, Bobby Evans, and Jason Ngai, and the layout wizardry of Sophie Mo (a wonderful designer who even let me win a few arguments about photo placement now and again). Thanks also to Ella Kemp for her excellent, accurate transcriptions of some very long interviews.

Special thanks to Roger and James Deakins, J. Todd Anderson, Mary Zophres, Carter Burwell, Jess Gonchor, Bryan Barber, David and Nathan Zellner, and Lisa Walker for agreeing to do interviews and contributing visual or other materials to our layouts.

I wrote the bulk of this book at the TIFF Film Reference Library, an invaluable institution which should be one of that organization's major points of pride. I want to thank each and every one of the FRL staff members who helped me along the way: Rachel Beattie, Fatima Mercado, Sagan Yee, Madelaine Wal, Chad Menard, and Michelle Lovegrove Thomson.

It is inadvisable, if not impossible, to undertake a book project and proceed without help from friends and colleagues.

For this one, I would like to graciously thank a few of the usual suspects for talking about the Coens and related topics with me at one time or another: Michael Koresky, Azadeh Jafari, Eric Hynes, Nick Pinkerton, Andrew Tracy, Alicia Fletcher, Jesse Cumming, Jason Anderson, Kiva Reardon, Bart Testa, Danelle Eliav, Darrah Teitel, Neil Badahur, Lydia Ogwang, and Violet Lucca.

My London pals Simran Hans, Sophie Monks Kaufman, Caspar Salmon, Paul Ridd, and Erika Balsom made me feel welcome while I was jet-lagged and working furiously away from home. Cool aunts Elena and Manuela Lazic both made spontaneous observations during that London trip that ended up sharpening several sections; Manuela also took a look at some chapters in advance of their completion and provided a wealth of honest, helpful, and occasionally hilarious feedback. Thanks, ML, and be a good Goy.

I've argued with Kevin Courrier about the Coens' films for years (and years) and some of those wonderfully dialectical discussions are basically re-created in the chapters that follow. Suffice it to say, I wouldn't have been able to write this book without him.

I'm always grateful to my family for emotional, moral and-in a happy new development-babysitting support. Thank you to Sandra and Vesa Koivusalo, who will make room on their shelves for a third book by their son-in-law; Matt Nayman and Suzie Lowe, who will have to buy their own copy because brotherly love only goes so far; and David Nayman and Evelyne Michaels, who always made sure I had a good breakfast.

Finally, I would like to co-dedicate this book to my wife, Tanya, my partner in every venture, big and small, who understood before I did that *Burn After Reading* is really, really funny, and our daughter, Lea, who's already really, really funny, and is going to see all these movies when she grows up. I guess that's the way the whole darned human comedy keeps perpetuatin' itself, down through the generations.... Aw, look at me, I'm rambling again...

The Editor would like to thank...

FIRST UP, BIG thank you to Abrams' Eric Klopfer, whose discernment, humor, and comforting sense of precision helped to make this not only a smooth but highly enjoyable project. From an art perspective, a shout-out to Oliver Stafford, Laurène Boglio, and Timba Smits for their sharp creative insights, and a glass (of coffee) raised to Sophie Mo for her gorgeous layouts. Thanks to Bobby "Telegramme" Evans and Jason Ngai for supercharging this volume with their sublime illustrated concoctions. Big love to Helen Jackson, the master fixer and celebrity wrangler, vital picture research from Andrew Webb and Abbey Bender, and ace transcription from Ella Kemp. A big thanks to Andrew Male, who was able to comb through the text at very short notice, and to Jonathan Butler at Alamy image archive for just being a massively helpful person. Loretta Ayeroff was massively helpful in allowing access to Jeff Bridges's photo archive and Justin Mitchell who was able to photograph Mary Zophres's design archive. Thanks to Alex Wade for legal advice.

Shout-out to all at TCO: Vince Medeiros, Wendy Klerck, Simon Baker, the Huck team, and everyone at 71a Leonard Street who makes it fun to come to work every morning. Super special mentions to the Team Little White Lies: Adam Woodward and Hannah Woodhead. And for all those who helped us along the way: Luke Norton, Martin Venezky, Lauren Thompson, Ewan Cameron, Caroline Middleton, Mark Allison, John Wadsworth, Rebecca Speare-Cole, Lena Hanafy, Dan Einav, Jack Godwin, Sophie Wyatt, Eve Watling, Amy Bowkey, William Carroll, Juliette Cottu, Courteney Tan, Josh Howey, Louise Busfield, Isobel Raphael, Emily Bray, and Joe Boden.

Finally, big love to the man with the original plan, Toronto's finest, Adam Nayman. We met in 2008, in the departure lounge of Zurich Airport, and our first conversation covered a mutual love of the films of Kelly Reichardt and *Showgirls*. The term "committed" doesn't stretch far enough to encapsulate his intense, some may even say cheerily antisocial, dedication for this project and the cinema of the Coens. Working with him was a simple joy. Every time I see a lengthy hyphenated internal clause containing a beautifully articulated digression, I will think of Adam.

THE

END

FOR LITTLE WHITE LIES

EDITOR: David Jenkins
ART DIRECTOR AND COVER DESIGN: Oliver Stafford
LEAD DESIGNER: Sophie Mo
PROJECT MANAGER: Helen Jackson
HEAD OF BOOKS: Clive Wilson
PUBLISHER: Vince Medeiros

FOR ABRAMS

SENIOR EDITOR: Eric Klopfer
PRODUCTION MANAGER: Denise LaCongo

Library of Congress Control Number: 2017956796

ISBN: 978-1-4197-2740-5
eISBN: 978-1-68335-319-5

Printed and bound in China
10 9 8 7 6 5 4 3 2 1

Abrams books are available at special discounts when purchased in quantity for premiums and promotions as well as fundraising or educational use. Special editions can also be created to specification. For details, contact specialsales@abramsbooks.com or the address below.

Abrams® is a registered trademark of Harry N. Abrams, Inc.

ABRAMS The Art of Books
195 Broadway, New York, NY 10007
abramsbooks.com